SCHOLAR GYPSY

A Christian Journey down the road less traveled

By Russ Head

EABooks Publishing
Your Partner In Publishing

Scholar Gypsy, A Christian Journey down the road less traveled

Names and details of some stories have been changed to protect the privacy of individuals.

Cover design by: Robin Black
Cover photo: iStockphoto/Freeartist
Author photo by: Luke B. Haney

ISBN: 978-1-963611-14-4
LCCN: 2024906753

Published by EA Books Publishing, a division of
Living Parables of Central Florida, Inc. a 501c3

EABooksPublishing.com

This book is dedicated to
the Father, Son, and Holy Spirit
and too all those who have been and
continue to be a part of my journey.

ACKNOWLEDGEMENTS

So many people played a part in the realization of this book. In particular, I would like to thank EAB Publishing. They have been wonderful with their love and support in walking me through this project. Rebecca Ford, Peter Lundell, and Jeanette Littleton at EA were so supportive with their editing and encouragement. I would also like to thank Emily Cromer for her help and encouragement.

WHY THE TITLE *SCHOLAR GYPSY*

"Scholar-Gipsy" is the name of a poem by the British poet Matthew Arnold. That poem resonates with me because the central character mirrors my life in many ways. I see so much of myself in the "Scholar-Gipsy."

I love learning, and I am the eternal student, the eternal scholar. I feel I have been blessed with the heart of a scholar in that I have an insatiable curiosity and passion for learning. There is no subject that I cannot find interesting.

In the poem, the narrator tells wistfully of the legend of the Oxford scholar who had to leave school and his schoolmates because his family didn't have the money to pay for the rest of his education. The scholar then leaves school and joins a band of gypsies he says have learned the true mystical meanings of life. He hopes that, when he learns these mystical lessons, he will return to his friends and impart these lessons to them. Because he took the road less traveled, the scholar's mind stayed innocent and young and his mind was not jaded by the drive of his schoolmates for the illusive life goals of the masses.

In the pages that follow, I express how I feel that God has, in many ways, preserved in my mind the innocence and joy of youth. God has taken me on a journey down the road less traveled and taught me so many of the great lessons of life. And now, I wish to lead you on a journey and to impart to you the lessons I have learned.

HOW THIS BOOK IS SET UP

I mean this book to mentor the reader. The first two hundred pages tell the story of my life and the spiritual journey I have taken. They include lessons learned. The next hundred pages are divided into a variety of topics: "Godwink" stories, funny stories, significant quotes, and spiritual essays. Look in the table of contents and skip around if you wish, and read what piques your interest.

Contents

PREFACE

THE YEAR OF COVID–19

The year of 2019 was a great year for my tour company. It had been blessed and booming for years, and 2019 ended a year of almost perfect tours. We had been to Alaska, Normandy, the Canadian Rockies, the French and Swiss Alps, Italy, and Scotland. In October, we had a magical tour to New England for fall foliage, and we rounded out the year with two holiday tours to New York. I couldn't have asked for a more wonderful year.

While I was truly thankful for the way my business was flourishing, success has its own set of complications, and for years, I had thought that I needed to cut back and take a break. In this business, you have to stay a year ahead, so, for me, that meant keeping up with the details of ten trips for the current year and ten for the next. That is a demanding mental exercise when you consider that any given tour has about twenty or so working parts, and with a group of twenty to thirty people, there are no "small" mistakes.

So, for years, I told myself I needed to cut back to six or seven tours. As each year rolled by, I got on that wonderful merry-go-round of travel, and I never cut back. I loved what I was doing, and I would always think of all the tours I wanted to repeat. It wasn't about the money. I had been to all those beautiful places, and I wanted everyone to see the amazing sites that I had seen and to have their own wonderful experiences.

By the end of 2019, I had led 290 tours, and by the end of 2020, my tour total would stand at 300. Maybe 2021 would be the year that I would finally cut back.

As the New Year began, we were busy managing the details for all the coming tours. In January and February, we began to hear about a virus that had started in China. Slowly, with each passing week, it seemed to creep nearer and nearer. It made its way to Seattle and the Pacific Northwest. As the months progressed, the news got worse. We slowly realized we would have to cancel a few trips in the first part of the year. Then the 2020 COVID–19 pandemic struck in full force, and the entire travel industry shut down.

As we saw that we would have cancel all our trips, and that we could do nothing about it, a calm actually filled my spirit. I fell back on the same basic Bible verses and spiritual truths that had carried me through the years. This would be another journey, and God would be with me and send his angel before me. God would still use both good and bad experiences to refine my faith and sculpt me into the image of Christ. So, God gave me a peace in the midst of the storm, and I looked to see what would be the highest and best use of this free time I had suddenly received. I had plenty to do in winding down the year's tours and building new tours for the following year, but I still had room for more activity. As I thought about the extra time, I realized this gave me time for something I had wanted to do for years—write an account of my own life journey.

I love biographies, and I always loved looking at others' fascinating journeys to help guide me along my own path. As I read the stories of others, I noted the key doors that opened, which ones shut, and what bridges led people forward on their journey through life. Now I had time to look at my own journey and write about it to help and guide others. So here it is. I hope it will be a living experience in your life and an active agent, helping you on your journey. I pray that God will bless you and be to you the pathfinder and provider that he has been to me.

Russ Head
Thomaston, Georgia, July 31, 2020

INTRODUCTION

The vehicle of travel has shaped a lot of my life. Without a doubt, some of the most formative years of my life were my post-college years of working around the country in resorts. I look back on those years as "the great graduate school of my life." During those years, I was always reading history and biography. What I read was not dead history or biography from the past. It was a living agent God used to show me who He created me to be. As I read others' biographies, I saw these people as vicarious mentors to challenge me and push me to be all God had created me to be. I saw biography as a mirror in which God defined who I was, sculpted my mind and my spirit, and shaped the course of my life.

In all my readings, whether of Teddy Roosevelt, FDR (Franklin Delano Roosevelt), William Borden, or Henry David Thoreau, I was defining who I was. At the same time, I was also seeing how travel played an important part in others' growth. This confirmed to me the importance of what I was doing. I always saw those years of resort travel as an experiential "university of life" that was preparing me for the future. Now, as I am living that future of creating and leading tours, I seek to make travel and the things we do on a tour an active agent in shaping the lives and thoughts of those who go with me.

The following pages include some of the significant moments in my life's journey. Some moments were funny, some were sad, some confusing, and some were heartbreaking. This is the stuff that our lives are made of. I hope this biography will not only mentor you, but will also inspire you, challenge you, and cause you to look within yourself. I hope it will show you how God's presence has been part of my life from the very beginning. And I hope this encourages you to see how His presence is laced through your life, too.

Russ Head
Thomastón, Georgia

1

BIRTH AND EARLY YEARS

I was born on September 14, 1955 in the small southern town of Thomaston, Georgia. My father was a doctor, and as was the custom, he deferred the lead of my delivery to his friend Dr. Justice Gower while my father assisted. But I was not the only one born. My identical twin brother, Doug, came out before me. Maybe because I was left alone in the dark of the womb for seven minutes, I developed a penchant for seeking the solitude and sanctuary of a quiet place, a place to think, reflect, and make sense of the continuing journey of life.

Being an identical twin would shape the course of my life. Doug and I have always been very close, and we have always had a symbiotic, supportive relationship. That relationship has acted as a mirror image that I could always approach to test out theories, to confide in, and to look to as an ever-present source of love and support. Yes, we often irritate each other and are combative, but that also shapes us.

My father was Douglas Lamar Head, and my mother was Sara Ann Kilpatrick. She was dynamic and creative and lived a life of the emotions and the spirit. He was loving and just and kind and possessed a heavy dose of logic and reason. While Daddy had a soft and loving side, he was also stable and steady and unemotional when it came to making decisions.

Science says our brains have two sides and that most people lean one way or the other. The right side of the brain is the artistic, creative, aesthetic, emotional side, and the left side is the logical, steady, practical side. If this is true, and I think it is, Daddy was predominantly left brained, and my mother was predominantly right brained. In turn, I think I am predominantly right brained and got more of Momma's characteristics, and my brother Doug was born predominantly left brained and got more of Daddy's characteristics. In the end, Doug gravitated toward banking, and I gravitated toward art, literature, and creating tours.

Momma, being artistic, was always making scrapbooks, and early on, she got interested in and learned all about sixteen-millimeter film. Because of momma's love of film, she documented a good bit of our early life on silent moving pictures. In those films, I can see the day Doug and I were brought home from the Upson County Hospital, where we'd been in incubators for a few days because we weighed just over five pounds at birth.

SUSAN

Waiting at home, along with Gert, Daddy's trusty hunting dog, was our sister, Susan. Born five years earlier, Susan always looked over us as a kind of loving, surrogate mother. In the early days she loved us, but from time to time she could get a little fed up with all the attention that the two little twins received. Once she got so fed up that she blurted out, "If y'all don't stop talking about those twins, I'm going to throw them in the trashcan!"

In spite of that threat, she has been a true north star, ever faithful, always there, a constant stream of love and support. Susan is very thoughtful, kind, and loving, and a holiday or birthday never passes without our receiving a card from her in the mail. In our later years, our bond with Susan and her husband, Darryl, has grown more with the passing of time. They have been not only a great source of love and support, but they have raised two wonderful children, John and Katie, who are a blessing to us all.

MY FATHER

As we grew up and got to know our parents, we saw that they were distinctly different personalities. For my father, everything seemed easy and simple. Decisions in life seemed clear and logical, not cluttered with the fog of emotion. He was a great and skilled doctor in all the ways a doctor can be great. He was a gifted diagnostician with a loving common touch that gave him a wonderful bedside manner. Everyone seemed to love my daddy, and as my life's journey played out, people were always willing to give me a chance based on their love and deep respect for my father.

How often has someone told me how much they loved my daddy and how he delivered them or their children. How many times have I heard, when someone was sick, "I wish Dr. Head were here." Once a man brought his wife, who was not feeling well, to my father's office. My daddy examined her and was a little puzzled about her illness. During the following night, my father woke up from his sleep and began to think about what might be wrong with the woman. He suddenly had a *Eureka* moment and called the man the next day, telling him to have a certain doctor check his wife for cancer. It was done, and she did have cancer.

A number of years after Daddy's death, I took walks with Dr. Mac Dallas, a surgeon in my town. Dr. Dallas loved and respected my father. On one of our walks, Dr. Dallas made a point to tell me what a brilliant doctor my father had been and that if he had devoted more of his time to medicine, he would have been known throughout the southeast as one of the greatest doctors of his time. But Daddy chose to lead a more balanced life. He devoted good portions of his time to family, friends, golf, hunting, and playing poker and gin rummy. This balanced life and common touch was why he was so beloved. He had a beautiful gift of being equally comfortable talking to the wealthy and poor alike. There was not a pretentious bone in his body.

It seemed as if everything was easy for my daddy, I know it wasn't, but it sure seemed that way. He was a great golfer, and if he had devoted his life to golf, he could have been a professional. He, along with a few others, held the lowest score of 63 at our local country club. He and his best friend, Bethel Ingram, both won the club championship five times.

When I had trouble with the mechanics of my swing, he would say, "Boy, just go ahead and hit the ball!"

It was as simple as that for him. I would reply, "Daddy, apparently you don't have a central nervous system. The rest of us do, and it's just not as simple as you think for the rest of us."

My father loved hunting dove and quail. His father had raised bird dogs, and he was raised on hunting. He was a natural and gifted shot. Just as I was never the golfer my father was, I was never the shot my father was either. God gave me my own talents, but daddy was so gifted in so many areas that it was a bit intimidating to live up to the expectations I thought he and others had for my potential.

He was a great father. He was loving, just, and kind. He was strong where he needed to be strong and loving and caring when he needed to be loving and caring. He was secure enough in his own masculinity that he did not shy away from the softer side of his character. Till the end of his life, he always hugged us, told us he loved us, and kissed us on the forehead.

In 1974, I came to make the decision I pray everyone will make: To accept Christ and embrace a loving, just, and kind heavenly Father. That step of faith was made easier than it would otherwise have been because every day I saw before me a loving, just, and kind earthly father.

In addition to logic and reason, my father had a good sense of humor. Sometimes he creatively combined these qualities. While I was in college, I felt listless and tired all the time. I was falling asleep in my classes. A friend of ours said that he'd read that a certain Dr. Erdmann, who ran the Erdmann Clinic in Philadelphia, had developed a treatment of cold packs that, when applied to the back along the spine, would stimulate the patient, renewing energy and clarity. I told Daddy about this treatment and felt that daddy would find merit in its efficacy. He quietly and patiently listened and then said, "Well, if that's true, then an ice-water enema should do you wonders!"

For quite a while, my father was the doctor for the local football team. The love and respect the coaches and players had for him went beyond the field. Often, one of the coaches, Clint McAbee, and a star player, Ronnie Lowe, would come over to our house at night to talk and listen to music on daddy's state-of-the-art stereo system. As a little boy, I enjoyed being in the room with them and listening to their conversation with the music in the background. People loved my daddy for the whole of who he was, especially for the common, down-to-earth person he was. They loved to be with him, play golf with him, hunt with him, play poker or gin with him, or just sit around a den and laugh and joke with him.

My father was always a steady part of our lives. While his work required a lot of time, he was there for meals, and he was there at night after he did his rounds at the hospital. I always knew my father loved me, even during my high school and college years. We never went through times when I felt like, "He just doesn't get it!" I received a great advantage in life by growing up with a strong, sensitive, and loving father.

MY MOTHER

My mother died when I was ten years old, so I did not get to experience a life-long relationship with her. However, during those ten years, she imparted to me many of the things that make up the person I am today.

In my memory, she seems a tragic heroine. On one side she was smiling and charismatic, full of creative energy, dynamic, full of life, and with an unfulfilled desire to see the country and the world. She was very loving to my friends and me. Everyone loved her in much of the same way my daddy was loved, but she was loved for her own distinct personality and qualities.

She was always working on projects. She had a stamp collection, which she meticulously organized in big books. She learned all about 16mm motion pictures and closely documented our lives. She had a collection of travel material, mostly about the USA, and we would get out maps and travel files and plan a trip to go see our Aunt Flora in Kalispell, Montana. We laid out a driving plan that took in many of the country's great national parks. We never took those trips, but years later, life came full circle when I, through the tour company I developed, would visit all the places we had planned to go. Being around Momma, and caught up in her kinetic energy, I absorbed the wanderlust, the collector, the organizer, the dreamer, and the traveler that radiated from her persona. I so wish she could have lived to see me leading tours all over North America and Europe.

My mother was a driving force of nature. She got us to play football and baseball. But we also loved putting together model airplanes and cars, so she got us models at Maxwell's Dime Store on the square in downtown Thomaston. She once called Mr. Maxwell after closing hours and got him to open the store just so we could get a model. Sometimes when we went to get a model, Momma said, "Now get David Short one too." David was our good friend who lived down the street.

Momma also had a tragic side. Shortly before Doug and I were born, Momma became addicted to prescription drugs. She would get very groggy at night, and sometimes we found her passed out in the kitchen. This didn't happen every night, but when it did, we would go get Daddy, and all together, we would roll her onto a towel and drag her through the house to their bedroom where daddy would get her in bed.

Once when we were seven or eight years old, Momma, Doug, and I were sitting at the table for lunch, and Mattie, our loving maid, was in the kitchen. All of a sudden, Momma started screaming. I'm vague on how it ended, but I think Mattie calmed her down, and we called Daddy. I do remember that our next-door neighbor was sitting outside, waiting on us to go and play. He asked us what the noise was, and we just said Doug and I had been playing.

Another time Daddy must have been at the golf course, and Doug and I were in the den. Whether Momma called or we heard a noise, we went and looked into the bedroom and saw her standing in the middle of the room, holding one of Daddy's pistols to the side of her head. How we handled that is again a bit vague—the mind seems to blank out certain memories—but I assume we begged her to stop.

Children, I think, are far more resilient than we expect. They are more emotionally and psychologically malleable than adults are. These experiences had to have been traumatic, but for some reason, they never had a dark or negative effect on me. The Bible says in Romans 8:28 that God uses all things, both good and bad, for good in the life of those who love Him and are called according to His service. I am so thankful that this early trauma did not result in my going down a dark road, but heightened my sensitivity and made me more introspective. Like the electric pads used to restart the heartbeat of a heart attack victim, the shock of these traumatic events, combined with Momma's passion for life, jump-started in me a ravenous, insatiable curiosity and passion to experience and taste all the richness and vibrancy of life.

Momma died during the night on Labor Day, September 5, 1966. She had not done well the previous night, but there was no real cause for alarm. When I woke up early that morning, the door to our room was closed. For some reason, my first thought was that Momma was dead. I don't know why I thought this because she had not really been sick the night before, except that I had seen her in the bathroom with a bit of blood coming from what must have been a puncture made by a hypodermic needle. Doug, who had also seen the blood and the puncture wound, said that, later that night, Momma had come through the den, looked at him lying on the floor, and said, "Did you think that I was going to die?"

Maybe God was preparing me that morning. I got up and walked down the hall. The whole house was quiet. I looked into Momma and Daddy's room and saw Daddy and his mother, whom we called Adele, with their backs to me. A doctor's bag sat on the floor by a chair, and the bed was still unmade. Then Daddy said, "Well, I'd better go tell them."

I tried to get back to my room before he could see me, but he saw me in the hall and told me to go to the den, that he had something he needed to tell us.

Daddy got Doug up, took him to the den, and sat us down on the sofa. Susan was still sleeping, and he chose to tell her later. When Daddy told us that Momma had died, I felt a mixture of sadness and relief. Sadness because I loved her and relief because all of the trauma that we had been through with her addiction would no longer be an unpredictable intruder that would walk onto the stage of our lives at any given moment.

We also asked, in that moment, if Adele could come live with us. She was my father's mother, and our only surviving grandparent at the time. She lived with us for about two years to help out. Two years later, when daddy remarried, Adele returned to her house. in Zebulon, Georgia.

The Bible says that God can use all things for good in the life of a believer, even when bad things happen. I can now see a silver lining in the trauma that was laced through our early lives. One is that, quite often, a young child is sailing along, not thinking about this thing called "life." Later, through various experiences, he begins to think more about what life means.

As I have said, the trauma acted like shock pads on the chest of a person whose heart has stopped beating. Traumatic events early in my life shocked me out of obliviously cruising through life to awaken within me a deep passion to know life and to know its importance, to know the interior landscape of people's lives, who they are, what they think, and why they do what they do. This led to my fascination with biography.

The early trauma also developed in me an inner spiritual life, a desire to look deeper within myself and others, to discover life itself and to explore why things and people were are the way they are. This retreat into, and love of the mental journey and the life of the mind might also have been my intuitive attempt to retreat into a world I could control. I am so thankful that this early trauma didn't send me down a dark path.

In thinking of my growing passion for life, I can really relate to the words of Henry David Thoreau. In Thoreau's great philosophical work, *Walden*, he said,

> I went to the woods because I wished to live deliberately, to front only the essential facts of life, and see if I could not learn what it had to teach, and not, when I came to die, discover that I had not lived. I did not wish to live what was not life, living is so dear, nor did I wish to practice resignation, unless it was quite necessary. I wanted to live deep and suck out all the marrow of life, to live so sturdily and Spartan-like as to put to rout all that was not life, to cut a broad swath and shave close, to drive life into a corner, and reduce it to its lowest terms, and, if it proved to be mean, why then to get the whole and genuine meanness of it, and publish its meanness to the world; or if it were sublime, to know it by experience.

I think I got a lot of Momma's personality, her outgoing passion for life, her curiosity about life and the world, her love of people, and her desire to travel. In the trauma of her life and death, she jump-started in me a passion for life, biography, and introspection and a desire to drink deeply from the spiritual reservoir created through the journey of life.

MATTIE

Mattie Cleola King, our loving maid, started working for our family probably before Doug and I were one year old. I can see her in Momma's 16mm movies, overseeing our playtime on our big terrace. She would stay with my family even after Doug and I left for the University of Georgia in our junior year of college. Mattie loved us as if we were her own, and we loved her dearly. Mattie's husband had died early, and she had never remarried and never had children. She always referred to us as "her boys."

Mattie knew that Momma's health was precarious, and she promised momma that, if anything ever happened to her, she would stay with us until we went off to college. Mattie kept her promise in what she no doubt felt was a commission from the God she loved and served with all her heart.

When we were babies and ready to move from baby food to more solid food, Mattie asked Daddy if she could give us some more substantial food. Daddy trustingly replied, "Mattie, I don't care what you give them; just don't kill them."

Mattie was proud of us, and when we played peewee football, she always made sure our uniforms were clean and in good shape. When we went to a parade uptown, she made sure we looked nice. She would inspect us and make sure we were presentable and proclaim, "I don't want y'all to go uptown looking like ragamuffins!"

Mattie was a Jehovah's Witness, and she was devoted to her God and her church. When we were older, she always wanted us to attend a special communion service held only once a year.

If possible, we would go, and she would introduce us with a big beaming smile as "her boys."

When we graduated from high school, Mattie prepared us for college by teaching us to cook the full array of Southern dishes: fried chicken, biscuits, cornbread, country fried steak, pork chops, green beans, mashed potatoes, and butter beans. We knew that most meat, pork, or chicken made its way to the table only after the obligatory stop in the black cast-iron skillet, properly prepared with a big dollop of Crisco.

One Saturday morning, when Mattie was teaching me to cook, my girlfriend came over. When she walked in the door, Mattie looked at Jennifer and said, "Now, Jennifer, Russ can't be studying you this morning, because I am teaching him to cook!"

Mattie proved to be a good teacher, and we ate well at college.

Mattie watched over us through the years. Even beyond college, she kept in touch with us, and we visited her after her retirement all the way to the time she died in the mid-1990s.

MATERNAL GRANDPARENTS "MISTER AND NANNIE"

My mother was an only child, the daughter of Herschel and Gertrude Kilpatrick. We called them "Mister" and "Nannie." It is interesting to learn how children develop names for grandparents. Mister and Nannie owned a hardware store just off the main square in downtown Thomaston, Georgia. Although it was called a hardware store, our grandparents sold almost everything. The store was divided into two main sections—a gift shop my grandmother ran and a hardware/variety section that my grandfather ran. On the hardware side you could buy anything from a hammer and nails, to a baseball uniform, glove, and ball. On the gift shop side, Nannie sold everything from Madame Alexander dolls and bridge club supplies, to china, and everything a person might need for a bridal registry.

Mister died very early in our lives, in the early 1960s, so I only see him in my mother's films. After he died my grandmother moved the gift shop to a front room in her house on West Gordon Street. Everyone loved my grandmother, and they loved shopping at her gift shop.

Nannie was a notoriously bad driver. She was short and plump and drove a big Buick with a big steering wheel. To see over the dash to drive, she had to look through the steering wheel. Early one morning, she put the car in reverse instead of drive and hit the gas. The car careened backward over a seven-foot wall and down to the street below. The car then swerved left across the street and into a house, knocking a young boy out of bed.

It was around eight o'clock in the morning, when people were going to work and school, and it is a miracle no one was hurt, not even the boy who got knocked out of bed. He later said he could see the front fender of the car sticking into his bedroom.

Nannie later executed a fantastic wreck downtown in which she managed to damage eight cars. To this day, she holds the downtown driving record for the most cars hit in a single wreck. I can only imagine this feat was fueled by a full tank of panic, requiring both forward and reverse gears, and a steady foot on the gas. Then she refused to exit the vehicle until her son-in-law, my father, arrived at the scene. After that wreck, a man named Buster drove for Nannie, and the streets of Thomaston were a good bit safer.

Nannie had a wonderful maid named Evangeline Stinson, whom we called Auntie. Like Mattie, Auntie loved us and treated us like her own. Auntie was a great cook, and we always ate with Nannie on Thursday nights.

Nannie was sweet and loving. She died in 1965 when we were nine years old, so I have limited memories of her, but I do remember spending a night at her house. Before bed, she insisted on taking a warm, wet handcloth and wiping the "klinkers" out of our eyes.

PATERNAL GRANDPARENTS DOC AND ADELE

My father's parents were Douglas Lamar Head Sr. and Adele Smith Head. Daddy became Douglas Lamar Head Jr., and when daddy had twins, he split his name. He named me Russell Lamar and my brother James Douglas. James came from our paternal great grandfather, and I was named after Russell Johnson, who lived beside us. He traveled all over as a salesman for Thomaston Mills, the cotton mill that was a major employer in our town. He and his wife, Virginia, had a matchbook collection from all the places they had visited, either through business or for pleasure. That match collection added a spark to the flame of my dreams fostered an excitement of travel.

We called daddy's mother Adele. I don't remember why we starting calling my grandmother by her first name, but that does not seem to be so odd.

We called our grandfather "Doc" because he was a doctor, and his father before him had been a doctor. Later, when neither Doug nor I became doctors, we ended a proud and admirable family tradition that had lasted for at least three generations.

Daddy's father had pretty much determined that daddy would be a doctor. By the age of twelve or so, Daddy was going to wrecks and helping his daddy sew people up. Doc was the town physician in Zebulon, which is about twenty miles from Thomaston. He not only had an office on the town square, but he also built a clinic there which served as a small hospital. Patients could stay overnight at the clinic in the care of a night nurse.

Doc also loved hunting and raised bird dogs. When Daddy was a small boy, it was his job to take the dogs out and run them. Daddy got his love of hunting, fishing, and medicine from being immersed in these three pursuits from birth.

To prepare Daddy for the rigors of medical school, Doc sent Daddy to one post-high-school year at Darlington, a preparatory school in Rome, Georgia. He then sent Daddy to Little Emory at Oxford in Covington, Georgia, which further prepared my father for medical school. Daddy then finished undergraduate school at Emory in Atlanta before going to the University of Georgia School of Medicine in Augusta.

Because Daddy's life was so planned by his father, and worked out so well, I think it is remarkable that Daddy kept his hands off the steering wheel of my career path. I am thankful that he did, but I think it required a lot of patience and self-control, especially since I took such an unconventional path.

Daddy gave us a lot of freedom in what we did. We were never really questioned, even when we were going to rock concerts at a time when drugs were a big part of the music culture. I later marveled at his courage and patience to give us that freedom. When I asked him about it in later years, he replied simply, "I was willing to trust you until you gave me a reason not to."

Again, based on how my grandfather, Doc, had planned out my daddy's life, I think it was a remarkable facet of daddy's parenting that he gave Doug and me so much freedom to find our own way.

My grandfather, Doc, was beloved by the town of Zebulon. Just as they have done with Daddy, people through the years have always come up to me to say how much they loved my grandfather, exclaim about his wonderful personality, and explain that he delivered them and their children.

Later in life, in the 1950s Doc began to have heart attacks, and then he had a crippling stroke, which caused him to give up his medical practice. Those who knew him said the stroke took the wind out of his sails and changed his sunny personality. They still loved him, but the old Doc was changed forever.

The Doc I knew used a crutch with an arm brace and had a brace on his leg and foot. He was quiet, but he still went dove hunting. He would find a stand on the edge of the field, sit in the shade of a tree, and shoot using one arm.

I also remember Doc and Adele coming to visit on Sunday afternoons. Doc walked slowly with his crutch, got inside, and sat on the sofa. He would ask for a small glass of tap water, because he believed it was bad to put cold water in your digestive system.

Doc died of a final heart attack in February 1965, three months before Nannie died. So, before I was eleven years old, my mother and three of my four grandparents were dead. We were left with Daddy and his mother, Adele.

Adele was a sweet, quiet person. She loved us and was so pleased whenever we visited her. She lived with us from when Momma died in September of 1966 until Daddy married my stepmother, Mary, in June 1968.

GOD ADDS TO AND EXPANDS OUR FAMILY

After our mother's death, through daddy's rock-solid love and character, our grandmother Adele's coming to live with us, and the devotion of Mattie, God provided the security in which our lives could move forward, grow, and evolve. Our family found a new structure and orbit through the next two years.

God is always working in unseen ways behind the scenes in our present to prepare us for our future. In those days, the east coast of Florida was a very popular vacation destination for people in Thomaston. For many, Daytona Beach was the place to go. The Reef Motel was a modest, seafoam greenish-blue, two-story hotel that was simple but just right as the place to stay. There is a lot of footage on Momma's 16mm films of us at The Reef. Those films show us swimming and playing in the ocean with many of our Thomaston friends.

In 1967, Doug, Daddy, and I went on a vacation to Daytona Beach. When we were driving down, we asked him if any people from Thomaston would be there. Daddy said a patient of his and her two daughters who would be there. Hmm. . . .

We met Mary and her daughters, Cindy and Kim, outside of Daytona at a filling station. This vacation would be the beginning of God's adding to our family. Daddy and Mary dated and finally married on June 8,1968. Adele returned to live in her home, and we began our lives as a new blended family.

God is always working with a big overview of our lives. He sees who we are in the present, but he also sees who we will become in the future. One day while Daddy and Mary were dating, Daddy asked Doug and me what we thought about his marrying Mary. I thought (but did not say), "If you want to marry Mary because you love her, you should marry her; but if you are marrying her to give us another mother, we don't need one."

In my twelve-year-old mind I was not against it; I was just being practical and thinking about the basic reality of what I saw and felt. God knows us better than we know ourselves; He knows what we need. I am now thankful that God was taking care of us at that time and in our future. In the years to come,

Mary provided for Doug and me, as well as Daddy, in so many ways I couldn't appreciate at the time.

In the years to come, our blended families would adjust to our new situations and find our way as a family and as individuals. I think Mary was the quiet heroine of the whole bunch. Daddy was already settled, and children are resilient, but Mary was joining a challenging family and social dynamic. Momma had been a dramatic force of nature who was well known and loved in the town. Mary was quiet, and had to try to settle into her new place with us, with daddy, and just as challenging, in the community. Mary didn't try to replace Momma; she was just who she was, and in the long run that was best. In any situation, it is always best to be your authentic self and draw on your own unique identity, and that is what Mary did.

Mary was a quiet, strong survivor with a good sense of humor. As our lives moved forward, Daddy and Mary built their lives, both together and in their social life.

We children did the same thing. Susan was older, and her journey was different from ours as she went away to the University of Georgia. Doug, Kim, Cindy, and I all got to know each other and settle into our new family life. As I later learned when Daddy died, any big changes that occur in life take you out of an established orbit. It always takes a while to find your new place in the social and psychological solar system.

In life, we always find security in an established orbit, controlled by the gravitational pull of those in whose social and familial orbit we find ourselves. When Daddy and Mary married, as when Momma died and when Daddy would later die, we were all thrown out of the life orbit we knew, and in time, we eventually settled into our new orbit as life restarted.

As our new family evolved, we worked through the initial awkwardness and, through the years, grew to know and love each other on deeper levels. When Daddy died in 1999, our love for Mary took on a new perspective as Doug and I tried to honor Daddy by taking care of Mary. Doug used his business acumen and compassion to reassure Mary in her sadness and uncertainty.

Through the years, I have seen God's overarching wisdom of the past, present, and future revealed again and again. When Doug married and had children, Mary became a loving grandmother to Sarah Ann and Mary Kathryn. They have loved her, and no one could have loved them more than Mary.

2

GRAMMAR SCHOOL AND HIGH SCHOOL

In spite of the traumas, I would say I had a happy and stable childhood. Daddy was always the steady rock.

GRAMMAR SCHOOL

In grammar school, I was an average student. I began to make Bs in the second grade. I have always probably had attention deficit disorder. Or maybe I was just lazy and undisciplined, or perhaps a mix of all three things. I tried my best, but math, science, and even grammar and composition were hard for me. I was a slow reader, and I had difficulty concentrating on what I read. In the second or third grade, students were divided into three groups—advanced, average, and slow. I was never in the advanced group, but at least I held my own in the average group. There was one time I fell to the slow group, but I worked hard and pulled myself back to the average group.

In second grade, we had to do book reports. I usually did my reports on a state in the United States. I can see in my memory my book report on Texas. I told everyone about Texas, drew a map of it in color, and drew the state flower and the state bird. Momma's interest in travel and her travel files probably had a good bit to do with my developing a travel-leaning mind.

Because of my trouble focusing, I stayed in a confused state of comprehension. In fourth grade, the school had a reading program called the SRA Reading Lab. We read stories and then answered questions based on what we had read.

We progressed through various color-coded levels at our own pace. The beginning levels were drab colors, like brown or gray. When we finished one level, we progressed through green and yellow and red, and finally ascended to the glorious heights of reading excellence in silver and gold.

My confidence took a big hit with the SRA Reading Lab, as I stayed mired in the mental quicksand of brown and gray, moving in slow-motion while seeing the pretty girls disappear in the distance on their smiling way to silver and gold.

I started making Cs in the third grade. It wasn't because I didn't try. Math and science were hard for me, and I only enjoyed stories in English and history class. I always had a good imagination, so I quickly began to live in the magical world of literature and history. I remember living in the idyllic world of Alice and Jerry as their lives played out in our reading books. This gift of imagination and a burgeoning sense of the spiritual magic of the mental journey were being born in me very early. It also became a place of escape from the sense of failure and low self-esteem I faced in math and science.

Momma died when we were in the sixth grade, but I don't think it significantly affected my schoolwork. I simply continued to struggle. A highlight of my seventh grade was when Mrs. Mary Freeman read to us for the last forty-five minutes or so of the day. She read Majorie Kennon Rawling's book, *The Yearling*. Mrs. Freeman was a great reader, with a soft clear voice, and I entered the magical world of the story. It was wonderful. Through this, a love of storytelling captured me from an early age.

Another good memory of grammar school was eighth-grade Georgia history. My imagination would kick in, and I would lose myself in the story. I was marching with the Spanish on Desoto's exploration of Georgia. I was there with General Oglethorpe as he laid out the city plan of Savannah. This was magical, but all the rest of the classes brought me out of the fascinating mental journey and back into the drudgery and difficulty of math and science.

SPORTS

In grammar school, Doug and I played farm team baseball and peewee football. We were pretty good, but we were small. I never got into baseball, but I really liked football. However, early on, I found that I didn't like the pain of football, whether through getting hit or delivering a hit. Drills like "bull in the ring" and "red and blue" served the purpose of getting you used to being beaten to a pulp. Due to our size, those drills never worked out too well for either Doug or me.

For a while we practiced on the same field as the next level, and that level looked even more painful. In our last year of peewee football, Doug was a halfback, and I was the quarterback. The town youth were divided into a number of teams, and we played each other. We had fun and did pretty well. Doug's first touchdown was a long run down the sideline where he jumped over a dog sleeping in the field. When Doug jumped over him, the dog got startled, jumped up, and knocked down the only little defender who had a chance of catching him.

In spite of our modest success, because Doug and I were small, we usually found ourselves on the painful end of most transactions. We decided to hang up the football and baseball cleats after peewees. We looked for a kinder and gentler sport. And there it was, a sport our father loved—golf.

When we were seven or eight, Daddy bought us our first set of golf clubs. We spent most summers in the last half of grammar school at the golf course, either playing golf, swimming at the country club pool, or working behind the counter in the pro shop.

OUR EARLY ATTEMPT TO RUN OUR OWN BUSINESS

The house Doug and I came home to was on Avalon Road, across the street from the beautiful home of George Hightower Sr. Our house had two stories. Momma didn't want to climb stairs with twins, so in that first year Daddy built a new house nearby on Cherokee Road. This was near the hospital and the neighborhood became popular for doctors. Six doctors, including our family, lived within three blocks of each other, and the neighborhood became known as "pill hill."

Two of our best friends were also twins. John and Jim Edenfield's father was a Tom's candy distributor who supplied cookies, crackers, and candy to stores and vending machines all around the region. In our first ten years, we did almost everything with the Edenfield twins. They lived next door, and we played golf and army together. We also had a band that did a few "concerts," pretending to play and sing the songs of Herman's Hermits. We had one real acoustic guitar, and the rest of the instruments were fake. Stools and cushions acted as a set of drums.

When Daddy bought land for the new house, he bought three lots. The two lots on the backside of our house were at first open woods where Daddy could take his beloved bird dog, Gert, and go quail hunting right out of our back yard. Over the years, a new neighborhood began to develop in that direction. As it did, Daddy held on to those lots. Gradually they were cleared, and the main lot behind us became an open field where we would play.

Over time, Doug and I and the Edenfield twins would build a football field and a baseball field in that open area. We took shovels and scraped the grass away to make the baseball field. We bought lime and lined everything off and even got some old discarded base bags to use as bases. There was a big backstop, and with this in place we had a first-rate baseball field. The neighborhood had plenty of kids to come and play. One of them, David Short, has continued to be a good friend to us through the years.

With the same sense of industry, we also built a football field. We also lined it off with lime. We got long, straight limbs and made two sets of goal posts. On one Labor Day, we had a big football game. Word got around the neighborhood, and cheerleaders showed up; then someone showed up with a set of chains to mark off first downs. That game almost ended on the opening kick-off when Chuck Thompson, a bruising running back, caught the ball, came down field like a freight train, and was met midfield by David Short. David's older brother, Steve, was our coach, and just before the titanic collision, Steve yelled, "Lower your head, David!"

Both players were laid out by the great head-on impact. Thankfully, neither was seriously hurt, and eventually, each got over his pains, and play was resumed.

As wonderful as our football and baseball fields were, our greatest creation in the "back field" was when we took shovels and scraped off grass to make greens. We designed a nine-hole pitch-and-put golf course. We took some discarded wood from a nearby construction site and built a store to sell drinks, candy, and crackers which we got at Mr. Edenfield's Tom's distributorship. After school, neighborhood kids would show up and buy something to drink and eat, and maybe pay to play a round on the pitch-and-put course.

We also offered golf lessons. The lessons didn't last long because someone hit a long drive that landed in a street on the backside of the course, took one jump, and hit a big bay window of a house beyond. It didn't break the window, but the incident ended the lessons.

THE IMPACT OF JOHN KENNEDY'S ASSASSINATION

When I was in the third grade, John Kennedy was our president. He, his wife, and their children were a living vision of beauty and love of life. Television was coming of age, and the combination of that image of life and beauty made a big impact on me, as well as much of the country. Television made the Kennedys seem like an extended part of our family. For a young person, that vision wasn't affected in any way by whether we were for or against his political views.

Then on Friday, November 22, 1963, a sunny and beautiful day in Dallas, Texas, John Kennedy was shot and killed. Suddenly something happened that I had never considered to be possible. That vision of beauty and light and life was destroyed and silenced forever.

Psychologically, it was like having a beautiful painting that you lived with as part of your life, and suddenly, a madman slashed it, threw paint on it, and destroyed it beyond recovery.

I was left concussed by that psychological and emotional explosion. Later, an image in *Life* magazine of Kennedy's two rocking chairs stacked on a dolly and being rolled out of the Oval Office poignantly confirmed that the fairy tale was over, leaving only a memory in its place.

I was in Mrs. Doyle Ward's class that day. The assassination took place at about 12:30 p.m. Dallas time. That would have been 1:30 p.m. our time. I was on the playground when I first heard about it. We later sat at our desks in the classroom and listened to the radio commentary of the final moments in the emergency room and of the priest being called to give the last rites.

That psychological trauma and the nonstop TV coverage over the next days and weeks seared my mind with the first shock of an emotional, white-hot effect that made me come fully awake from the drowsy sleepwalking of youth. Two more life-altering events would happen in those early years. What was going on with momma, and her death, was the next. And the third was a visit years later to the Little White House, the home Franklin Delano Roosevelt built in Warm Springs, Georgia.

WORKING AT THE GOLF COURSE

My first real job experience was working at the local golf course. Our father was a great golfer, and we naturally had a desire to play. When we were about seven or eight years old, Daddy gave Doug and me sets of Ben Hogan junior clubs. My daddy loved Ben Hogan, and those clubs were really nice. He gave us a few pointers to get us started, but he mainly let us develop a natural swing on our own.

When you start playing golf at a young age, it is easy to watch, imitate, and develop a natural, fluid swing. I never took a formal lesson. I do remember Daddy watching every now and then and giving a few instructive comments. He played with a group of good players, and we played with our friends.

As a result of being at the golf course a lot, we began working behind the counter in the pro shop. We were about ten or eleven years old when we started working. We sold drinks, crackers, balls, and gloves, and kept the shop in order.

Over time, we caddied for our father and other players, and eventually we cut the greens and fairways, raked traps, and drove trucks and tractors. All these jobs were a great introduction to the working world. We learned to be dependable, conscientious, and courteous.

These jobs also taught us the feeling of a job well done, and they instilled in us the good feeling of monetary gain through disciplined work. We continued to work part time at the golf course, even through the time we commuted to our first two years of junior college. We went to Gordon Junior College in the morning and worked at the golf course in the afternoon. Numerous people worked with us, but Johnny Wells, Dale Straughn, Doug, and I were a working core for a good while.

It seems that during all of my working life before travel, odd things seemed to happen. After college, these odd occurrences would follow me into resort work. The four of us at the golf course were dependable, focused workers, but we managed to tear up a good bit of equipment. One time Doug was spraying the fairways with a tractor and a spray rig which included a big barrel of chemicals on the back of the tractor. The chemicals were sprayed through two long spray booms, or wings. You had to look back as you sprayed the broken and rolling landscape to make sure that the wings didn't hit the ground and cause a spray-nozzles to malfunction. Doug was spraying and looking back to make sure all was running smoothly when he ran into the only pine tree within thirty yards. Fortunately, the old tractors were built tough, and the only thing damaged was Doug's pride.

Another time, I was cutting the fairway on the fifth hole, driving a tractor and pulling a big gang of reel mowers behind me. I felt something burning my rear end. The tractor was a typical green John Deere with a yellow seat. I would drive a short way and then feel the burn. This happened a few times, and I kept looking at the seat but saw nothing. Finally, around lunchtime, I pulled the tractor over, shut it down, and walked to the clubhouse. After lunch, when I returned, all that was left of the yellow seat was springs and ashes. I guess a shorted-out wire somewhere was making contact with the seat. Weird things just seemed to happen.

At the end of one day's work, I drove the tractor to the big old corrugated barn. I was daydreaming as I approached the barn at top speed. I suddenly realized that I needed to hit the brakes—fast. I took my foot off the gas pedal and slammed it on the brakes. In my panicked reaction I hit the clutch instead of the brakes, which sent me into the tractor stall, where I slammed into the corrugated metal on the back of the barn with a bang. What seemed to be the entire back of the barn bowed under the blow of the tractor. I finally found the brake. Oddly enough, as I put the tractor in reverse and backed up, the back side of the barn just followed it back into place. I just had to dust off the skid marks, and no one ever knew there had been an accident.

We also used the big gang mower to mow the fairways and the area near the greens. J. M. Caldwell was a wonderful boss, and we all got along well. One day, as Johnny Wells was mowing the fringe of the ninth green with the gang mower, J. M. flagged him down. Johnny pulled up and shut the tractor down. J. M. said, "Johnny, we need to be really careful when we mow around the greens. We are running over the water hoses and tearing them up, so just be careful and keep an eye out for the hoses." Johnny replied, "I sure will. Got it!" Then Johnny cranked the tractor and drove no more than twenty feet when he hit a hose and sent it spiraling into the air. He looked back to see J. M. with his hands on his hips, shaking his head and staring up to heaven. J.M. was, no doubt, uttering a few unheavenly words.

Another time Johnny dropped a wrench into the gas tank of the tractor. I am not quite sure how that happened, but we were all adept at doing things people would think couldn't be done. Good ole J. M. patiently figured out how to fish the wrench out and had it almost out of the tank when Dale Straughn slapped him on the back, exclaiming, "Mr. J. M., there's more trouble on the western front." Of course, this jolt caused J. M. to lose hold of the wrench, sending it back into the depths to the darkened tank. The trouble, Dale explained, was that, while trimming the bushes on the front of the clubhouse, a short in the cord running to the electric trimmers had set the bushes on fire. This sent everyone immediately around to the front of the clubhouse to find a small bushfire sending smoke into the air. The smoke had alerted everyone at the club pool, and all the children were bringing little cups of water to try to put out the fire. In the end, at least we were dependable and showed up sober.

HIGH SCHOOL

High School was a quiet time for me. I didn't play any of the major sports, so it was like walking through a movie set, watching the stars live out their big parts. I think there are moments in life when, like the slow growth of a tree, you are in the process of becoming, but nothing dramatic seems to be happening. That would all change in my sophomore year.

THE LITTLE WHITE HOUSE PLAYS A MAJOR PART IN THE COURSE OF MY LIFE

My grandmother Adele always talked about President Roosevelt, Warm Springs, and the Little White House. She said one day Doc came into the house after having been to Greenville, Georgia on a house call. This would have been in the mid-1920s, after Roosevelt began coming to Warm Springs to get treatment for his polio and before he ran for president. Doc told Adele, "I just met a man from New York at a filling station in Greenville, and I think he will be president one day." Hearing stories like this and others, Roosevelt captured my imagination.

Later, when Doug and I were in high school in about our sophomore year, and after Adele had moved back to Zebulon, we decided to go with her to see the Little White House, where Roosevelt had lived. This was my first visit there and, just as importantly, it was my first visit to any kind of historical site. I cannot underestimate the impact that visit had on the course of my life. When we walked around the grounds and stepped into The Little White House, the whole experience was absolutely magical. It electrified me and seized my imagination. I saw the den where Roosevelt had the cerebral hemorrhage, the bed where he died, the antique feel of the whole house; it was all shrouded in a transformative excitement. I thought, "This is where it all happened." Everything I saw was alive with the romance of real history, living history. It has continued to live in my memory in a sort of dream-like state. As I walked around, I thought, *Roosevelt touched this. What I am seeing and touching, he saw and touched.* The emotions were so intense that that experience was a watershed event God would use to shape my future. These moments happen throughout our lives. Unexpectedly, we turn a corner on the road of life, and we have an experience that shapes us forever.

When I combine the impact of John Kennedy's life and assassination, the trauma of Momma's life and death, and then this experience at the Little White House, it all awakened an introspective mindset which led me to the living sacred wells of the mental journey in life. That, in turn, led to my love of history, and the magical transformative nature of biography. I began to live in biography as if I were really there. The men and women I read about became my mentors as they challenged me, inspired me, pushed me, and defined me.

Slowly, the people I met through biography began to shape how I saw things and transformed the vision and landscape of my future. That love of history and biography led me to study history and eventually led me into a love of travel and my tour business. I wanted to see, stand in, and touch the places I had read about. I wanted to commune with the spirits of the people I had read about and let them shape me. Today, on my tours, when I take people to a historical site or a beautiful national park, I am trying to recreate for then the magic and the romance I felt that day at the Little White House. Let me say that again. Today, on my tours, when I take people to a historical site or a beautiful national park, I am trying to recreate for travelers the magic and the romance I felt that day at the Little White House.

For most of my high school years, life was slow and easy. We were either on the golf course or hanging out with close friends. Most girls went for the big sports stars, and I didn't have much confidence to make a play for anyone. Like the movie set, I was on the sidelines, watching the game and lacking the confidence to see what would happen if I got in the game.

FALLING IN LOVE FOR THE FIRST TIME

That all changed my senior year when I had study hall during fifth period. Study hall was in the auditorium, where people could spread out. A beautiful freshman girl named Jennifer sat in a section ahead and to the right of me. She needed help with her math, and I began trying to help her. That was a joke because I was never good at math, but we both liked me trying to see if I could help her. Our chemistry was just right. We were comfortable together, but with all the excited energy of experiencing love for the first time. A friend had a Honda 175 motorcycle, and I started borrowing it after school to take Jenny for rides. I had never ridden a motorcycle before, but we had fun learning.

The first time I borrowed it, we rode outside town to a creek. We walked along the creek until we came to a spot where there were big smooth rocks where you could sit by the stream and talk. Up until this relationship, I had always been shy and awkward with girls, but with Jenny I felt relaxed and comfortable. On our way back, when we tried to cross a difficult part, I fell in the creek. We were comfortable enough with each other that it didn't really embarrass me. I just stood in the creek, helped Jenny across, and we rode back home with me soaking wet.

My relationship with Jenny was the perfect one for a first love. Her parents loved me and Daddy and Mary loved her. It was wonderful. It was what I would call a "free-fall" love, where you emotionally jump off a cliff together. Since it was my first love, it never occurred to me that it could ever end or that anything could ever happen to what we felt for each other.

Our relationship had started in March, and I graduated in May. Doug and I had been accepted to the University of Georgia, and we went for orientation that summer. We quickly realized that we were not ready to go to college. We shifted gears and enrolled in Gordon Junior College in nearby Barnesville. Over the next two years, we commuted to Gordon and worked at the golf course. This was a great transition for us as it gave us time to grow up a little more and then go off to Athens and the University of Georgia.

Jenny and I were cruising along that summer with my getting ready to begin college and Jenny getting ready for her sophomore year in high school. Jenny was a popular cheerleader. One of her friends convinced her that if she continued to date me, she would miss all the fun of high school. I never saw the breakup coming.

The confidence and trust of that freefall love was suddenly shattered. I was lost for weeks with no interest in dating, while she reentered the fun of her busy high school life. Within a month she wanted to come back—and we tried—but I couldn't get over the shattered feeling and the shock of what we had gone through. I felt as if we had created a beautiful bowl together, and we had dropped it. It had shattered into a thousand pieces, and we couldn't put that bowl back together.

The Bible says that all things work together for good for those who love God, and looking back, I now see that it worked out for the good. We had a great first love, and now she is happily married with children and a wonderful husband. On the other hand, God opened a path for me to an incredibly wonderful and fulfilling life that would be so suited to the person I would become. In the words of Marilyn Monroe, "Sometimes, good things fall apart so better things can fall together." In looking back over my life, I can certainly agree with the wisdom of that philosophy. In other life events this youthful experience has also been instructive. This has become one of many examples to me of how God knows us better than we know ourselves. Psalm 139 describes how God knows us intimately. He knows who we are, who we are becoming, and the person we will become, and his dreams for us are far better than our dreams for ourselves.

All of us experience moments we don't see coming, which will forever change life as we know it. These moments can be both good and bad. The night I first believed in Christ, I was cruising along and didn't see it coming. All the spiritual ingredients were in place, but I had no idea that I was about to turn a corner in life. What God revealed to me changed me forever in the best possible way. Other moments are not so nice, like the year of COVID–19. I finished the year of 2019 cruising along, my life and business were booming, with every expectation of a big 2020. Then suddenly, what seemed so sure was knocked down. Some people are shattered by a divorce they never saw coming. Others receive a cancer diagnosis or the sudden loss of a child or unexpected financial ruin. All these things can rock our lives, and, in some cases, permanently change the way we look at life, relationships, and God.

What have I learned over the passing years that I suggest to help others prepare for these moments? One thing, even for the devout believer, is to realize that the Bible should give you no expectation that your life in this world will be a bed of roses. Jesus prayed in the garden that he would be spared the cup of the cross, but it was not to be.

I am always amazed when someone rejects their faith because of a tragic event in their life. If they have read the Bible at all they should realize that the believer is not always spared difficulty and tragedy. While tragic events may rock our world, they should not leave us disillusioned. After all, the central event of the Bible and history is the cruel death and crucifixion of God's Son at the age of 33. Jesus was killed after only three years of a what, in earthly terms, seemed like such a promising future, lived out in the loving service of others. But we need not forget that the crucifixion is followed by the resurrection and the revelation of what all that meant in the course of history and eternity.

What does this tell us? That God is working out our good for eternity. In this world, we are assured of his love and presence. We are assured that he will not leave us nor forsake us. But he does not necessarily protect us from harm or difficulty. He allows bad things to happen to good people. In eternity, the believer is assured of a happily-ever-after, but what can we hold onto in this world? Romans 8:28–29 assures believers that whatever happens in our lives, whether good or bad, God will use it for good. In concert with this verse is 2 Corinthians 3:18 which tells us that the Holy Spirit is using all things to shape the believer into the image of Christ. God is shaping us not just for this world, but also for eternity.

In light of all this, we need to be making daily deposits into a spiritual bank account so that a life event, even a serious one, does not change our identity. Our identity is found in Christ first, not our health, our wealth, our social status, or our marital status. First and foremost, every day, if possible, we need to pray, study the Bible, and meditate and marinate on who we are in Him and what that means.

Jeremiah 1:5–10 tells us that God knew us and had a plan for us before we were even a thought in our parents' minds. Colossians 1:16 tells us that we are made by God and for God; therefore we are meant to find our meaning and purpose in relationship with Him. The Bible is His owner's manual, giving us all we need to know to take that life journey with Him. We are to make daily deposits into a spiritual bank account from which we make withdrawals on a daily basis.

Our identity and self-worth must be defined by Him. If we place our identity in others or wealth or physical health, we are in for a roller coaster ride that cannot ultimately satisfy us because we were created by Him and for Him. The Bible also shows us the big, eternal picture to help us sort through the often-complicated question of "How could a loving God allow that?" A good starting point would be that a loving God, for eternal purposes, didn't even spare His own Son the cup of the cross in his efforts to make a way for us to get back to Him. There are so many questions that are unsolvable or in which we can find no peace outside the perspective of eternity.

3

COLLEGE YEARS

Many people consider their years in high school and college to be their glory years. For me, that was not so. While my years in high school and college were fine, they were a time of quietly growing, evolving, and preparing me for the rest of my life. I think of that time like the silent growth of a tree when nothing much seems to be happening, and later you look to find it has evolved into a big, beautiful tree. Also, I was a slow reader who had to study hard just to make average grades.

GORDON JUNIOR COLLEGE

I spent my two years at Gordon Junior College commuting, studying, and working at the golf course. I actually went through my whole college career in a low-key and disciplined manner. Most people experience fun and freedom in college, but I would later experience that in my post-college years of resort work. I simply wasn't smart enough to play and study at the same time.

I was also a late bloomer. I sought the safety, comfort, and security of trying to do the right thing and keep the rules. I didn't do this from a religious sense, but out of an intuitive sense of safety and security. Within me was an unexpressed fear of the scary, dangerous, and unpredictable consequences of breaking the law, breaking rules, or breaking societal norms. Now I also see clearly that I so loved and revered my father that I intuitively felt that any action or activity outside of the light of his approval was a dark and dangerous place I dared not venture.

Even so, during my freshman year at Gordon Junior College occurred the most pivotal event in my life.

CONVERSION

In February 1974 I was a freshman, and a lot of things were working and conspiring toward a spiritual awakening in my life. Maybe I was like that tree where nothing seemed to be happening, but internally things were lining up for a change.

Because of my loving father, I desired to be good, but it was more out of love and admiration for him rather than any knowledge of Christianity or Christ. I also had a vague romantic desire to seek the truth. Sunday school and church had little effect on me. I never gave much thought to the possibility of knowing God on any intimate level. Christianity seemed to be more a philosophy of doing good in memory of God and Jesus. I think I was reading a little of the Bible, but it wasn't having much impact on me.

During the summer of 1973, after high school graduation and before I went to junior college, I took a step closer to something spiritual when a Billy Graham crusade came to the Atlanta stadium. I had seen Billy Graham on TV, as my father liked to watch him, but we never talked about what we saw or heard, and nothing seemed to make any substantial impact. I must have absorbed a vague sense of what he was saying, and maybe this was floating around in my subconscious, waiting for what the Bible would call "the fullness of time." The Bible talks about seeds being planted, watered, and bearing fruit. When Mr. Graham came to the Atlanta stadium, I attended and even answered his call to come forward to receive Christ. But I don't believe it was yet the fullness of time. I would call that night a "creeping closer."

Then one day, months later, during winter quarter at Gordon Junior College, George Ford, my neighbor and friend from high school, asked me if my brother, Doug, and I would like to meet with a few people at West Side Park in Thomaston to talk about the Bible. He pitched it more like a chance to talk rather than a formal Bible study. We went that night, and maybe five of us were there. I'm not even sure any believers were among us.

In the end it didn't matter whether or not any believers were there because we were honest seekers, and the Holy Spirit was there. That night I heard a lot of the things I had heard many times before—that God wanted to have a personal relationship with me and that it was possible through Christ.

As I sat there, what I had heard so many times before suddenly meant something. It was as if I were beginning to see, hear, and believe the truth in a way I had not before. That night, I guess you could say Jesus performed a modern miracle. I, who had been blind to spiritual truth, could suddenly see it for the first time. I, who had been deaf to spiritual truth, could suddenly hear it for the first time. In the twinkling of an eye, I believe God gave me the gift of belief, and I realized that Jesus was the answer to life's questions. It was as if I had been living in a dark room, and God had suddenly turned the lights on. An image came into my mind: If the cup of life was half full of mystery, Jesus was the only thing that could fill the cup of mystery with a yes. Even today I realize that I don't know all I might want to know about life, but I am satisfied with what was revealed to me that night and in the years that followed. God may not tell us all we want to know, but He tells us all we need to know to have peace, purpose, love, forgiveness, and perspective.

That night God gave me the gift of faith in Jesus Christ. I heard what I had previously heard so many times, but this time God revealed Christ to me. It was as if a veil had been taken away, and there was Christ, "the way, the truth, and the life." The first chapter of Galatians describes this perfectly where Paul says, "For I neither received it of man, neither was I taught it, but by the revelation of Jesus Christ . . . *when it pleased God*, who separated me from my mother's womb, and called me by his grace, to reveal his Son in me" (Galatians 1:12, 15,16, emphasis added).

That night I went home and knelt beside my bed and prayed, "Lord, I don't know if you are in my life or out of my life, but I know you are the answer. If you are in, stay in, if you are out, come in now." And He came into my life that night; He took up residence in my heart, and nothing has been the same since.

In John 17:3, Jesus said, "And this is life eternal, that they might know thee, the only true God, and Jesus Christ, whom thou hast sent." That night a new relationship was born in my heart and mind and being. Something that had not been in me before was born in me that night. That night Jesus came in through the Holy Spirit and took up residence in the manger of my heart.

In John 14:23, Jesus talked about how he and his Father will come and make their abode with the believer. Before that night, it was *me*. After that night, it was *us*. In a very real way, I had been "born again," and in the best possible sense, life would never be the same again. This is the single most important event in my life, and it came out of the blue when I least expected it. It was like walking along on a dusty, endless plateau through scrub pines and rocks, and suddenly coming upon the Grand Canyon of life. What an incredible blessing. It happened in college and would radically change the rest of my life.

When the Holy Spirit comes in, you begin not only to desire to read God's Word, but through the guidance and interpretation of the Holy Spirit, the Bible suddenly means something, and you can understand it.

The group of people I was with had come together with no expectation to meet again, but something dramatic had happened, and now we wanted to meet regularly. But we needed a teacher to lead the Bible studies, and there was just us. And so, lacking a leader, Doug and I became the initial leaders. That was an incredible blessing because it forced us to study the Bible and teach it to others. We were babes in Christ feeding on the "milk of the Word" and growing. In time, others like Steve McGuire, would help lead the Bible study. I think there was a tremendous outpouring of the Holy Spirit during this time. Many people we knew were coming home from college and they too had become believers. They would hear about the Bible study in the park and just show up. One night we met down by the creek and there were about sixty people. I think the Bible study lasted about six months, but it fed us and others, and when it ended, we were strong enough to walk on our own.

As I said before, sometimes in life you are walking along with the days passing in a seemingly uneventful way, and then you turn a corner, and *bam*! Something happens, and you are never the same again. When George Ford asked Doug and me to come to a meeting at West Side Park in Thomaston, I had no idea that that night my life would change forever. George thought enough of Doug and me to invite us, and I am forever grateful for his acting on his impulse. For him, at the time, it may have seemed like a very small thing to ask us, but God used him to change both Doug's and my life forever.

THE UNIVERSITY OF GEORGIA

After graduating from Gordon Junior College in the spring of 1975, Doug and I transferred to Georgia in the fall. Again, I wasn't smart enough to play while I went to school, so my years at Georgia were low key with my nose to the academic grindstone. At Georgia I had a second watershed spiritual moment in my life.

WILLIAM BORDEN: A WATERSHED MENTOR IN MY CHRISTIAN LIFE

When we first believe, we are "born again," and we begin a journey of spiritual growth. The Bible says, "Desire the sincere milk of the word that ye may grow thereby" (1 Peter 2:2). Just as in the physical life, God does not intend us to remain babies. Colossians 1:16 says we are made "by him and for him." God wants us to grow and mature in him so that we can evolve more and more into the image of Christ. In doing so, we also evolve more and more into the unique image of the person He created us to be—and in that process, we experience the deep meaning and fulfillment of living out His unique purpose for our life.

Along the journey of our spiritual life, there are watershed moments when we seem to see or learn something significant in our walk. God is always working with the big picture in mind, and sometimes when we least expect it, He sends a person or a book or an experience that makes a big difference.

One such person in my life was William Borden. You may have never heard of him. He died in 1913 at the age of twenty-five.

I never knew him in the conventional sense, but through the wonder of written biography, William Borden had a tremendous impact on my spiritual journey.

When I first became a Christian, I tried to be as good as I could be—to be like Christ. I still do, but Satan can often take the best of intentions and pervert them into something bad. Second Corinthians 11:14 says that Satan masquerades as an angel of light. I believe that is true, and that his temptations are clothed in a bit of truth and light. Love is good, and God intends us to love others, but Satan can also take love and twist it into a variety of sins. When someone becomes a Christian, he or she tends to swing toward either legalism or liberty. Paul often talked about the bondage of legalism, but he also warned about using God's grace and forgiveness as an excuse to indulge in the pleasures of sin.

When I first believed, my personality leaned more toward legalism. I wanted to be as good as I could be, and Satan took that good desire and twisted it in such a way that he slowly and subtly turned my focus away from Christ and my relationship with Him into having me focus on rules and spiritual details. Mind you, I had the best of intentions, but Satan took that and began to lead me to a place where I was focusing on the rules rather than the relationship. Over time, he slowly bound me up in a spiritual straitjacket of legalism. Jesus said, "I am come that they might have life and, and that they might have it more abundantly" (John 10:10). But my increasing focus on legalism slowly and subtlety sucked all the joy and freedom out of my life.

And this is where William Borden, who lived nearly a century before me, came in with a ray of hope that I could break free from the straightjacket of legalism that bound me. In my desire to be good, I would examine everything I said or did, looking for what seemed to be sins and driving me into guilt, saying, "Was what you said totally true? Was what you did right?" I was constantly looking at everything I did and assessing whether it was good or bad. I would find myself in the library, torn between trying to study and thinking that I should witness to everyone within sight. I was definitely not living the abundant life.

My history courses were on the north campus at Georgia, which abuts the downtown area of Athens. Sometime during my time at Georgia, I walked into Logos Bookstore a couple of blocks from campus. I wandered around, looking at the titles, and eventually looked over some books on a sale table. Suddenly my eyes fell on a yellow book with a title that intrigued me, *Borden of Yale '09.* The thought of Yale conjured a romantic sense of virtue mixed with the pursuit of academic excellence. I picked it up, and the mustard-colored cover listed the title and a drawing of a sailboat with its sails outstretched and seagulls flying low over choppy seas. On the back cover was another sailboat and a saying, "Tis the set of the sail, and not that gale that determines the way we go." The book was written by Mrs. Howard Taylor, and it was a biography of a man named William Borden. I had never heard of him, but the cover intrigued me enough that I bought the book. Little did I know that it would be a shining light to lead me out of the repression and darkness of my legalistic bondage.

William Borden had accepted Christ as a young boy and lived a passionate and devoted life. A key to his charm and popularity with almost everyone he met was his authenticity and passion for life and the Lord. He did everything with passion. Whether it was wrestling, sailing, playing golf, or pursuing his faith, he did it with passion and without the least bit of half-heartedness or affectation. Borden died at a young age of cerebral meningitis, and a tribute was published about him in a Toronto newspaper.

That piece offers a great description of the beauty of his life and his way of living:

> It was a natural life. Someone has said that every Christian needs two conversions, first from the natural to the supernatural, and second from the supernatural back to the natural. But it was not so in William Borden's case, for though he was thoroughly converted to the supernatural, he was never converted away from the natural. From first to last, he remained as God had made him, not trying to be anyone else however distinguished that one might be, and not thinking that sanctification meant *can't* or morbidness or denial of the pure and wholesome pleasure of life. Strong of body, he loved to live.

As I read the book, a hope and joy flooded my mind that God meant what he said. We were meant to have a joyful and abundant life. He meant to set us free from the guilt and the bondage of the law. I felt this was a direct message from God, and I slowly gained the spiritual confidence to break free of my legalism and to revel in the joy and freedom of who God had created me to be.

GRADUATING COLLEGE—WHAT'S NEXT?

As we approached our graduation, believe it or not, neither my brother, Doug, nor I had thought much about what we would do when we got out of college. Doug had a business degree, and mine was in history. My very vague plan was to teach high school, but before that, I wanted to invest in a few post-college years of travel in what I would later come to call my "experiential extension to an academic education." I funded those years of travel by working around the country and seeing first-hand the historic places I had studied about. But as I approached graduation, I could only see a few feet down the road of God's plan for me. That plan would slowly unfold over time.

In February 1978, during my final year at Georgia, Elizabeth Smith, a beautiful girl I had an interest in, asked me what I was doing after I graduated. We studied in the library at the same time, and while nothing ever became of my interest in her, the casual question she asked me became a God-appointed door to my future.

I suddenly realized that I hadn't thought much about life beyond college. After all, that was four months away, which was an eternity at my age. I said I thought I might go to Cape Cod and find a job. I had an interest in the Kennedys, and I wanted to see Cape Cod. She said she would work on Mackinac Island in the Great Lakes. I had never heard of Mackinac Island. A month or two later, some other friends of ours, Montie and Peggy Hendricks, who were in the same sorority as Elizabeth, said they too were going to Mackinac Island. And just like that, through seemingly insignificant events and others' plans, the next chapter of my life began to take shape. Here was the boy who was reluctant to leave the security of home and the things he knew. Now a new dynamic was taking place. A slowly evolving vision of what travel could add to the person I was becoming began to gain momentum and help me break the bonds of insecurity. But bonds and grave clothes sometimes come off in stages. I was not quite free of some of my old insecurities, and I began to think that as long as I wanted to travel, I might as well start out with people I knew. You never know in life when a "chance" conversation, such as the one I had with

Elizabeth, becomes a door that God opens into the next chapter of your life. For me it would become "the great graduate school of my life."

THE GREAT GRADUATE SCHOOL OF MY LIFE

After graduating from the University of Georgia, for about five years, I worked in seasonal resorts around the United States. This time was invaluable in sculpting the person I was becoming. Herman Melville referred to his time spent working on a whale ship as his "Harvard and his Yale." Theodore Roosevelt talked about what some considered his "wasted time" out west, but he concluded that without that invaluable experience, he would never have become president of the United States. I consider my five post-college years of resort work to be the great graduate school of my life preparing me as nothing else could for the work of designing and leading tours.

When I graduated with a degree in history from the University of Georgia in 1978, I thought I was headed toward a future of teaching history. Sometimes, when your life's road twists and turns, you get only a partial view. From reading history and biography, and to prepare for teaching history, I developed a desire to see the places I had studied. I wanted to visit the places where historical people who meant something in my life had lived. I wanted to see what they saw and touch what they touched and commune with the spirit of those people in those places where they had lived. I wanted to drink deeply from those experiences, to take it all in and let those places and settings have their effect in sculpting the person I was becoming. I wanted to think about life, to take it in and let it make its mark on my individuality.

I wanted to travel, and I paid my way by working in seasonal resorts. I worked a summer and fall on Mackinac Island in Michigan, a winter in Palm Beach, Florida, two summers and falls in Bar Harbor, Maine, two winters and a summer in Big Sky, Montana, and a summer and fall on Nantucket Island, twenty miles off the southern coast of Cape Cod.

As Corrie ten Boom said, "Every experience that God gives us, every person He puts in our lives is the perfect preparation for a future that only He can see."

These five years of "migrant work" were the best preparation in so many ways for the main work of my life, which would be teaching. But instead of teaching in a conventional classroom, I would eventually have the best of all worlds: teaching to a willing, rather than captive audience—and doing it on location!

During the years when I worked in resorts work years I kept journals. Keeping a journal of the experiences and things I learned during those years proved to perfectly prepare me for the rest of my mental, spiritual, and work life. I cannot say enough about the education I gained by keeping those journals.

Three things converged and worked together to make my resort years such a rich experience:

1) *I did the beginning resort years alone* and therefore it was a rich time of introspection, journal keeping, and communing with the Lord. I was by nature a bit fearful and insecure, so finding myself alone heading out of the harbor of the safe and known into the great sea of an unknown future forged in me an intense, personal moment-by-moment walk with the Lord. The wonderful result is that today that moment-by-moment walk, which was so intense then, became an ingrained reality that is the preeminent feature of my walk of faith today.

2) *I had become a Christian* in the winter of 1974. The spiritual truths I was learning and my relationship with Christ provided a spiritual/psychological framework from which to interpret what I was reading, what I was writing, what was happening, and who I was becoming. The Christian perspective helped me make sense of what I was experiencing and learning. Assimilating all I was experiencing and learning within this Christian superstructure helped me define my true, divinely related character and identity. Rather than my living in a darkened room and trying to figure out who I was and what life was about, God had turned the on lights of His eternal truth giving me peace, purpose, hope, unconditional love, and perspective.
3) *I kept a journal.* The journals began in Palm Beach. At first these journals recorded what I did, what I ate, what I thought, and what I spent money on. But soon I began to record deeper thoughts about what I was reading, what I was thinking, what was happening, and who I was. During these years, with the help of the journals, the Lord and I built a psychological/spiritual house I would live in going forward. We built that house plank by plank, nail by nail, and shingle by shingle, and it was so fundamental, so spiritually sound, so balanced in the way of logic, reason, and imagination, that it is essentially the same psychological/spiritual house I live in today. While I am subject to mistakes, bad decisions, or depression, like anyone else, this house has served me well in all the years since that time. It was a house that God was building for all eternity because He intended to live there with me.

Writing the journals also trained my mind to think, organize, gather information, and assimilate what I learned. Thinking through what I was doing while traveling by the seat of my pants would train my mind to assess a situation and make decisions on the fly, a skill that would be vital in leading tours in the future. My five years of travel and resort work prepared me as no other experience could have for my future career of creating and leading tours to Western Europe and North America. These years were truly the great graduate school of my life.

A TIMELINE OF MY TRAVEL, DIARIES AND BUILDING THE SPIRITUAL HOUSE OF THE FUTURE

I worked at the following places:

- Mackinac Island, Michigan: June–October 1978
- Palm Beach, Florida: January–April 1979
- Bar Harbor, Maine: May–October 1979
- Big Sky, Montana: December–April 1979 / 1980
- Bar Harbor, Maine: May–October 1980
- Big Sky, Montana: December–April 1980 / 1981
- Big Sky, Montana: May–August 1981

Then I briefly returned to pursuing degrees, first at the University of Georgia, working on an English degree September–December 1981. Then I continued working on my degree in English through Tift College with Teresa Lowe doing private studies in the winter quarter of 1982. Spring quarter of that year found me student teaching under Ruth Pressley in history at R. E. Lee Institute March–June 1982.

I then returned to my pursuit of the world:

- Nantucket Island, Massachusetts: June–November 1982, hotel/fish market
- Trip to Africa: Summer 1983

I taught in the classroom for a year, then got into my career of travel:

- August 1983–June 1984: teaching English at Pike County High School
- Summer 1984–Present: working at The Travel Connection

4

MACKINAC ISLAND, MICHIGAN

1978

Mackinac Island is a small island in the Straits of Mackinac; the slim body of water that connects Lake Michigan to Lake Huron. The state of Michigan is divided into two pieces, the much bigger lower part, which looks similar to a left-hand mitten, and the upper peninsula, an elongated piece that borders the top of Wisconsin and extends east into the Great Lakes and borders on its northern side with Canada.

The lower part of Michigan is a wide peninsula embraced by Lake Michigan on the west and Lake Huron on the east. Interstate 75 runs through the center of the lower peninsula of Michigan to the northern tip and crosses the straits of Mackinac over the Mackinac Bridge to the upper peninsula. If you were to cross the "Mighty Mac" bridge and look east, you would see Mackinac Island.

Doug had not thought a lot about what he would do after college, so to buy a little time before setting off on his career and to have an interesting experience, he decided to go with me to Mackinac Island. We graduated in May, and waited until July 15 for the wedding of our good friends Pete and Debbie Cavan.

Doug and I planned to drive to Mackinac after the wedding. Montie and Peggy Hendricks, friends from UGA who were also twins, were going to work at the beautiful and historic Grand Hotel, and through them we had communicated with the hotel about mid-summer job possibilities. They basically said to come on up and that they would have jobs for us. A large number of their employees were in college and had to return to school in August or September so the fact that we had graduated and could stay into October to help them close up made us invaluable as employees.

When we arrived on the island, we interviewed for jobs, and the Lord provided great situations for both of us. We would live together in a private room in the pool house, which was on the beautiful lower grounds of the hotel, right beside the pool. Doug worked in the kitchen and then as pool manager, and I was a "porchman." Doug managed the huge pool area with its lawn and lounge chairs, and I wore a uniform and made sure the longest hotel porch in the world was clean and that all its rocking chairs were in place and in good working order.

WORKING AT THE GRAND

"Mackinac" ends with a "*c*". It is a French word meaning "turtle," which was what the Native Americans called it. Contrary to the island's spelling, Mackinaw City on the Michigan mainland is spelled with a "*w*", which is how the word, whether spelled with a *c* or a *w*. is phonetically pronounced. So, phonetically, you would pronounce it "Mackinaw Island."

Part of the island's history is tied to the fact that it was a major base of John Jacob Astor's fur trading empire. Today, Mackinac Island is a wonderful tourist destination with a magnificent fort, stunning Victorian-era homes, a great harbor, and a lost-in-time feel with wood frame buildings. The centerpiece of the island is the magnificent Grand Hotel which is an architectural masterpiecc. The extra icing on the cake that makes Mackinac so special is that all transportation, except emergency and construction vehicles, is horse-drawn, bicycle, or foot traffic. To further preserve the atmosphere, construction vehicles must be used only between midnight and 6:00 a.m.

The Grand Hotel is a stunning wooden hotel on a bluff overlooking the Straits of Mackinac. Its magnificent columned façade has a wonderful porch, which takes full advantage of the incredible view overlooking the straits. Because of its dramatic position and architecture, the Grand Hotel generates a lot of romance and excitement in the hearts and minds of visitors as they approach the island by ferry.

During my time at the Grand Hotel, I got promoted from porchman to doorman and finally to assistant head of food and beverage. As doorman, I helped load and unload carriages with arriving or departing guests at the grand stairs which led up to the porch and the hotel's front door. I had no qualifications for my final position as assistant head of food and beverage except that I was college educated, responsible, and could stay the season. They must have really valued my other qualifications, because they promoted me in spite of the fact that I didn't drink and didn't know how to mix a drink.

I had a great summer and fall on Mackinac. This was the first semester of the great graduate school of my life. I met great people, reveled in being free, and let my mind run in regard to what I wanted to read. I had been academically disciplined in college, and now I could enjoy the feast of life set before me. It felt so wonderful to be in a gorgeous place with no need to study and where all the possibilities of the future lay before me. I realized that this could be the template for all my future stops. As I saw the hotel's constant need of good employees, I realized that, being free from the restrictions of returning to school, I was a much-needed commodity in the seasonal resort world. As a result of my free schedule, my biggest question in the future would be: Where would I like to work next?

One of the most influential books I read on Mackinac that summer was Rose Kennedy's, *Times to Remember*. That book was an exciting history of the Kennedy family, and it inspired me as I contemplated my future. It also convinced me that travel should be an important part of my education in preparing for that future.

So, by the time I left Mackinac, I was convinced that working in resorts was a logical way to pay for travel and work for an extended time in different areas of the country. With school behind me, I reveled in the incredible joy and excitement of who I was becoming. My decision to go to Mackinac was such a great first experience in this way of life.

At the Grand, we worked seven hours a day, seven days a week. Yes, seven days a week! All the other places I would work I would have days off, but not at the Grand. We could arrange days off, but working seven days a week was the norm. This may sound burdensome, but it really wasn't. Everyone was working, we had half a day off, the island world was small, and we were making money, so it was fun and exciting. Even though the entire circumference of Mackinac Island was only eight miles, we never lacked for something fun to do.

The social life on Mackinac was great. The pool house had a number of rooms, and Montie and Peggy Hendricks, our UGA friends, also lived there. We had a great group of friends to go out to eat, to go dancing at night, and to explore the interior of the island during the day. I had a girlfriend, Tomison Wilson, a Michigan girl, whose father was the legal counsel for the hotel, and we had lots of fun. Jim Duffy, the pastry chef from Cleveland, Janet Hutto from the University of Mississippi, Julie Chrysler from Atlanta, and many more people made this the perfect first-semester experience . Later, I would read about the life of Corrie ten Boom, whose words would prove prophetic for me, and I paraphrase her again, "**Every** experience God gives us, **every person** He puts in our lives is the perfect preparation for a future that only He can see."

Everything I was learning and feeling on Mackinac was the exciting first phase of the incredible and formative time in my life.

AFTER MACKINAC, WHAT NEXT?

When I got home in the fall, I assessed my options for continuing travel that would finance itself. I came up with two choices. One, I could work at resorts, or two, I could work for an airline. I decided to apply for employment with Delta Airlines and continued to evaluate which mode of travel would best serve my goals. My father had a former patient who worked in the Delta employment office, and he called her. She said I should come up, fill out an application, and then ask to see her.

In November of 1978, I went to the Delta office at the Atlanta Airport. I filled out an application and asked to see this lady. I immediately got an interview, was seemingly given a green light, and then went to see the company psychiatrist the next day, which many said was the final hurdle before being offered a job. Then I went home and waited.

By January, I had heard nothing from Delta, and I was getting restless for an answer. Then something happened that was to occur a number of times in my life. God is so practical. He gave me a vision of what I should do and followed that with a conviction that I should pray and lay the decision before him.

While I prayed about my decision, God directed me to make a practical list of pros and cons of how each job would lead me to my goals. When I did this, all the pros fell to resort work and few fell toward working with Delta. After all, these years were to prepare me for a career in teaching, not a career in the airline industry.

My immediate vision was to live in an area, get to know it, and learn the lessons life had to give. While working in a resort for six months or so would accomplish that end, flying in and out of locations with Delta clearly would not.

When I saw this, I had a sinking feeling. Daddy had helped me get an interview at Delta, and I felt sure I would get the job. But at the same time there was no question in my mind which way I should choose. The very next day—yes, the very next day—a letter came from Delta, dated January 4, 1979. I still have it, and it said,

> Thank you very much for coming to our office for personal interviews. All persons with whom you came in contact enjoyed meeting you and talking with you.
>
> We have carefully reviewed your application for employment, and I sincerely regret that we will be unable to offer you encouragement for a flight attendant position with Delta. We have relatively few openings and an extremely large number of well-qualified applicants; therefore, the competition is extremely keen.

> Again, let me personally thank you for your interest in Delta Air Lines, and I wish you much success in your future endeavors.

That rejection was a wonderful answer to prayer and a confirmation of my strong feelings about what was the best path for my future. The rejection was a great relief, as I wouldn't have to explain to daddy why I would decline a job offer from Delta. A door had clearly shut and another had opened.

During the time I was waiting on the reply from Delta, I had been thinking about Plan B. I decided that a winter in Palm Beach, Florida, would be a place to further explore my fascination with the Kennedy family, who had a winter home there. So, in mid-January, I was off to Florida.

5

PALM BEACH, FLORIDA

1979

I first heard of Palm Beach because of President, John Kennedy. As a little boy, I knew nothing about Kennedy's politics, but I was drawn by the vision of a vibrant, youthful, and beautiful family that always seemed to be smiling and living life to the fullest. To a young boy or girl in the early 1960s, John and Jackie and their children were an image of wonder, of a sheer love of life, and beauty that you were drawn to and wanted to be a part of.

After Kennedy's assassination, I began to read biographies about him in an effort to keep that dream alive. In the pages of a book, that image of truth and beauty still lived vibrantly, still laughed, still played football on the front lawn in Hyannisport, and still sat smiling and clapping in the Oval Office as his young children danced and played around the room. Through biography, I could still be a part of that truth and beauty.

And so, biography began to be a wonderful, vicarious way to live in the presence of charismatic and interesting people, people whose lives challenged you. In the pages of a book, you could live with them and be shaped and challenged by them. Also, in the pages of a book, you could look at the person and compare yourself and your ideas to them to help you define who you are.

Along with the Kennedy winter home, Palm Beach was unique and different. My friend Jim Duffy, who had been a chef at the Grand Hotel was living in a nice condo on Marco Island and offered me a place to stay and to help me get a job. Another friend, Jim Edgecombe, who had been a doorman at the Grand, lived in Boca Raton, and said I could get a job there, but, in the end, I chose Palm Beach because it had a unique, one-of-a-kind feel. The other places by comparison seemed homogenized. I wanted to be shaped by the unique and different. I wanted to mine the riches of the road less traveled.

INTO THE UNKNOWN

I left for Florida on Tuesday, January 16, 1979. So here was that sheltered boy who hadn't wanted to leave home, going not just to a faraway place but into a great unknown with no job at the end of the line. I had only the Lord to accompany me as I walked into the future. In the end, this uncertainty would forge a deep and intimate bond with the Lord.

The great thing about living spontaneously was that it forged my intensely personal, moment-by-moment relationship and dependence on the Lord that would serve me well then and into the future. When I look back into that past, there seems to be an unbroken lifeline of His presence in both good and bad times. Psalm 139 speaks about how deeply and intimately God knows us, and how He is with the believer in good times and bad.

> Thou hast beset me behind and before, and laid thine hand upon me. Such knowledge is too

> wonderful for me; it is high, I cannot attain unto it. Whither shall I go from thy spirit? Or whither shall I flee from thy presence? If I ascend up into heaven, thou art there: if I make my bed in hell, behold thou art there, If I take the wings of the morning, and dwell in the uttermost parts of the sea; even there shall thy hand lead me, and they right hand shall hold me. (Psalm 139:5–10, KJV)

In spite of feeling vulnerable and insecure, I knew I was meant to follow this path. My passion and conviction that I wanted to travel and learn from life first hand moved like a tidal wave in my vision and overwhelmed and pushed through my insecurity, my feelings of vulnerability, and the uncertainty of what lay ahead. As I left home, I strongly sensed that God was sending His angel before me and that whatever the day brought, it was allowed by God, and He would be with me to help me walk through it. As I set out, God gave me two verses to cling to. I went over them every day, and I put them in my journals. They were:

> And we know that all things work together for good to them that love God, to them who are the called according to his purpose. For whom he did foreknow, he also did predestinate to be conformed into the image of his Son. (Romans 8:28–29)

> And he said unto me, "My grace is sufficient for thee: for my strength is made perfect in weakness." Most gladly therefore will I rather glory in my infirmities, that the power of Christ may rest upon me. Therefore, I take pleasure in infirmities,

> in reproaches, in necessities, in persecutions, in distresses for Christ's sake: for when I am weak, then am I strong. (2 Corinthians 12:9-10)

Through the coming days, amid the uncertainty, I held to the promises in these verses and the deep sense of the nearness of the living Christ. This was living faith in real time. A real sense of God's presence was seared into my mind, spirit, and body like a psychic brand giving me a peace and security because I felt His closeness in a very intense way. This was all like food to feed my spirit.

At first, when I arrived in Palm Beach, I considered working at the beautiful Breakers Hotel, but then I accepted a job at the Palm Beach Country Club, where the Kennedys had been members. I worked in the pro shop and on the small practice range, keeping it in order and picking up the balls. Also, Ann Pinto, a lady who worked in the pool and cabana area, rented me her son's empty room in the back of her house. The rent was $25.00 a week. The room did not have a tub or shower, but it did have a sink and toilet. The room was tiny, nine feet by six feet, and it had a small single bed, a chest of drawers, and a nightstand. At first, I looked for a bigger place with a bathroom, but over time I saw the benefits of where I was. My little place was clean, in a nice neighborhood, and cheap. Other places I looked at were more expensive or in a neighborhood that wasn't safe. And so, I stayed in my little room for my entire three months in Palm Beach.

Food was cheap. When I look at my daily spending entries, I see one night I ate a hamburger, tea, apple pie, and ice cream for $3.35, including tip. On another night, I went to Testa's, an upscale restaurant in Palm Beach, and paid $10.62 for steak, baked potato, salad, a glass of milk, bread, and a tip.

On most days I got up about 6:30 a.m., did pushups and sit-ups, ran, stopped by the 7-11 to get milk for my cereal, bathed, and went to the club. Arriving early to work, I would read my Bible across the street by a seawall on the ocean before going in. I spent the day either working in the pro shop or on the practice range, picking up balls. I got off about 4:30 and then played golf at the club or explored Palm Beach. At night I would write in my journal which, in the end, was 654 pages.

It is amazing how you can get used to a routine. I was obsessive about this disciplined life. Some days the schedule would get messed up, but I saw the good in that too. I would write,

> My missing these parts of my schedule will test me to see if my joy is stemming from just keeping a schedule or from my relationship with the Lord. Just because I didn't pray at a certain time shouldn't hurt my joy with Christ, for he is always with me. Sometime in the future I may be put in a situation where I can't jog or do exercises or pray on a certain schedule, but I hope my relationship with the Lord will keep right on growing, and I pray it will be him that brings me joy and not a meager little schedule. He must be the continual living water that refreshes my life, not an uncertain man-made schedule or routine. You can pray anytime, anywhere, and I hope also that I get just as much peace and assurance out of a quick, unstructured conversation with the Lord as with a structured one. I hope to grow in my relationship with this Friend I can call and depend on any time for he is always there within reach.

THE IMPORTANCE OF A CHURCH FAMILY

By January 27, I was feeling a bit lonely. I wrote in my journal, "I have been feeling kind of blah. I guess it's because I don't know anyone too well. If I make it till my job is over, I will have more self-respect for myself in that Christ and I did something kind of on our own in faith. He sent lots of people to help, but they were mostly new strange faces."

It is amazing how God provided in his time. The very next day, on Sunday, January 28, after work, I went to a Sunday night youth service at Memorial Presbyterian Church. I met a number of people who became friends and the church became an important part of my social and spiritual support system.

God gives us what we need when we need it. In the other places where I would work, I would not have a church home, but I needed one in Palm Beach, and God gave me the perfect one. I would later write in my journal, "I can see the Lord working in guiding me to a good church on the first shot."

If I had had a mediocre or bad experience, I might not have made a second effort at finding a church home. I went to covered-dish suppers, regular services, and Bible studies. I can't say enough about what a great support and influence it was during my time in Palm Beach. Besides going to church on Sunday, I met with Alan Cochet, the associate pastor, for study on Tuesday night, church and supper on Wednesday night, and Bible study on Thursday night. Alan and Anne Cochet, the Toothman family, Dan Hall, and the church family at Memorial Presbyterian provided incredible support to me.

My experience at Memorial Presbyterian brought home to me the importance of good friends. God created us as social beings. God knew, even in our relationship with Him, it was not good that we be alone. Not only did I notice how my friends in Palm Beach lifted my spirits and mentored me, I was also to see another side of my long-time friends back at home. I felt I was learning so much, but this all took on an even richer meaning when I returned to Thomaston and shared my experiences with those at home.

PALM BEACH

I spent a lot of time studying the history and personalities of Palm Beach. Palm Beach is a long, skinny island bounded by the Atlantic Ocean on the east and the Lake Worth Lagoon on the west. Three bridges connect the island to West Palm Beach on the mainland. The name Palm Beach came from all the coconut palm trees in the area. In the beginning, the island was nothing but a big sand bar. Over time, a village developed there.

Around the time of World War I, Palm Beach began to grow as a resort. During the war, the French Riviera and the spas of Europe were closed, so wealthy Americans turned to Palm Beach and the Flagler Hotels, built by Henry Flagler, who had made a fortune as a key player with John D. Rockefeller in Standard Oil.

Later in life, Flagler developed a lot of Florida by building railroads down the east coast, punctuated along the way by very nice hotels. In Palm Beach, he built the Breakers and the Royal Poinciana Hotel. Wealthy Northerners took their personal Pullman train cars, attached them to a regular train headed south, and traveled from the northern cites to Palm Beach. Then they parked their train cars on a siding for "the season," and stayed in one of Flagler's hotels, where they socialized and networked with other wealthy people. They would have lots of social gatherings, play golf, polo, croquet, and enjoy the warm weather. In late spring, when the weather got better up north, they took their Pullman train cars back north. Eventually, the wealthy built large mansions on grand estates. In the early days, these estates extended from the Atlantic Ocean on the east to Lake Worth Lagoon on the west.

One of the few estates to survive through the years in Palm Beach was Mar-a-Lago now owned by Donald Trump. *Mar* means "sea," and *Lago* means "lake," so the estate's name is a memory of an earlier time when most grand estates went from the sea to the lake. Mar-a-Lago was originally the estate of Marjorie Meriweather Post. She owned the Post Cereal Company and then combined it with Birds Eye to create General Foods. She was married to E. F. Hutton, a match that united two great fortunes. The mansion had 122 rooms and took four years to build. It opened in 1927. It had seventeen acres, a nine-hole par-three golf course, and an underground tunnel linking the main house and grounds to a private beach on the Atlantic Ocean. Mrs. Post left Mar-a-Lago to the U.S. government for presidential use and to accommodate foreign heads of state. It was never used for that purpose until later when Donald Trump bought it.

ADDISON MIZNER

Wherever I went during my resort years, I always studied the lives of the great personalities of the area. One fascinating person in Palm Beach's history was Addison Mizner, whose name is synonymous with the city's architecture.

Addison Mizner was born in California in 1872. Early in life he fell in love with architecture. Prior to 1918, he traveled extensively, making architectural notebooks as an inspirational source and "idea book" to help him in his work as an architect. I looked at a lot of these fascinating notebooks in the Society of the Four Arts Library in Palm Beach. There were books with photos and drawings for cloisters, stairways, loggias, doors, and much more. He was drawn to Latin America's Spanish architecture, particularly in Guatemala. On his travels he would buy doors and other architectural features and then store them until he was inspired to incorporate them in a new project.

Early in his work life, in an effort to build his business, he moved from California to New York, where he met Paris Singer, an heir to the Singer sewing machine fortune. When World War I came, Mizner's architectural business died, and most of his skilled laborers were sent to the war. Also, at this time, a series of events conspired to send him south to Palm Beach. His beloved mother died, his leg was seriously injured, and the severe heating fuel shortage of 1917 made his bed-ridden convalescence in the cold of New York intolerable. To help lift his spirits and give him a change of scenery, Paris Singer invited Addison Mizner to visit him in Palm Beach.

By the time Mizner came to Florida, he had traveled widely, learning all he could. He even spent time in the Yukon during the Gold Rush. Mizner arrived in Florida in full command of the arts needed for his craft. With the war going in 1918, the United States was practically without skilled craftsman, and building supplies were scarce. Here, Mizner's travels and learning came to the fore. As written in *Palm Beach Entertains*,

> In all of his wanderings over the world, studying buildings, looking, sketching, he had never been content until he knew how the thing that attracted him was made. He studied with the hands as well and his eyes, not satisfied until he could do the thing. The result was that, when he went

> to Florida, he was, as he says himself, "as good a bricklayer as any man I ever had. I can plaster as well as any plasterer I have ever seen. I am a fairly good carpenter, and a better than ordinary electrician. . . . One has to know these things, otherwise you cannot get done the thing that you want done for there is the eternal objection, 'It can't be done that way.' I know enough to say, 'We will do it that way. I know how to do it.''

He started Mizner Industries in West Palm Beach to make the tiles and home wares he needed. Whether using iron or wood, Mizner had learned the methods of style and production in his far-flung travels, so he could train unskilled people to make almost all the things he needed for his homes. He even mixed his own paint colors. His factory was called *Los Manos*, which indicates, "hand made."

Mizner's many adventures had prepared him for his future work. According to *Palm Beach Entertians:*

> There you have the man-the man who won't be stopped in getting what he wants for his work. No tiles? Mold them over his thigh as he had seen it done in Latin America. Build a kiln, bake them yourself. No bricklayer? Teach someone. Your furniture falls apart? Go across the sea for the wood you want and peg the parts together. No blue that suits the scene? Mix one—and so it goes, and if there is no one to build a chimney properly or plaster to suit one's need or mend a pipe, do it yourself. To know these things and to be able to show others

> how to do them is as much a part of your profession as planning, designing, and adapting.

Reading about Addison Mizner was thrilling. I cannot overemphasize the importance of my experiences and my reading. This was far more than reading about someone's life. My readings and my passing moments were a laboratory, creating my future from the history I read and the experiences I had each day. In the years to come, the inspiration of this kind of artistic knowledge would give me a ravenous desire to create the type of transformative tour experiences I experienced myself.

Like Mizner, though I did not know it, I was digging out of each passing moment the materials to build my future. In my vision of the future, a tour would not be mere sightseeing. It would be so much more—a spiritual site-experience to affect the way people thought and felt, and to design a new space in their mind, their house, their garden, or their menu. I could never leave the creation of such a magical thing to someone else. I would scout the area myself. I would hand pick the hotels, the guides, the things to do and see and store them in the warehouse of my mind, awaiting the process of inspired creation. I might take a number of different local tours or walks found in guidebooks. In the end, I would take all these things into my mental and artistic laboratory, and then craft a unique, one-of-a-kind, handcrafted creation—not so much a tour as an experiential work of art to feed one's spirit. Just like Mizner, whose factory was called Los Manos, I was later to have my own dream factory, with unique designs that were also "handmade," dug out of personal experience and hours of observation, thought, and design.

Today, the people who take my tours may have no inkling that I have this vision or that I look at my tours this way, but my tours are better because I put this much thought and time into their creation. Like an iceberg, there is so much more than what people see.

When Paris Singer brought Addison Mizner to Palm Beach, Singer had turned his homes in Paris and near London into hospitals for soldiers, and he wanted to build a hospital in the United States for convalescing officers. At first, Singer did not envision a permanent structure, but Mizner convinced him that it was better to build something well that could later be used as a club when the war was over. Today, that building is the posh Everglades Club.

Addison Mizner was not only a great architect, he was also a master in all areas of building. He felt architecture should be built from local materials. In Florida, this meant plaster made from coquina shell, sand, and water. He felt the Spanish style suited the tropical setting far better than the styles chosen by wealthy patrons who wanted their Florida home to look like their homes up north. Mizner wanted his buildings to look as if they had developed over centuries. He wanted a building to look as though it had fought its way from a small unimportant structure to a great rambling house that took centuries of ups and downs to accomplish.

As I read all this, it affected my life and my vision for the future. Like the evolution of Mizner's buildings, I would be shaped by the ups and downs and the many experiences I would have. As I read about Mizner's life, I was discovering how interesting the world of the arts could be and how what I learned could shape my life. It was thrilling to read about Mizner's creativity and genius in *Palm Beach Entertains:*

> Mizner's unorthodox manner of giving the kiss of centuries to his creations was the despair of his

> workmen. He would take a hammer to newly constructed statues and mantelpieces. He would burn tarpaper in a freshly painted room in order to soften the colors and make them look centuries older. His men would be instructed to spray condensed milk on newly painted frescoes and then wipe down the walls with steel wool. Worm-eaten timbers for ceilings were his favorite, but if he ran short of these, he used pecky cypress, filling the holes with paint pigments and then scraping them out again. Anything to achieve the effect of deteriorated magnificence.

Despite all this, when the bottom fell out of the Florida land boom, Addison Mizner assumed the personal responsibility of his company's debts, which ruined him financially.

THE PALM BEACH COUNTRY CLUB

I worked at the Palm Beach Country Club, which was organized as a private club in 1953. When I was there in 1979, it cost $25,000 to join, with extra fees for golf and pool cabana privileges. It had the reputation of being the premier Jewish club in the South. In town, at that time, it was known as the Jewish Country Club, and the Everglades Club was the Gentile Club. Most of the South at that time still thought in terms of black and white, but in Palm Beach, people thought in terms of Jewish and Gentile. The Joseph Kennedy family were charter members and one of only three Gentile families who had been members in the whole history of the Palm Beach Country Club.

The club drew membership from all over the U.S. and Canada, and always had a waiting list. Many members were from

Cleveland, Boston, Manhattan, or the Hamptons on Long Island. All the members were very wealthy. One member regularly flew in from New York on Thursday, played golf through Sunday, and then flew back to New York on Sunday for a four-day business week. Members tended to be older; they played for exercise and used the club for social experiences as much as golf. The atmosphere was relaxing, and days were slow and lazy compared with the stress of the big cities up north.

Four car valets were on duty at any one time. The more expensive a car was, the closer to the front door the valets parked it. As the club membership was very wealthy, valets had a section for Rolls Royces, a section for Cadillacs, a section for Mercedes, and on it went. Needless to say, my Oldsmobile Cutlass Supreme was parked a long way from the front door—down by the maintenance building.

On busy days, the man at the valet podium would announce who was leaving over a loud speaker. Two valets on a golf cart would bring the cars to the front door for whoever was leaving.

The valets had a phone, and relayed messages to the caddie master, who was informed as to who was arriving and who was leaving. At the first tee, there was a starter's station with a check-in book and a phone to relay messages to Doc, the caddie master, as to who was teeing off and whether they were teeing off from the first tee or from the tenth tee. Caddy fees were $6.00 per bag for nine holes and $12.00 per bag for eighteen holes, and the caddies usually carried two bags.

My foremost duty was to pick up balls on the practice range, keeping the pros supplied with balls for lessons, and the ball machine full for members who wanted to practice on their own. I sometimes helped Doc get bags off the practice tee or out to the caddies. I also cleaned clubs and put on new grips. Sometimes I worked in the pro shop, selling merchandise. To end the day,

I was supposed to clear the practice range of balls, turn off the ball machine, and take the money out. My last daily duty was to vacuum the pro shop and the pro's office, and my day was usually finished by about 4:45 p.m.

THE CADDIES

When they were not caddying, the caddies usually gathered in a small room and played cards. They all seemed to have nicknames. A chauffer named J. C. usually showed up a few times a day and played a few hands while waiting on his boss. He dressed formally in a black coat, black pants, black tie, and a white shirt. He also wore a black cap like a policeman's cap, but with no insignia.

Doc Black, the head caddie master, took great pride in his position and his work. He told me that he had been President Kennedy's personal caddie, and that he knew about the Bay of Pigs invasion of Cuba a week before it happened.

Freddie Spitrini or "Boston Freddie" was the assistant to Doc Black. Freddie worked the summer season at the Belmont Club in Boston. He told me that he had received some scholarships to go to college but left as he had no real interest in college and felt he was just taking a scholarship from someone who was more deserving. He preferred the easygoing life at the club in Palm Beach and his summer club in Boston.

The caddies were a diverse bunch and each had a unique and colorful personality. "Big Jim" said he got his name not from his size, but from carrying four bags at a time. He claimed all the caddies used to do that. He loved to boast about the pros he had caddied for. "45th Street Jack" got his nickname because, from time to time, he had to check into a "crazy house" on 45th Street. "Scorecard Dave" collected scorecards from the various places he had worked. He was a sad figure to me because he seemed to have bitterness etched into his face from working in establishments that allowed him to enter some sections and didn't allow him to enter other sections because of his social status. "Pantry" got this name because he stopped at the Pantry Pride convenience store every morning to get breakfast. Pantry was a large man who, in his earlier years had polio, so now he had a brace on one of his legs and walked with a limp. Pantry had a sweet and kind spirit. You couldn't help but love him. "McGoo" had a goatee and fancied himself as a lady's man. As such, he had a suitcase of aliases: "The Brain," "The Goat," "Superstar," "Sweet Papa Bass," and "Handsome Slim." "Short Stick" was a pool player. "Peek-a-Boo" was always looking for golf balls. He was a sidekick of "McGoo." "Racetrack Nick," or "Dog," was so named because liked to go to dog races. I didn't know the origin of "Sporty Pop's" nickname. "Headache Red" was a pain in the neck when he was drinking. "Rabbit" James' nickname was obscure but probably had to do with the way he moved. "Red Cap" always wore a red cap. "Carolina" Johnny was from Greensboro, North Carolina. And "Stuttering Johnny" was a man from West Virginia. Needless to say, the caddies were a world unto themselves, a fascinating collection of personalities with an endless stream of stories.

LIVING AND LEARNING DAY BY DAY

Every day, I seemed to be living and learning the fundamental things of life. I learned the history of the place, soaked in the beauty of my experience, and got a lot out of my church, prayer, Bible reading, formal Bible studies, and the people I met. I once wrote, "It is nice to be able to have these experiences and be free to enjoy them. This is typical of the way God has so richly blessed my life—the richest of which is the salvation He has given me."

I was allowed to play the course after work. One afternoon I wrote about playing and just soaking in all the beauty of the passing moments and the atmosphere. I always walked the course after the caddies were gone and the carts had been put up. I wrote,

> It was a beautiful time of day. . . . The setting was beautiful, a beautifully manicured course with a smooth carpet of green grass . . . a quiet breeze . . . causing small ripples on the quiet ponds. The white crane-like birds and the ducks in the distance feeding and sleeping or resting. The rolling hills, the oaks with moss hanging from them . . . the sprinklers in the distance making one of the few sounds to be heard in the stillness. The fifth fairway where they say the presidential helicopter used to pick up President Kennedy. . . . Leaving the sixth tee, I thought to myself of the many blessings the Lord is giving me here. A rich experience. I am glad to be here instead of Marco, or Boca, or Delta Air Lines. He (God) knew what I really wanted (and needed). This is the life, beautiful course, beautiful time of day, sharing it with the Lord.

I was to have many of these beautiful, atmospheric moments. How many times do most people, amidst the responsibilities, the rush, and the worry of life, have the chance to really live in such moments of sacred beauty? God not only gave me these moments, but also gave me the mind and sensibility to appreciate them, live in them, and feed on them. Experiencing the intensity of all that beauty alloyed with the deep sense of God's presence, caused these moments to become a part of me. As I write this, I am so grateful and thankful for these special moments that were shaping me and transforming me. In these and other moments, God was building the spiritual/psychological house that would weather the storms ahead. The Lord and I would continue to build that house over the next five years. As I have said, we built it plank-by-plank, shingle-by-shingle, nail-by-nail. In the end that house was so sound and fundamental that it is essentially remains the psychological/spiritual house I live in today.

It is hard to impress upon anyone reading or hearing me of the cumulative spiritual power of moments like these. In his book, *Abandonment to Divine Providence*, Jean-Pierre de Caussade said, "There is nothing trivial about our passing moments, as they enclose the whole kingdom of holiness, and [they are] the food on which angels feed."

When you combine my personality, my imagination, a sense of taking a spiritual voyage alone with only the Lord to commune with, the saturating power of such moments fed me in an incredibly intense way. In my journal I reveled in the joy of the intersection of my will and His will and how I felt God was giving me, as He had promised, the desires of my heart.

Here is a passage from my journal in regard to my incorruptible inheritance: "One thought that God revealed to me is that, in this town of Palm Beach, where the wealthy heirs and heiresses of America and the world come to relax, there is no one who has a greater inheritance than me. And the majority, sooner or later, would give all they have and more for a part of the inheritance that I have."

I was thinking of my inheritance as a believer with a relationship with the God of all creation—to know that I was forgiven and that I would spend eternity in heaven. I knew I had all this and so much more, and that nothing could separate me from either His love or that future.

THE WAY FORWARD

As my time in Palm Beach passed, I began to formulate a plan for the future. I would later describe these years on a resume saying, "The following five years were an experiential extension to an academic education." In a letter home to my father, I talked about working in hotels in other areas of the country. I felt that over time, through meeting people and working in hotels, the Lord would shape my future and give me the desires of my heart. I felt that doors of opportunity would open and shut as way led on to way. I had faith in God's providence and an unwavering confidence that His plan would work out for me. I wrote Daddy and Mary and described what I was thinking and what my plan for the future would be:

> This is a rough outline of the places I want to visit and when I might do it.

My Age	**Time**	**Place**
23	Summer	Cape Cod
24	Winter	Wyoming
24	Summer	Greenbrier, WV
25	Winter	Pebble Beach, CA, or Augusta, GA
25	Summer	Maine
26	Winter	Maybe Europe

"I know this is what I want to do now. If this schedule goes as planned, at twenty-six I will be ready to settle down and work my way up in a hotel."

In the end, my years of travel went like this:

My Age	**Time**	**Place**
22/23	Summer 1978	Mackinac, Mich.
23	Winter 1979	Palm Beach, Fla.
23/24	Summer 1979	Bar Harbor, Maine
24	Winter 1979/80	Big Sky, Mont.
24/25	Summer 1980	Bar Harbor, Maine
25	Winter 1980/81	Big Sky, Mont.
25	Summer 1981	Big Sky, Mont.
25/26	Fall 1981	UGA / English degree
26	Winter 1981/82	Tift / English degree / Teaching degree
26/27	Summer /Fall 1982	Nantucket, Mass.
27	Winter 1982/83	Tift English degree
27	Summer 1983	Africa trip
27/28	1983/84	Pike County High 10th grade English
28	Summer–Present	The Travel Connection

My study of Addison Mizner and how travel prepared him for his future gave me the confidence that maybe that was a path of preparation God would use in my life. Though it would not necessarily take the path I thought, in general I pursued that path, and it did work out for me. Some people felt I was "searching for something," or they may have thought I needed to get on with a career, but I felt confident that this was right for me. I thought about this and wrote, "I don't feel I am searching for something. I feel I know what I want to do now, and as I feel the Lord has given me these desires, I am doing it. The proof of it to me is the peace I have and the joy I am experiencing. Also, I am learning a lot of very good lessons, and the Lord has used them to draw me to himself."

I mentioned to Daddy about reading how Addison Mizner had traveled and that it prepared him perfectly for his great work, which he could never have done without the things he learned in those years that some may have called "wasted years."

MEETING ROSE KENNEDY

As a little boy, I was fascinated with the Kennedys. I had gone to Palm Beach after hearing about it from its association with the Kennedys. When I was working on Mackinac Island, I read Rose Kennedy's book *Times to Remember*, and it had reinforced my idea that travel needed to be a part of my education. It convinced me to commit to a number of years of travel, and my experience at the Grand Hotel on Mackinac Island had convinced me that seasonal resort work could finance that education.

One day, during my time in Palm Beach, I walked down the beach and found the Kennedy home. Many days I saw their maroon Lincoln Continental pass down North County Road; I knew that most mornings Rose Kennedy attended mass at St. Edward's Catholic Church. One day a friend who owned a bookshop suggested that I try to get her to autograph her book *Times to Remember*. Mondays were my day off, so on Monday, April 2, 1979, I wrote in my journal,

I set out to St. Edward's Catholic Church to see if I could get Mrs. Kennedy's autograph. I got there a little early, and only moments later I saw the reflection of the maroon Continental in the big glass windows of a grocery store across the street. It rounded the curb, and the chauffer parked the car on Sunset Avenue. He got out and helped Mrs. Kennedy into the church. I now waited for her to come out. As people started coming out of the church, I got my book out, ready to the page I wanted signed, and got my pen ready, making sure it would write. At about ten till nine, she came out with her bodyguard-chauffer. As they approached, I was standing beside my car. She was walking and holding his arm for strength in case she tripped. I caught her eye and walked slowly toward her, and she walked toward me. I asked her if it would be too much trouble to get an autograph. She obliged and I told her I enjoyed the book. She asked me what I liked about it. I said a lot, particularly the part she wrote about John after he got out of college and didn't know what he wanted to do, so he traveled some. I told her I was in the same position. She talked about how it's hard for young people to know what they want to do and asked me if I had anyone to guide me. I said I had a firm faith that the Lord would guide my desires and draw certain people to me to guide me. I told her before I told her this that I was a Christian and enjoyed her talking about her faith in the book. She said how her children listened to their father and felt if he said it, it was a good idea. She said how I was young and had a lot of life ahead of me. She then walked on, and I got in my car, looked at my newly acquired autograph, and left.

CAMDEN, WILLIAM BORDEN, AND THE DECISION TO GO TO MAINE

Five days after telling Rose Kennedy that I felt God would bring people into my life to help guide me, I was talking to a young guy who worked at the club. His name was Bob Winchenbach, and he was from Camden, Maine. I had planned to go to Cape Cod for the summer, but, little did I know, but Bob Winchenbach was the person God would use to show me my next step in life. As he talked, I began to get excited about Camden and the coast of Maine. It was surprising how the biography I read often intertwined with personal contacts to guide me.

My mind was already filled with images of the rocky coast of Maine from my reading William Borden's biography when I was in college. Borden's family had summered in Camden, Maine, where he loved to sail. Also, through my readings I had come to know about Campobello Island, where the Roosevelts had summered. Though Campobello was actually a Canadian possession, it lay off the northern reaches of the Maine Coast. The Roosevelts had loved Campobello because of its great sailing waters.

So now visions of the Maine coast which had been planted years earlier were awakened by my conversation with Bob Winchenbach. Bob suggested summer work that he thought I might like. Camden was the summer home of a number of schooners which made weeklong cruises along the Maine Coast. These schooners needed crew to help, and the crew lived on board the schooner. The cruises left on Monday and returned on Saturday, giving the crew Sunday off.

Over the following days and weeks, I talked more to Bob, and my interest in the Maine Coast grew. Bob gave me his address when he went back to Camden and said he would check on a job for me.

I had also thought about going to Monterey, California for the summer with my friend Jim Duffy, but Jim decided not to go. The more I thought about Cape Cod, the more commercialized it seemed, and so I thought more about the coast of Maine. On Monday, April 16, I wrote in my journal, "The Lord has really gotten me excited about it, and I've decided to go even if I don't get the job." And so I ended my time at Palm Beach and set my sites on the Maine Coast.

WHAT PALM BEACH TAUGHT ME

What were the ways Palm Beach shaped me?

1) Traveling alone and keeping a journal forged in me a deep, intimate, moment-by-moment relationship with the Lord.
2) The Lord is always preparing you in the present for a future that only He can see
3) The Lord sees what you will become as well as what you are now, and He is constantly working on both your present and your future.
4) The value of relationships. We are created social beings. In the beginning, God saw that we needed not just fellowship with Him, but also fellowship with others. In the beginning, He said, "It is not good that man be alone." The people I met in Palm Beach made a huge difference in my experience.

5) The church is a good place to find and build relationships.
6) The Lord created you as a unique being, and he wants to feed your uniqueness and bring it to its fullest fruition.
7) Biography, and the example of others, can help define who you are and be instructive in teaching you about life.

On the day I drove home from Palm Beach, it took all day. I arrived home at night and daddy took me out to the Golden Corral for a steak dinner. As I told him all I had experienced, I was so full of joy and felt so fulfilled I said, "Daddy, if I died tonight, I will have lived a full life."

I felt that then, and as each year passes, I continue to feel that, should I die at any time, I will have lived a full life.

6

BAR HARBOR, MAINE

1979

When I left for Maine, I was more apprehensive than I had been when I left for Florida. When I left for Florida, I was focused on working in Palm Beach. When I left for Maine, I didn't know where I would end up.

I did have interests in Campobello Island, with its Roosevelt connection, and in Camden, Maine, with its William Borden connection. And I did have Bob Winchenbach as a contact in Camden, but still everything was up in the air. Because I wasn't praying much, my spiritual focus was very lax, leaving me spiritually unsure and, as a consequence, unsure about the road ahead.

Steve Rogers, a long-time friend, had a few days off from his job, so he rode along with me to Maine. We first stopped in Camden, where I met with Bob Winchenbach and then went to the harbor and talked with a few shipmasters. They already had their crews for the season, but one took my name in case something opened. I would find out later that the shipmaster had tried to find me through Bob, but they had lost my trail. It would be just as well. For some reason, I didn't look for openings at any of the hotels in Camden.

Next, Steve and I drove north along the Maine coast to Campobello Island, the Canadian Island just across a bridge from Lubec, Maine. There I looked at possibilities at the Roosevelt Home, a small golf course, and a herring packing plant. No jobs were available, and as we left the island, I felt down because of the uncertainty and lack of job openings.

We returned down the coast to Bar Harbor, where I went to the best hotel in town. The Bar Harbor Motor Inn overlooked the harbor, Frenchman's Bay, and the islands. It was a beautiful, shingle-style hotel that had started its life in an abbreviated version in the late 1880s as a gentleman's club called the "Reading Room." It was said most of the members did their "reading" through the bottom of a glass. When I spoke to a girl at the front desk, she said there were no openings, but that I could fill out a job application. As I filled out the application, the manager, Lottie Butters, walked in. She said there was an opening for a bellman immediately, and, in a week, there would be an opening for a front desk clerk. She told me to come back at 3:00 p.m. the next day.

Suddenly the skies of life brightened, and I felt I had a great chance at a job. Steve had to fly back to Atlanta that night, so we went uptown to a mom-and-pop restaurant and had a lobster dinner for $5.95 each. I then took Steve to Bangor to fly home, and I returned to Bar Harbor.

I had been told I would have to find my own housing, so the next morning I inquired at the YMCA and other places. I then interviewed with the Motor Inn's owner, Barry Harris, and the manager, Mrs. Butters. They offered me a job on the front desk as long as I agreed to stay until the hotel closed in late October. I hesitated, but then said I would if I could find appropriate housing. She said to check back with her at 10:00 a.m. the next day. As a side note, Mr. Harris, the owner, was a historian and loved

Teddy Roosevelt. During my interview with him, we talked about "T. R.," and I believe that conversation sealed the job offer. Don't ever underestimate the power of your non-business interests to enhance your overall resume.

The next morning the manager said there was some employee housing at a place called Pineo Court. I went down in the drizzling rain and found a place that was rundown, filthy, and where the water hadn't even been turned on. A maid named Velma came in and said the boss had told her to clean up the place. When her crew came back later that day, they refused to clean it up, as it was in such bad shape. Between the drizzling rain and the depressing housing situation, my feelings began to sink.

As we stood around, a maid said a man named Roger Cunningham rented nice rooms for $25.00 a week, but he had started with girls and probably wanted to keep it that way. I checked anyway. The rooms were clean and nice, and he agreed to rent me a room for $25.00 a week. Now I had a job and a place to stay.

Around noon, I headed back to the hotel to tell them I had found a place to stay. Mr. Harris said I could start learning the front desk on Friday—and that I could stay in an attic room in the hotel for free as they liked to have front desk staff nearby. I could have my employee meals for free, and my salary would be $150.00 per week. Wow! Free room, free food, and a $150.00 a week. Could my situation get any better? Yes, it could. The attic room had the best view in town!

Velma took me to the attic and showed me a few huge, rambling rooms with basic beds and places to put my clothes. The views out the windows were incredible. In every direction were boats, islands, water, and on the horizon, either the sea or distant blue hills. My bed was under two casement windows with incredible views. I would room with the night auditor, but the room was huge, so space would be no problem. In the end, I positioned my bed beneath those two windows so that when I sat up, I looked out on the harbor, the boats, the islands, and the distant hills of the northeast Maine coast. The windows faced east so if I woke early, I could see a beautiful sunrise with the black silhouettes of the islands set on a silver sea.

On top of everything else, I could go wherever I wanted in the hotel. That was an employee benefit that most resort hotels did not offer. So, I had a number of pleasant lounges within the hotel, as well as a second-story deck that overlooked the harbor, where I could read, write, and just drink in the incredible beauty spread out before me. I couldn't have dreamed up a more perfect situation. I am so grateful to the Lord for this incredible gift and the memories that helped fill the deep reservoirs of my spirit, from which I still drink.

As would prove true time and time again, the Lord had sent His angel before me and set me up with a job and a place to live that was far beyond anything I could have imagined. As happened in Palm Beach, I would learn important things about God, life, and myself that continue to be an integral part of who I am.

DAILY LIFE

Duties at the front desk of the Bar Harbor Motor Inn involved check in and check out, working the switchboard, and taking reservations. It took a while to learn the various duties, but, over time, I got the hang of things and began to enjoy the camaraderie of the other front-of-the-house workers.

There were three shifts, 7:00 a.m.–3:00 p.m., 3:00 p.m.–11:00 p.m., and 11:00 p.m.–7:00 a.m. The overnight shift basically involved the night audit. Most days, I worked one of the day shifts.

I worked five days a week and then had two days off, usually together. I often took side-trips up and down the coast, sometimes spending a night away from Bar Harbor.

Bar Harbor is on Mount Desert Island. Knowledgeable scholars pronounce "Desert" in one of two ways. Some pronounce the name of the island like the desert in Africa. Others pronounce it like you would the final course at dinner. I pronounced it like the dessert at the end of a meal, as did the park rangers and most people, but the other way was also acceptable.

I spent my free days exploring the natural beauty all around me. I took sailing lessons and went out with a lobsterman. Many days I read history, took walks, and enjoyed the many sites around the hotel. Sometimes I visited the island villages of Northeast Harbor, Southwest Harbor, or Seal Harbor. Everywhere there were interesting shops and sites, and always, there were the mountains and the sea.

More often, with beautiful Acadia National Park at my doorstep, I visited places in the park, like Great Head, Sand Beach, Mount Cadillac, and Thunder Hole. I could scramble around on the ledges of the dramatic rocky coast with the wind whistling and the waves crashing before me. It was thrilling to be in that setting. Sometimes I might do a hike by myself or with a friend, or I might take a ranger-led walk. Every once in a while, I would visit the Jordan Pond House with its famous tea and popovers.

Once I ventured with a friend as far as St. Andrews in the Canadian province of New Brunswick. Another time I took a trip to Moosehead Lake far in the interior of Maine. There I climbed Mt. Kineo in the pouring rain and crossed a stretch of open lake in a canoe, bucking the wind, waves, and rain to return to land. A number of times I went to Campobello Island or other places along the coast, such as Camden or Kennebunkport.

My summers in Bar Harbor were amazing from both a travel and spiritual viewpoint. I can't say enough about them. God had set a great spiritual foundation in Palm Beach, and my Bar Harbor summers took that to another level. How fortunate could a young person be?

A GOOD LESSON LEARNED AND A SPIRITUAL WATERSHED EXPERIENCED

Over the summer in Bar Harbor, I enjoyed the books I read, whether they were Bar Harbor or Acadia history or biographies about Franklin or Theodore Roosevelt. As always, whether I was reading about people or nature, I drew parallels and insights about the sculpting of my life's views. As can happen, my enthusiasm in my general reading seemed to burn hotter and brighter than that of my Bible reading. I seemed to be learning as much spiritually from biography as I was from the Bible. This bothered me and finally led to a true spiritual revelation.

As I had previously been in Palm Beach, here also I was very disciplined in my physical and spiritual routine. Every day I ran, did push-ups and sit-ups, read my Bible, prayed, and read for pleasure. In Maine I also took nature hikes and learned from ranger walks. I took these years of resort work very seriously. This was a thrilling time. It was both a serious and joyful endeavor. C. S. Lewis talks about this kind of life and the joy associated with it in *The Weight of Glory*, "We must play. But our merriment must be of that kind (and it is, in fact, the merriest kind) which exists between people who have, from the outset, taken each other seriously."

I struggled with the fact that I found more excitement and joy from my "secular" interests than from my "spiritual" interests. One morning, as I got on my knees to pray, a revelation of the

Lord came to me. I said in response, "Lord, I know you are leading me in this thought path. You said you came that we might have life and have it more abundantly, and I don't feel that I am feeling an abundant joy in my Bible reading, but I do feel an abundant joy in my reading of biography and my walks in nature. I have more of a desire to read biography than the Bible. I have always been taught to consider all *my* desires guilty until proven innocent. I have also fallen into the view that certain activities such as reading biography, running, or taking nature walks, are non-spiritual in nature, and others pursuits, like reading the Bible and praying, are more spiritual in nature. So, I feel guilty about my joy in the secular activities and my lack of enthusiasm in my Bible reading and prayer.

"From this day forward, I will assume all my desires and interests, unless strictly forbidden in the Bible, as God-given and an integral part of your process of sculpting my identity in Christ. From this day forward, I will assume my good desires innocent until proven guilty instead of guilty until proven innocent."

Yes, God means us to pray and to read His word, but he is also shaping our lives through the other desires and interests He gives us. As I worked through these thoughts in my prayer, an amazing joy of assurance welled up within me; an assurance that this was God's will for me, that this was God's way for me.

Since then, I have thought that this revelation was pictured in the story of Lazarus. When Christ raised Lazarus from the dead, it is a spiritual picture of Christ saving someone for eternity, and that's wonderful, but Christ wants so much more for us. Everyone was joyful when Christ raised Lazarus from the dead, but he told the people to take off the graveclothes that were binding and preventing Lazarus from living a full life in the full blossom of both his spiritual and secular potential.

That morning, in Bar Harbor, God was helping me shed some of the graveclothes of my legalism and freeing me to love and revel in my passion for biography, art, and history. He was showing me that He wanted to use all those interests in His process of shaping me. That revelation brought such a feeling of joy and freedom. In the future years, as I led my tours, all those interests enhanced the quality of my commentary and the experiences I was able to give others.

Christ is to be our Savior for all eternity, but He is also our Lord both now, in the immediacy of our passing moments. Eternal life is not just *then*; it is *now*! In our present, passing moments through both our spiritual and our secular interests, we are being sculpted into the image of Christ so our personal potential might blossom into its highest fruition. There is, in fact, no separation between the spiritual and the secular. All of our life and interests are being used to sculpt us. God is also working *through us* to sculpt others' lives. In his book, *Abandonment to Divine Providence*, Jean-Pierre de Caussade said, "There is nothing trivial about our passing moments, as they enclose the whole kingdom of holiness and [those moments are] the food on which angels feed."

The potential of this thought is amazing when we realize that God wants to work in concert with us, His creation, to both achieve His ends and in bring our personal potential to its fullest joy and realization. This is the true source of fulfillment in life because it is what we were created for. We can't download these things into our spirit. We can't buy them or get them from reading about someone else's experience. This is a *process of becoming* that we work out in concert with the Lord through the Holy Spirit.

The Bible talks about working out our salvation in "fear and trembling." This is a process in which the Holy Spirit changes us from "glory to glory" into the image of Christ, through the seemingly insignificant passing moments of our life. We need to meditate and marinate on this because, if it is true—and I believe it is—this is the true source of our passion, our fulfillment, and our reason for being. Colossians 1:16 tells us we are made by Christ and for Christ.

This watershed moment in Bar Harbor is closely linked to my earlier discovery of William Borden. God used both to lead me out of the bondage of spiritual legalism and into the freedom and joy of my relationship with Him. Sometimes in life it takes a while to take off all the graveclothes that bind us and keep us from the joy, meaning, and fulfillment God has for us. This side of heaven, we will always be a work in progress.

And so, I began to see my love of biography, art and literature as part of God's plan for my life. I embraced these interests. I reveled in them rather than fought them. Today, as I lead my tours, I draw on this vast storehouse of knowledge taken in over the years, and this knowledge enhances my commentary whether I am in Europe or the United States.

RANGER WALKS IN ACADIA AND LESSONS LEARNED

Though I was having fun, I was constantly learning lessons from both biography and my walks with park rangers in Acadia National Park. By the time I left, I had sampled every nature walk offered. I found these walks to be both beautiful and fascinating. Here are some examples of some of the things I was learning and how they translated into everyday life lessons.

The Maine coast, in its shape and geology, has been affected by the forces of nature. During the Ice Age, the glacial ice sheet may have been from a mile to two miles thick as it moved down, scouring and shaping New England. The ragged Maine coastline, as well as the Porcupine Islands in Frenchman's Bay, were all shaped by the great ice sheet thousands of years ago. Also, the plant life of coastal Maine is shaped by the harsh and changing weather along the coast.

As you move to higher altitudes, the height of the same type of tree may be stunted by exposure to harsh conditions. Two fir trees may both be ten years old, but one in one place may be five feet tall and one in another place may be fifteen feet tall because it was situated in a setting with more favorable growth conditions.

Also, a natural phenomenon called "flagging" is caused by the harsh winds and weather, especially where plants are exposed on the side of a mountain or along the coast. When the winds blow predominantly from one direction, over time, the limbs of a plant on the windward side will be stunted, whereas the limbs on the leeward side will be stretched out and elongated. As a result, the plant or tree may take on the shape of a flag. Thus, the term "flagging."

My spiritual takeaway was that God was using everything in my life environment to challenge me and shape me into the image of Christ. The Bible teaches that God can use all things, whether good or bad, to shape and change us from "glory to glory" into the image of Christ (Romans 8:28 and 2 Corinthians 3:18). This learning was never forced drudgery; I reveled in the beauty, the wind, the waves, and the joy of God's incredible creation, and I absorbed amazing lessons along the way

Don't think my life was all fun and games. I had plenty times of frustration at work or complications with relationships. As in everyone's life, I went through times of depression, sadness, frustration, and unhappiness. But because of a life view based on my faith and my relationship with the Lord, I had an overarching sense that the glass of life was half full and that all things—good and bad—were being used by Him and shaped with His good intentions and purpose.

My coworkers made life pleasant at work, and people like Doug Engstrom and Linda Carter made my free time fun and interesting. Linda and I spent a good bit of time together and enjoyed a great whitewater-rafting trip down the Kennebec River. There were also others, like Gerry Mitchell, the well-known Bar Harbor personality who started Geddy's Pub near the waterfront. The first time Linda and I went to Geddy's, Gerry embraced us as if we were family. He came in the hotel from time to time, so he already knew me, but he refused to let us pay cover charges, gave us free drinks, and showed us around as if we were VIPs. All along the way there were wonderful people like Gerry who loved me, embraced me, and made life fun and exciting.

GEORGE B. DORR

In reading about Acadia National Park, I came to know the life of George B. Dorr, a dynamic and inspiring figure in the park's history. Dorr inherited a fortune and spent the rest of his life, energy, and money promoting the creation of Acadia National Park. Dorr would set out on long hikes in the park with nothing but an apple or a biscuit in his pocket. He was passionate that the lands of Acadia be preserved and protected from development. Often, he spent his own money or worked with John D. Rockefeller to make his vision for the park become a reality. In the end, he so depleted his fortune in this noble cause that he would show up at board meetings in shop-worn clothes with threadbare and tattered cuffs.

It was inspiring to read about Dorr and to immerse myself in his passion. So many of the people, like George B. Dorr, who the Lord has used to drive and shape my life, are people who died before I was born or whom I never knew. In spite of this, their lives entered my life in an incredibly way and animated the ever-evolving vision of who I was becoming. I encourage you, dear reader, to find great role models, whether living or dead, and let them move you and shape you along the course of your life's journey.

LESSONS IN INDIVIDUALITY

With such astounding beauty and drama in Acadia National Park, I was constantly learning about the incredible diversity in nature and the dynamic forces and themes that run throughout God's creation. One amazing opportunity I had was to visit the gardens of the Ford family in Seal Harbor. The Ford Gardens are an amazing combination of a Chinese and an English garden. There was an English wall, as well as a Chinese wall with tiles from the Forbidden City. Everywhere you looked, beautiful flowers complemented and enhanced the architectural styles of the two diverse cultures. As a result of my experience there, I meditated and wrote in my journal about diversity and uniqueness as part of God's plan for humanity. Here are some of my thoughts.

> All nature is an example of the genius, creativity, and immense diversity of God. At the Ford gardens you see flowers with so many different colors, patterns, and structures that enable them to adapt to differing environmental conditions.

God has also made humans just as glorious with delicate and intricate parts to adapt to their changing environment and yet remain rooted in the living faith. Every person is "fearfully and wonderfully made." Each, like the variety of flowers and trees, is beautiful and delicate. No two people are alike, and each has his or her own uniqueness and adaptive ability. Each has his or her own strengths and weaknesses. Each, because of his or her sinful nature, is not perfect. Some are stronger in one area, and others are stronger in other areas.

Christ, in his economy, rightly integrates believers as they give themselves to him into a working interrelationship, which is his body, the church. The thumb, as the Scripture says, has no right to say to the foot, "I have no need of you," for all the parts are necessary, and each part is important to the health of the whole."

Also, it is important that each person works out his or her faith in fear and trembling, for we are all desperately in need of each other to be authentically and genuinely who Christ made us to be—not anyone else, however seemingly important that other person may seem. God created each of us differently for a reason. We are to rejoice and revel in that uniqueness and strive, through abiding in Christ, to allow The Holy Spirit to change us from "glory to glory" into the image of Christ" (2 Corinthians 3:18). When we do that, God brings our uniqueness to its fullest realization. Here is

> found the true source of joy, meaning, and fulfillment as we find ourselves evolving and becoming who we were created to be.

These thoughts were prompted by the gardens and the park and then worked out in discussions with Doug Engstrom, orchestrated and moderated by the presence of the Holy Spirit. Throughout my Bar Harbor journal, I worked, finessed, and meditated on these central themes again and again until they were a part of me. I reveled in discovering and embracing my unique identity. In the years to come, this would be one of my passions, to encourage others to get to know themselves, love themselves, and be themselves. Later, on September 14 of that year, I wrote in my journal, "Well, I'm twenty-four years old today. I feel great about my life so far . . . if I weren't myself and I met myself, I would want to be like myself."

JODY

I have dated a good many women in my life and have really fallen for a few. One was Jody Smith, a waitress in the dining room at the Bar Harbor Inn. Jody was both a beautiful, delicate flower and a rugged, independent spiritual warrior. She had taken a three-month National Outdoor Leadership (NOLS) course in Wyoming, and as a result, she was highly skilled in outdoor camping and survival skills. She was also a songwriter and singer who led Bible studies. I fell hard for Jody, and though we became great friends, she never really felt the spark of love. Over our time together, we helped each other along our spiritual journeys as we took walks and spent time together. She shared her songs, and I would share my love of poetry.

A WONDERFUL GIFT FROM MY FATHER

One of the great values of travel is meeting people and putting our faith in the crucible of diversity to separate the truth, what C. S. Lewis called "Mere Christianity," from superstition or provincialism. In all my readings, whether of Teddy Roosevelt, F. D. R., or Thoreau, I saw how travel played an important part in the growth of people. This confirmed the importance of what I was doing.

Sometime during these years, when I was home between trips, Daddy—the doctor whose life had been planned out by his father—came down to my room to talk.

Maybe he was having doubts about allowing me to find my own way. In reading one of his letters to Doug and me, I now know there were moments of doubt, but it is a testament to his wisdom, and his wonderful loving and kind nature, in the way he spoke to me that night. He pulled up a chair, and his question was short, concise, and brief. "Tell me a little bit about what you are trying to do."

I saw the answer to that question very clearly. "Daddy," I said, "I see what I am doing now as an experiential extension to an academic education. I am not sure what I will do in the future, but I am sure that, whatever I do, I will be better at it because of these years."

He was quiet for a moment; then he said, "Okay."

He put the chair back and walked upstairs. Later I asked him how he was able to trust us in high school and college, in going to rock concerts, and in traveling on our own. This was a time of drugs, and Doug and I were charting our own way, and he never really had a "sit-down" with us. His reply in later years would be, "I was willing to trust you until you gave me a reason not to."

For that I am so thankful. Through his faith and trust, he kept his hands off the steering wheel of our journeys. This couldn't have been easy. It was a journey so different than the one he had taken. He had to have had doubts, but Doug and I found our way—a way that had to have been plotted and planned by us. It was unconventional, it was the road less traveled, and it's been no better than anyone else's road. But it was our road, and our journey had to have been done our way.

In my Bar Harbor journal, I wrote, "Spiritually, this summer, I have grown a lot in many ways and also in trying to define truth from provincialism. I've made some mistakes . . . but nevertheless we are moving and sounding the depths in search of the truth and of trying to separate Christian truth from insecure provincial dogma."

After my summer in Bar Harbor, I was bursting at the seams with pride and excitement. I was thoroughly convinced of what I had said to my father. I had been reading about how Theodore Roosevelt felt about his time in North Dakota. Edmund Morris, in his wonderful book, *The Rise of Theodore Roosevelt*, talks about the value and dividends that Roosevelt's time there paid back to him in the years to come: "Although his Dakota adventure had impoverished him, he was nevertheless rich in non-monetary dividends. He had gone west sickly, foppish, and racked with personal despair. During his time there he had built a massive body, repaired his soul, and learned to live on equal terms with men poorer and rougher than himself."

I was so excited as I felt that I, too, was building a spiritual bank account that would pay vast dividends in the years to come. And I was right. Roosevelt would later say of his time out west, "If it had not been for my years in North Dakota, I never would have become President of the United States."

On the surface, many who knew me may have been wondering why I was wasting these years when I should have been getting on with a career. Little did I or they know that I was in a great experiential graduate school, developing all the skills, the talents, and the knowledge that would be the heart and soul of the success of a tour business that still lay, unknown to me, in my distant future.

WHAT NEXT

As the summer passed in Bar Harbor, I began to start thinking about the next stage in my journey. With my interest in John Kennedy, I had often thought that I would like to do an internship with a senator or representative in Washington. I pursued that for a while, but an interview for an internship with Senator Herman Talmadge in Washington never quite materialized. Then, I started thinking about working in the American West at a ski resort.

The likely candidates should have been resorts in Colorado or Utah. That is where the best-known resorts were, like Vail, Aspen, or Park City. Nevertheless, for some reason, I started considering Big Sky in southwestern Montana, which was just north of Yellowstone National Park.

This time I felt no real biographical pull. I am not really sure when or why I started thinking about Big Sky. In retrospect, as I look back, the choice of Montana seemed to fit who I was. There was a sort of romantic quirk in my personality, which is still there today. I was never drawn to take the obvious choice; rather, the unique and different invariably tugged at my heart and spirit. Something in me was always drawn to the mysteries and riches of the road less travelled. It also fit my desire to seek a private, soulful, secluded, and quiet place—a sanctuary of the soul rather than a more well-known resort with a high-energy atmosphere.

My initial plan was to work geographically in areas in the north, south, east, and west. Nevertheless, in a journal entry for September 13, 1979, I mentioned Big Sky for the first time when I noted that I wrote a thank you note to Mr. Musser, the president of the Grand Hotel Mackinac, "for writing me a letter of recommendation for my job at Big Sky of Montana."

On Saturday, September 22, 1979, my future plans came more into focus. I wrote, "Got my letter from Senator Talmadge's office in reference to my job application. Thanks, but no thanks. Nevertheless, onward we go, for where the Lord closes one door, he opens another. Looks like I'm headed for Big Sky of Montana. Still waiting to hear from them, and feel sure I will get an offer. Never can tell, though."

On September 28, I mentioned in my journal about getting the Big Sky job, and for the first time, heading to a destination with a definite job at the end of the line. "I've decided to take the job with Big Sky after a brief period of cold feet. The pay is bad and benefits aren't great, but it's where I want to be, and I can know I have a job now. It will be nice leaving home and being able to enjoy the trip out, knowing there is a job at the end of the line."

Books I read in Maine:

Hunting Trips of a Ranchman, Theodore Roosevelt
The Rise of Theodore Roosevelt, Edmund Morris
The Threefold Secret of the Holy Spirit, James McKonkey (This book had been very significant in William Borden's life.)
The Beckoning of Destiny, Kenneth Davis (about Franklin Roosevelt)
The Maine Woods, Henry David Thoreau

At the end of the season, in October, Doug flew up, and we took a wonderful trip all through New England. He flew home from Boston, and I drove home continuing to see interesting sites along the way.

One wonderful spiritual shrine was Theodore Roosevelt's home at Sagamore Hill on Long Island. It was a beautiful Victorian house with a great veranda, and as you would expect, it was filled with hunting trophies from Africa and North America.

I got home in October and spent some nice time with my family and friends before heading out to Montana. The ski season would start before Christmas, and so I would miss my first Christmas at home.

WHAT BAR HARBOR TAUGHT ME

In my first season in Bar Harbor, what did I learn, and how did it shape me?

1) I continued to be reaffirmed about the importance of others, both from a spiritual and social sense. We are created as social beings, and we need others on so many different levels.
2) I further affirmed that we are uniquely created beings. We are created by Christ and for Christ. We can never be God, and though we are created in God's image, we are not God; we are not all things to all people. We should get to know and revel in our unique identity and through Christ, try to be the best version of ourselves we can be.
3) I developed the philosophy of "know yourself, love yourself, and be yourself."
4) If we abide in God, and trust Him, he will faithfully sculpt us and send His angel ahead of us providing for our needs.

5) I was living by the seat of my pants and keeping my journal. These activities trained my mind, as nothing else could, to think on the fly, access situations, and make decisions in a fluid and changing environment. The journals were helping me build a psychological/spiritual house for the future, but in building that house, I was also building a mind based on logic and reason that could build and access a tour itinerary. I learned how to make decisions on the fly and go with and trust my gut intuition when there was no rule book to work from.

7

BIG SKY, MONTANA

1979–1980

Big Sky of Montana is a ski resort in winter and a dude ranch of sorts in the summer. It is nestled in the Rocky Mountains in southwestern Montana, forty-seven miles north of Yellowstone National Park, which is in the northwestern corner of Wyoming. Because of its close proximity to Yellowstone, you can enjoy not only the skiing at Big Sky, but also snowmobiling into the beauty of Yellowstone, with its geysers, thermal features, buffalo, and other animals.

The ski season started before Christmas, so they wanted me there around the twentieth of December. The first question was how would I get there? Montana and the Western Rockies in winter did not seem to be the best environment for a driver from the sunny south, and this time, if I did drive, I would have to drive alone. Getting there could be treacherous, and, once I got there, I would have little need for a car. I could have flown, but there was another way to get there that people neither then, nor now, would consider a very desirable way— the Greyhound bus. Yes, the bus came through Thomaston in 1979, and it was possible to buy a one-way ticket and ride Greyhound or Trailways all the way through to Montana. To me, at that time, it seemed adventurous, and it held the advantage that I did not have to do the driving. So, in the end, I left the driving to Greyhound and Trailways. I still have the check dated December 4, 1979 where I bought my one-way ticket from Thomaston to Bozeman, Montana for $86.00.

THOMASTON TO MONTANA VIA GREYHOUND AND TRAILWAYS

All along the way to Montana, I saw a changing kaleidoscope of scenery and people, so I never got bored. It was a continuation of the great adventure I was living, and in my journal, I noted it all. My general route was north to Atlanta, west to Dallas, then north through the panhandles of northern Texas and Oklahoma. I then continued up through eastern Colorado and Wyoming, finally crossing the Montana state line and turning west for the home stretch to Bozeman, Montana. I found it fascinating and noted everything I saw both inside and out of the big bus windows.

The first night I got off in Tuscaloosa, Alabama, and spent a nice weekend with my good friends Pete and Debbie Cavan. This was a comforting weekend with friends as I spent my last nights on the frontier of my known world. On Sunday afternoon I was headed westbound into the great unknown from both a physical and a spiritual sense. The thrill of it all swept away any fear or uncertainty in my mind. It is hard to convey the excitement I felt, the sense of adventure, and the romance of it all!!

As we crossed Alabama and Mississippi, I noted beautiful farmland with cows grazing, stately homes, and stops at various bus stations. As night fell, I started talking to a guy whose grandfather had owned the first outdoor movie studio in Hollywood.

He would spend exciting summers with his grandfather and got to meet many of the movie stars. His favorite was Fess Parker who played Daniel Boone in a weekly series. He also said there were some hippies who had taken over one of his grandfather's run-down sets that he didn't use any more. His grandfather decided to live and let-live and leave them alone. The young guy would find caves in the mountains nearby where there was abandoned drug paraphernalia. That abandoned set was called The Spahn Ranch, and those hippies would make national headlines in 1969 when they went on a murder spree orchestrated by their guru-leader, Charles Manson.

We crossed state lines, stopped in both big cities and small, out-of-the-way, hamlets. We arrived in Dallas at 3:30 a.m., had a thirty-minute layover, and then headed north. As we went through Childress and Amarillo, I saw brick streets for the first time. The landscape was littered with oil wells. They were short oil wells, not the tall derricks you see in the movies, pumping away everywhere, even in parking lots.

I stopped at 10:00 p.m. on Tuesday night in Colorado Springs at the Antlers Plaza Hotel, having read of its connection with Theodore Roosevelt, who had hunted in Colorado. I woke up the next morning to my first view of the Rockies, and I saw Pike's Peak with snow on top of it. By 9:50 a.m. the next morning, I was headed north through Denver and Ft. Collins, and later we crossed into Wyoming, where our route took us through Cheyenne, Chugwater, Wheatland, and Douglas. I remember seeing the sign for Chugwater and its population of 10!!

That night I asked the driver if I spent a night somewhere, could he suggest a route the next morning that would be scenic. He said I should spend the night in Casper, Wyoming and catch the 9:00 a.m. bus the next morning which would head up through the dramatic Wind River Range. I took his advice. We wound our way through the picturesque Wind River Canyon where the Wind River cut its narrow way through a gorge with huge cliffs on both sides. I loved riding the bus. For me, each unfolding panorama was new and exciting, and I noted it all in my diary.

Later that afternoon, we crossed into Montana and had a four-hour layover in the small town of Laurel, waiting for a westbound bus to Bozeman. Our layover was in what seemed to be more of a house than a bus station. Ten to fifteen people sat around what seemed more like a room in someone's house. Some, including me, sat on narrow stairs, which led upstairs. It was dark outside, and the light in the room was dim. You felt as if you were in your grandmother's house, and I felt as if I were living in a short story.

Over the next few hours all the people in that room told a little about themselves and their lives. Everyone respectfully listened to one person tell his or her tale, and then the next person would talk. One guy said he was in the rodeo. The scene of that room and the people and their stories lives in my memory to this day.

We headed for Bozeman at 9:05 p.m. The bus was full, and it was dark, cold, and very windy. At one point you could feel the wind pushing the bus sideways and the driver struggling to keep it in its lane.

People get into conversations with each other on the bus. I was sitting on the aisle and I heard a southern accent two-to-three rows in front of me. This voice came from a guy who was also sitting on the aisle. He was from Albany, Georgia, and we realized we were both going to work at Big Sky. His name was Kevin Oliver, and little did I know that God, in his amazing way, had just introduced me to me to the guy who would be my dorm mate for the next three and a half months. Kevin and I were similar in disposition. Neither of us were partiers, so it all worked out well.

After three hours the bus pulled up to the Bozeman station, and Kevin and I agreed that since it was already after midnight, the best plan was to sleep in the bus station and catch the Big Sky Shuttle the next morning. When we told the stationmaster that, he said he was closing the station for the night and directed us to the Rambona Hotel just up the street.

WELCOME TO BIG SKY

The next morning, we had time to relax, as our shuttle did not leave Bozeman until 12:30 p.m. The drive from Bozeman to the Big Sky Ski Resort took about an hour and wound its way up the beautiful Gallatin Canyon, which followed the Gallatin River. It was unlike any landscape I had seen before. The day I arrived, I wrote in my journal, "Arrived at Big Sky! I think I am going to like it here. Snow is on the ground. There are some nice people here, and Kevin and I are rooming together."

The next day I wrote, "Today was my first day of work. As a convention setup person, I end up doing most anything they don't have anyone else to do. Today I set up tables and chairs, shoveled snow, cleaned out the hotel van, and went to pick up the mail. Tomorrow I will work as a bellman. Got my employee ID and bought my ski pass."

As the days rolled by, and I proved reliable, I was often tapped to set up morning convention sessions and coffee breaks. In between time, I might find myself painting lockers, scraping ice off the front steps, or shuttling guests and bags to outlying condos.

During my free time, I learned to ski, and this was long before the advent of snowboarding. In the first few days, I bought a pair of Boyne 180s with Spademan bindings. They were on the low end of ski technology and fashion, but they got the job done.

The learning curve for skiing was painful and frustrating, particularly because I taught myself and learned from friends instead of taking lessons. Fortunately, I soon caught the knack of it. I would ski maybe three or four days a week, depending on when I worked.

In the first days, other than Kevin, I had trouble finding a group of people to do things with. Being away from home during the holidays, I fell into a spell of self-doubt. Two days before Christmas, I wrote in my journal,

> I'm having a spell of homesickness. I will miss being home with all my family and friends for Christmas and New Year's. I'm also feeling a little down about my future. I think I will teach for a while, and if I don't like that, maybe I will try hotel work. I really think I would like to teach high school history and have Bible studies for students at night . . . helping them to know Christ, how to be saved, and helping them come to a healthy self-image through him.

On Christmas Eve, I wrote in my journal, "Christmas Eve. I'm kinda down and homesick. I hope I don't spend another Christmas away from home."

Nevertheless, slowly, with the camaraderie of Kevin and other co-workers, I began to pull out of my holiday funk. On Christmas Day, I wrote, "Christmas Day! . . . Today was my first white

Christmas. Last night, Kevin and I ate the buffet dinner at the Huntley Lodge. We sat with a girl named Cindy Smith, who works in the cafeteria." Cindy was from California and a political science major. We had a great conversation, and Cindy would become a fun friend. I would come to call her "Scout" because her face, petite size, and short, black hair reminded me of the little girl named Scout in the movie *To Kill a Mockingbird.*

CHARLIE RUSSELL

A few days later, I went to Bozeman and wandered into a used bookstore. There, I found a great biography of the western painter, Charles Marion Russell. Charlie Russell's story of how he went west from St. Louis and lived with both cowboys and Indians was fascinating.

The book was full of color prints of Russell's works with their clever titles. One showed a hunter who had killed a bighorn sheep, but the sheep had fallen over a ledge onto an outcropping that made the kill difficult and dangerous to get to. The painting showed the hunter, rifle in hand, scratching his head and pondering his dilemma. Russell named the painting, "Meat's Not Meat, Till It's in the Pan."

I was thrilled with how Russell went west and dug his education out of the ground of firsthand experience. He spent time herding cows, on cattle drives, and later he lived with an Indian tribe. He was seeing and learning his subject first hand, and as a result, everything in his paintings was authentic, whether it was the situations he depicted, the signs on the Indians' horses, or the dry and dusty Western landscape.

Once again, like Addison Mizner in Palm Beach, and George B. Dorr in Bar Harbor, Charlie Russell, though long dead, was alive in the pages I read and became as much a mentor and role model as any living person could be. It was, and still is, thrilling to live in the presence of those I admire, find fascinating, and seek to emulate. Another great advantage to these role models was that they were all unique and superior characters who had achieved great things. And with so great a host of high achieving mentors, I was living in a wonderful and rarified atmosphere that was calling me to make something unique and special out of my life.

FUN TIMES WITH A FAMILY FROM SOUTH AMERICA

Sometimes I would spend time with interesting guests. One family I really enjoyed was the Estaban family from Bogata, Columbia. They were very wealthy, with a second house in Miami. The father was in the import/export business. Their family included five girls and four boys ranging in age from seven or eight to the late teens or early twenties. They were a very loving and handsome family, and all the older children looked after the younger children.

The South American, Latin sense of family was wonderful. I was charmed at how they all loved and took care of one another. The middle daughter, Kim, said her little brother Filipe looked on her as his mother. She would hug him and tell him what to do just as if she were his mother. Kim felt she was the apple of her father's eye, and she expressed that sentiment as best she could in English by saying, "I am the daughter of my father."

I spent the most time with Kim. She, her sisters, and I would go skiing, dancing at night, and sometimes meet for lunch. On New Year's Eve, skiers came down the mountain holding torches.

Kim and I had a crush on each other, and on the last day she gave me a plaid scarf and said in her charming way, "You not forget me." And I haven't.

My attraction to Kim came from a different place than I was used to. She was very pretty, but also, she and her sisters, though young, were very cosmopolitan and sophisticated compared to young American women of a similar age. They also knew how to have a good time, have their drinks, and still not feel that they had to go overboard to prove they were having fun. American girls had their own attraction, individualism, and sense of fun and confidence, but this introduction into a different way was both charming and attractive.

When they left, I was sad. My time with them had done a lot to bring me out of my holiday funk. They left at night, and the hotel that night was busy as I helped them with their bags. Cute little Filipe had a wine skin hung with a lanyard around his neck. Every once in a while, he would drink from the wine skin. I thought it was probably water or soft drink, and I asked him for a drink. I took the wine skin and squeezed a good draft into my mouth. When I swallowed, I immediately felt the burning of what I would find out was cognac.

EXPERIENCES IN THE SNOW

As I met new people, learned to ski, and found new things to study, I felt better about my stay at Big Sky. I wrote home on January 7, "As with all the places I've been, it is taking a while to cultivate an appreciation for my new home away from home. . . . I have been reading some Jack London, Robert Service, and a biography on Charles Russell, whose print I have enclosed. I have met some really nice people and am learning to ski fairly well. . . . The dry air really makes a difference. I went skiing yesterday, and it was around minus 2 degrees Fahrenheit." (Later in my stay I would get off the gondola at the top of the mountain to be greeted by a warning sign that said, "Frostbite warning, wind chill factor 42 below zero!" Nevertheless, you dressed for it, and it wasn't as bad you might think.) I finished my letter home by saying, "Traveling has its ups and downs, but for me, I see it as an invaluable preparation for the future. I am so grateful to be able to be doing this and have these experiences."

In mid-January, I took a trip into Yellowstone all the way to Old Faithful. I went with two employee friends, Jeff Altizer, a houseman from West Virginia, and Marion Fisher, a front desk clerk from California. We had a great time taking a snow cat—an enclosed vehicle with tracks like a tank—from the small town of West Yellowstone into Old Faithful where we spent the night at Snow Lodge. We went cross-country skiing and saw bald eagles, coyote, lots of buffalo, two moose, countless elk, thermal features, the Firehole River, and of course, Old Faithful. Later in my life, I would see the beauty of Yellowstone in summer, but, on this first trip, I saw Yellowstone in its winter blanket of snow. What a wonderful time and experience with new friends!

SERIOUS READING

I enjoyed reading Jack London's stories about the great north and also the wonderful poems of Robert Service. Service was a vagabond poet, and his poems about the Yukon and the beauty of the wild backcountry trained my sensitivity to enjoy, on a deeper level, the beauties of the scenery surrounding me in Montana. Without a doubt, one of the great gifts of the study of art and literature is how the artist's or the writer's sensibility soaks into you and, in turn, your sensibility and way of seeing is heightened and enriched. The study of the arts helps you to see the colors and the richness of the passing moments of life on a deeper level. In reality, there are no ordinary moments. Each moment of life is sacred and full of the eternal grandeur of God's presence and glory.

At that time, I was also reading Henry David Thoreau's *Walden*. Thoreau sang the praises of the benefits of serious reading. I took the time to write down this pertinent quote,

> The adventurous student will always study the classics. . . . For what are the classics but the noblest recorded thoughts of man. . . . To read well, that is to read true books in a true spirit, is a noble exercise, and one that will task the reader more than any exercise which the customs of the day esteem. It requires training such as the athletes underwent, the steady intention almost of the whole life to this subject. Books must be read as deliberately and reservedly as they were written.

With each passing day—amidst the fun of working, meeting fellow employees and guests, skiing, and enjoying the beauty of wintertime in the west—life and God reaffirmed in my heart and mind the importance of the lessons I had learned in Palm Beach and Bar Harbor. I was reaffirming lessons about the importance of people in our lives, lessons about how God has created each of us as unique beings, and how through Him, we are to know ourselves, love ourselves, and be ourselves. I noted in my journal, "I think so often that we would know God's will for us if, instead of questioning our desires, we would just say, 'What would I like to do?'"

As to getting to know, love, and be ourselves, I wrote, "It is important to get to know ourselves. A good way is to write down your likes, dislikes, hopes, fears." God gives us strengths, talents, intuition, and interests, and He also gives us dreams all as part of His plans for our lives.

A SEVERE MERCY, *A WATERSHED READ*

On January 25, I noted in my journal, "Got a book today that Doug sent me. He says it's the best book he ever read. It's called *A Severe Mercy* by Sheldon Vanauken."

This book would become one of the watershed reads of my life. The book had two important focuses. It followed the spiritual journey of the author and his wife from atheist to agnostic to Christian believer. It also was an interesting exploration into love—what makes it stay and endure and what makes it fade.

The reading of *A Severe Mercy* would affect many areas of my life. It introduced me to the reality that Christianity holds up under the rigorous demands of intellectual scrutiny, it delved into a study of what makes love last, and it was my first introduction to the mind of C. S. Lewis. It also further schooled me on the idea of the sacred nature of our passing moments. *A Severe Mercy* helped define, crystalize, and confirm many of the thoughts I had been developing, and it began a relationship with the author, Sheldon Vanauken, that my brother and I would carry on through letters, as well as a visit for Doug and two visits for me. Also, the author's passion for literature and poetry would result in my buying a book on poetry, falling in love with literature, and later, getting a degree in English.

I finished the book on January 30. I immediately wrote to Mr. Vanauken, telling him how much I enjoyed his book and telling him about my spiritual journey and all the things I was learning along the way. I mentioned how his words defined many of the thoughts I had already been having. I talked about how I saw God's leading me through secular interests and reading as well as the Bible and prayer and how, over time, God was freeing me from a spiritual straightjacket of legalism into the wonderful joy of a relationship with Him.

I got a quick reply dated February 6, 1980. Mr. Vanauken, like his spiritual friend and mentor C. S. Lewis, felt it was his spiritual duty to respond to all correspondence sent to him, much of it from interested readers like me. Here is his reply.

> *"Thank you for writing. I'm glad ASM meant what it did to you. I am warmed to you because of your using the word "romantic" correctly—few do. I might mention that Harper and Row are publishing a novel by me next month that I describe as "high romance," Gateway to Heaven. The adventures and temptations of a young couple in the '60s. You have written with a good deal of self-insight, and you know the answers to many of your questions. I would not let what you call "legalism" bother you too much. In your heart and mind you know whether you are putting Him first, doing His will for Him. I don't myself pray as regularly as I'd like or read the Bible regularly. I'll read a lot one day, and no more for a week perhaps, and I pray lots of little prayers. You ask if I think it (love of Christ, not legalism) will come in time? Yes—if you keep it before you as a goal. You ask how I harmonize my romantic love of beauty with*

> *Christ. No problem. Christ is beauty, the trees and the mountains are him also. Sailing "Grey Goose" [Vanauken's sailboat] would be a way to be close to Him. Loving life and beauty, joyously knowing that God is joy, that God can grin, that God means us to drink of the wine of life outpoured . . . you see? Loving life joyously is worship."* Read the novel GTH. Write again if I can help.
>
> Under the Mercy,
> Sheldon Vanauken

This book and my subsequent correspondence and visits with Mr. Vanauken all came at the right time—what the Bible would call "the fullness of time."

All that had come before, and now Vanauken's book, conspired together in my life like the continual unwrapping of the graveclothes of the risen Lazarus. God was releasing me from the straightjacket of spiritual legalism, which had been a taskmaster of spiritually dead dos and don'ts. I was now being set free into the glorious freedom and joy that Christ meant for me. It was necessary to have known the bondage in order to truly appreciate the freedom. Wow! I can't thank the Lord enough for how He has used everything in my life to not only give me eternal salvation, but also the incredibly thrilling and freeing moment-by-moment relationship that has brought and is continuing to bring who I am to its fullest fruition. He means, dear reader, to do the same for you!

SNOW DIAMONDS

One of the most beautiful things was the sparkle of new fallen snow at night. Often, we went dancing at Mountain Lodge.

By the time we walked back, it was around midnight. On a clear night, when the moon and stars were out, the snowscape was lit in a dim, pale, glow so that we didn't need a flashlight. It was beautiful and completely silent. As we walked back to the employee dorms across a field covered by a foot or two of new-fallen snow, we would either blaze our own trail or follow in the tracks of someone who had gone ahead. This was a particularly beautiful experience if you were alone in all the sacred silence of the moment. As you walked through that field and looked around, the moon glow caused the snow crystals to sparkle like diamonds across the entire field. The sacred reverie of these moments was broken only by the sound of your feet plodding through knee-deep snow. The memory of those late-night silent walks across that field of sparking snow diamonds will stay with me as long as I live.

PICKING UP THE OWNER—WHAT COULD GO WRONG?

Because I was college educated and could talk with anyone, I was often tapped for special duties. One time the owner, the board of directors, and their wives were flying in from Michigan. Mr. Everett Kircher was the owner and Charles "Chuck" Moll was the chief financial officer. The mountain manager asked me to take a van into town and pick them up at the airport. They would be flying in by private jet, and I was told that the owner was obsessive about every detail of the arrival protocol.

Though I could carry on a good conversation, something unexpected usually went wrong when I got tapped for special duty. The problems usually weren't my fault, so I continued to get these special missions. When I was called up for this detail, and when I heard of the owner's obsession about protocol, I got a bad feeling. This sense of doom hung on the periphery of my consciousness, but I tried to ignore it and headed out with the hope that this mission would be successful.

The first part of the plan was to take the company van to the car wash in Bozeman and give it a thorough cleaning. Protocol one completed. Check!

The second part of the protocol was more complicated. I was to position the van at the private gate at the airport, which would give me access to the private jet parking area. When the jet taxied up, I was to await full shutdown, and then the gate would open. I was to drive into the jet-parking zone and approach the jet from the left side and park at an angle just forward of the left wing, with the front of the van pointing just ahead of the nose of the jet. I was then to open the doors of the van and help with luggage and boarding.

When the group arrived, all went well. Everything was done according to the specs. I introduced myself. Everyone was in good spirits, and the loading process went off without a hitch. Once everyone one was loaded, we were ready to leave the airport grounds for the hour-long drive back to Big Sky. Protocol two completed. Check!

Mr. Kircher sat up front with me, and the rest of the VIPs and their wives sat on the three benches behind us. As we rolled out, the ones in back entertained themselves in conversation, and I engaged Mr. Kircher, who I knew was a golfer. When he heard I was from Georgia and had both attended the Masters and actually played the Augusta National, I was golden. By the time we reached the resort entrance, we were having a high old time, and I felt I was home free. What could possibly go wrong?... Uh . . . apparently, quite a bit.

As we turned into the resort, the road ahead was nicely cleared. Tiny Bingman and his crew had done their snow and ice-clearing job well. Unfortunately, Mr. Kircher said, "Russ, take a right at the next road; I would like to show the board the progress on the new condominiums."

When we got to the next road, I only saw ice and snow and slush. I slowed to a stop. I said, "I don't think we should go down there. It looks pretty icy."

Mr. Kircher replied, "Oh, just go ahead. It shouldn't be any problem." And so, with this ill-fated directive, the doomed party proceeded.

Within twenty feet, the tires started spinning on the ice, and Mr. Kircher started giving orders in an irritated and excited tone. With his volume increasing as he delivered steady quick-fire orders, my blood pressure began to rise, and with it, my brain's mainframe quickly became overloaded and began to shut down. Everything was happening quickly now, and the easygoing atmosphere of the wonderful drive up the canyon now turned into chaos. The tires began to slide sideways and then the high whine of spinning tires gave the final commentary on our disintegrating situation. We were stuck!

Confusion and mild panic now spread from the cockpit back through the passenger cabin. The copilot, clearly irritated, immediately laid the situation in the lap of the pilot, "If you had listened to me, we wouldn't have gotten stuck!"

I was clearly in no position to register any rebuttal up the chain of command, but I heard the voice of an unlikely advocate coming from the passenger cabin. It was the copilot's wife! "Well, he warned you not to come down this road!"

This only seemed to incense the copilot, and he exploded. "All right! Everybody out of the van! Chuck, you get behind the wheel, and everybody else help push." We all got out and gingerly stepped into the icy brown slush of the mess made by the spinning tires.

Fortunately, we were not stuck that badly, and soon we were all headed up the mountain, having abandoned any attempt to see the new condos. I was stripped of command and bore the indignation of a view from the back bench. Chuck Mull, the oldest in the group, was now given command of the ship, and Mr. Kircher, despite being responsible for the ship's recent fate, retained his position as copilot. The party ultimately arrived safely at the Huntley Lodge.

Mr. Kircher did not mention the incident, so I was left with a clean record leaving me available for future duties, with only a stain on my confidence and self-image.

DOORS THAT OPEN IN LIFE AND DOORS THAT CLOSE

In our unique design, I am convinced that God creates us with interests and desires, talents and gifts—as well as life circumstances that He uses to guide us. Along the way, based on these things, doors will open and doors will shut. As a believer, I believe that all along my way, God has had His hand on my life and was using everything to sculpt me and to guide me. David assures us in Psalm 139:5 that God has "beset me behind and before and laid his hand upon me." This is not just what He was doing then; it is also what He is doing now and what He will do in the future.

I don't believe in luck, and I don't believe in random coincidences. I believe that God is a very personal God and is intimately involved in our passing moments, even those that seem insignificant. God, through the Holy, Spirit literally indwells the believer. (John 14: 16,17, 23) I also believe that He is always patiently desiring that we will engage and commune with him. He has made all this possible through Christ. He is continually knocking on the door of our hearts, but the key is on the inside, and we must choose to open that door. This potential is what makes our passing moments so epic as they are laced with pregnant possibility of communing with our Creator.

I believe God knows us as intimately as Psalm 139 says He does: "O LORD, thou hast searched me and known me. Thou knowest my downsitting and my uprising, thou understandest my thought afar off" (Psalm 139:1–2).

I think Psalm 139 also talks about doors in life. In verses 5–6, "Thou hast beset me behind and before, and laid thine hand upon me. Such knowledge is too wonderful for me, it is high, I cannot attain unto it," I believe David is saying that God besets us behind and before, that He allows both good and bad, that some things work out and others don't, that doors open and doors shut, and that in all these circumstances, God is there with His hand upon us. We may feel alone, but God is there, using both the good and the bad, the doors that open and the doors that shut, to guide us in life and to sculpt us into the people we are becoming.

While I was at Big Sky, I continued to pursue an internship with Senator Talmadge's office in Washington. This process had been going on for almost a year. In a letter to Senator Talmadge's office, I had written, "It has been a long desire of mine to spend some time working for a senator. I am very interested in getting an internship, and see it as a great part in my education for my future."

As it turned out, this was a door that would be closed in my life. Life moved on, and it never worked out. Now, with a bird's-eye view of my life, I can say that I am thankful not only for the doors that opened, but I am also thankful for those that shut. I can also say that we have many dreams over the course of our lives, and I am thankful for the dreams that came true, but I am also thankful for the dreams that did not come true.

I believe Romans 8:28 when it says, "And we know that all things work together for good to them that love God, to them who are the called according to his purpose." It never says that all things are good. It says that all things, whether good or bad, are used together for good. I am truly convinced and thankful that all along my way, a loving God has been there with His hand upon me, using the doors that opened and those that shut to guide me into the image of Christ, and in that process, He is changing me from glory to glory into the fullness of all He envisioned for me when He created me. Abiding in this truth is the place of joy, meaning, and peace…

And so, just like the job at Delta, I never got that internship in Washington. God had a different plan, and as I was to see, one that suited me far greater than any I could ever have imagined.

SETTLING IN AND PLANNING TO MOVE ON

By February, I had fully settled into social life at Big Sky. I had made lots of casual friends, but I spent most of my time with a few close ones. Outside of skiing and working, I spent a lot of time with Marion Fisher, Jeff, and Kevin. I had also made good friends with a girl named Lindsey McSwain. Marion and I loved to go dancing, we had great conversations, and we had a great time together. Lindsey and I had a different kind of relationship based on different interests. We loved to cook together, take walks, listen to music, and play cards. When I first met Lindsey, she seemed like an emotional stonewall, but as we got to know each other, I found she was very soft, tender, and caring. Like many people, it just took her a while to open up. Everything I experienced in travel enabled me to learn so much about people.

Marion, Jeff, and I decided to end our time at Big Sky a little early instead of staying until the original April 15 deadline. Jeff and I planned to buy thirty-day bus passes and tour the West before heading back east. Marion would first head home but join me later on a tour of the East Coast.

About this time, Doug sent me another book called *Dove*, by Robin Lee Graham. This book was about a young boy who became the youngest person to sail single-handedly around the world. This book reconfirmed my choice in taking the road less traveled, and highlighted the importance of how that road was preparing me for an as yet unseen future.

At the beginning of the book there was a letter that Robin's father had written to Robin's mother expressing the mixed emotions of letting their young son set off on such a dangerous and unpredictable journey. The letter resonated with me so much that I copied it into my diary in full.

> Dearest Norma,
>
> Our work is done, and Lee has sailed. I watched the boat until it was out of sight in the morning mist. I returned to the slip to pick up some things. All the farewell wishers were gone. The slip was empty.
>
> As I drove home without him sitting beside me as we had done for so many days, I had a great big empty feeling. We have been so close and so busy, and now there is nothing. I feel that

Lee has sailed out of my life. I have lost his boyhood companionship. When I see him again, he will be a man looking for a life of his own with friends and other interests where you and I are not included.

It happens to all parents, but it is so hard to take when it happens all of a sudden as it did to me as he moved out of his slip and down the channel. I don't think I would ever have let him go if I didn't love him so much. It would have been easier on me to have kept him at home.

In my heart, I know it is the right thing to let him go. He was happier today than I have ever seen him, or than he will probably ever will be, and happier at sixteen than most people will be after living a comfortable life stretching it to a safe end.

Lee knows the risk he is taking as he knows there are risks to those at home. Nobody can be entirely protected from the mishaps of life.

If anything should happen to Lee—and it would be the end of me if it did—I would still feel that I did the right thing for him.

Success or failure, he is fulfilling his destiny. We all have only one life, some are short and some are long. He loves life and wants a little more out of it than to follow convention out of fear of what others may think, or to be just another face in the crowd that follows the herd.

Please don't worry about Lee. The boat is safe as can be. He knows this is the greatest thing

that could happen to him and he appreciates what
we have done for him to make it possible.
With Love,
Lee[1]

When I read this letter, I realized how Daddy must have felt. And, the letter also highlighted how I felt about the long journey I was taking. As I have said before, I will forever be grateful to my father for letting me find my own path in life. It was not the path most would take, but it was mine. Everyone has his or her own unique path. I also want to say that I truly feel that everyone's life path is epic, no matter how conventional it may seem. It is not a matter of looking for a glamorous or flashy or dramatic path, it is about quietly and intentionally seeking to follow your authentic path, whether it is that of a doctor, a lawyer, or sailing around the world.

MY SEASON AT BIG SKY ENDS

At the end of March, we started winding down our time at Big Sky and going our own ways. Marion and Lindsey left, and Jeff and I prepared for our big bus trip. I mailed home some items, including a big elk horn that Lindsey had given me. On Tuesday, March 28, Jeff and I were at the Bozeman Bus station ready for the 4:50 pm bus heading for Butte, Montana, and on to Idaho Falls, Idaho. We were off on our grand adventure with a thirty-day bus pass and all of the American West before us.

SIGNIFICANT BOOKS I READ AT BIG SKY

Robert Service Poems
The Charles M. Russell Book, Harold McCraken

A Severe Mercy, Sheldon Vanauken
101 Famous Poems
Poems that Live Forever, edited by Hazel Fellerman
Call of the Wild, Jack London
Dove, Robin Lee Graham

WHAT BIG SKY TAUGHT ME

By this time in my travels, God was reconfirming the core truths I had learned in Palm Beach and Bar Harbor. Everything I learned and read reenforced the validity of what I had learned before. God was a close, intimate, personal God who loved me and wanted the best for me. He had His hand on me, and I could be at peace about the doors that opened and the doors that shut. Also, relationships, whether with God or with people, were what mattered most. Jesus had summed it up when He declared that the two greatest commandments were to love God with all your heart and soul and mind and to love your neighbor as you do yourself. Notice He assumed you would also love yourself.

---

1. Robin Lee Graham with Derek L. T. Gill, *Dove*, (Sydney, Australia: Angus & Robertson, 1972).

8

THE BIG BUS RIDE HOME FROM MONTANA

Jeff and I left Bozeman on Friday afternoon, March 28, 1980, just before 5:00 p.m. and wound our way through Butte, Montana, and on to Idaho Falls, Idaho. Part of the charm of riding the bus was seeing the small towns and the places used for bus stations. In Three Forks, Montana, we made a stop at Johnson's Drug Store. In Whitehall, Montana, we stopped at the Me Like Um Chief Motel. We crossed the Continental Divide, passed through Butte, and were in Idaho Falls at 12:30 a.m. Saturday morning.

Due to the bus schedules, we had to make quick decisions. We had planned to go to Jackson Hole, Wyoming, but scrubbed that when we found that the bus going that way would not leave Idaho Falls until 8:00 a.m. Monday morning. So we headed to Salt Lake City with a plan to go to Lake Tahoe after that. As small as this decision was, I now see it as God's teaching me to gather and assess information and schedules on the fly. I would do this numerous times on this trip, and this training would be very important to me thirteen years later when I began to create and lead tours.

We rolled into Salt Lake City at 5:30 a.m. and passed the Mormon Tabernacle, with its spires lighting the dark sky. We used our break in Salt Lake City to grab a quick breakfast before heading on. Later, we got back on the bus and were soon passing a huge Union Pacific rail yard and a Morton Salt plant. Breaking out of the west side of the city, we passed the Great Salt Lake, surrounded by low mountains and stretching north all the way to the horizon. It was nice to focus on what we were seeing and leave the driving to someone else.

Heading west toward Nevada, we crossed great stretches of salt flats with mountains in the distance. At the Nevada state line, we stopped at a casino. I put thirty cents into a slot machine and joked that it must be broken because nothing came out.

As we moved on, the landscape was that of vast, open expanses of nothing but low sagebrush and rocky, sandy soil with mountain ranges in the distance. It is hard to imagine the pioneers heading west in their wagons, not knowing what lay ahead and hoping that it would be better than what was behind them. In a landscape like this, doubts had to have crept into their minds. Think of it! They had left loved ones and all they knew in hopes of creating a better future for themselves and their children. For many, this desperate roll of the dice paid off, but for some, it did not. That is life. We make choices, and their consequences sometimes lead to life and good fortune, sometimes to disaster, and sometimes to death.

We pulled into Reno, Nevada, at 4:50 p.m. and got a room for forty dollars. In our room, we found two-dollar certificates both for slot change and for food at a place called Harold's Club. Jeff somehow had a certificate for an extra two-dollars in slot change, so we pooled our resources and managed to play our good fortune in such a way that we ate their food at their expense and enjoyed an evening of gambling on their dime. I walked out after playing and eating at their expense, having not spent a dime of my own money.

The next morning, we rose early and worked the bus schedules to spend a day traveling around Lake Tahoe. Important to traveling is picking up advice wherever you can. In South Lake Tahoe, the man at the bus station told us that, given our timeframe, the best way to see the most was to take the bus to the town of Truckee. And so we did. All along the way we had nice views of the blue lake below and the beautiful mountains all around. We also stopped at the Squaw Valley Ski Resort which hosted the 1960 winter Olympics. That man at the ticket counter's name was Don E. Lee, and he claimed to be the great-great-great grandson of Robert E. Lee. I had him put his autograph in my journal.

We then took the 4:00 p.m. bus to Sacramento, the capitol of California. It was a beautiful drive that wound through the High Sierras, down through rolling hills, and into the valley where Sacramento lay. I wrote, "The Sierras are beautiful, especially on a day like today! The sun is lowering in the sky and shining down through the huge pines. The road winds through the mountains, which rise on either side. Lots of pines leaving a carpet of needles. The rocky slopes are often covered in snow."

When we got off the bus, we talked to two policemen who said that the area around the bus station was dangerous, and they suggested we stay at the Vagabond Hotel. The next morning, we walked to the state capitol building, where the grounds were graced with palm trees and lots of beautiful flowers. As we left the city, to the east, we could still see the snow-covered peaks of the Sierras.

We headed south into the San Joaquin Valley and saw why this region is so well known for growing the fruits and vegetables of America. We rode east to Merced, gateway to the magnificent Yosemite Valley. The approach to the Sierra Nevada

Range was a beautiful drive through lush, green foothills covered in white oak trees. The green foothills were such a welcome vision after the brown, treeless expanses of northwestern Utah and Nevada. If we had been travelling later during the summer, these California hills would have been brown, but in early spring, this lush green was a welcome sight.

We followed the winding course of the Merced River, lined with brilliant rosebud trees that were a vivid purple in the shade. At 5:00 p.m. we arrived in the incomparable Yosemite Valley, a sacred cathedral of nature with massive granite cliffs on both sides and waterfalls everywhere. We stayed in a camp called Curry Village. The camp offered nice canvas tents built on elevated wooden floors with wooden doors. Each tent was furnished with two cots, a chest of drawers, and a chair. Bathrooms and showers were in a communal area.

The next morning, on Tuesday, April 1, I wrote, "Yosemite is beautiful! I got up about 6:15 a.m., before the sun rose over the mountain peaks. The first light hit the western peaks, and then, with the sun still hidden in the east, the yellow light began to trace around the valley rim and slowly flow down the sides of the granite walls." Experiences like the sacredness of this sunrise added another significant layer to the depth and richness of these passing days. All the experiences I was having combined to fill a vast inner spiritual reservoir from which I drink to this very day.

On that sunny day, we wandered the valley, enjoying the waterfalls and streams. Yosemite Falls was magnificent. It plunged from the top of the granite rim to some unseen pool and then plunged a second time to the valley floor below.

We stayed three nights and two days, enjoying ranger walks, nature hikes, and scrambling over boulder-strewn streams. We feasted our eyes in every direction on the beautiful valley floor, waterfalls and streams, and the granite walls and peaks of Half Dome and El Capitan. Seeing all this wonder for the first time—and with all the expectant joy and hope of youth—we knew just what the naturalist John Muir felt and meant when he called this valley a great cathedral of nature.

On April 3 we left Yosemite Valley and headed to San Francisco. It was exciting to see so many places we had always heard about. We crossed back through the great San Joaquin Valley with its beautiful rolling hills covered with orchards bearing everything from almonds and pistachios to peaches and every conceivable variety of fruit.

We arrived in San Francisco at 5:00 p.m. As we got near the city, we struck up a conversation with two girls on the bus. They told us they lived in a commune outside San Francisco and thought we should live there too. The Charles Manson murders had happened about ten years earlier, so with that image still in my mind, the idea of a commune took on a whole different meaning. I declined! We stayed at the Powell Hotel, and, from there, set out to see the sights of the city by the bay. We went to Chinatown and the next day we went to Fisherman's Wharf and Alcatraz.

From San Francisco, we caught the 5:15 p.m. bus heading south for Santa Cruz. We rode an inland route through a landscape of green mountains and lakes. When we arrived in Santa Cruz, we took a local bus and then walked three blocks to New Brighton Beach. The weather had turned pretty by the end of the day, and though we had a cheap twenty-five-dollar tent, we decided to sleep in our sleeping bags on the beach under a canopy of stars. The night was pleasant, and we figured we had the sound of the surf to lull us to sleep.

At first the surf sounded so nice, but with the incoming tide it got louder and louder, and closer and closer. Finally, we decided to move to the official campground on a high cliff overlooking the beach. There, we set up our tent and had a good night's sleep. The next morning, we took showers at the campground and enjoyed the spectacular view of Monterey Bay from our cliff-top viewpoint.

We then rode the bus back to town and ate breakfast at the Lost and Found Café. Across the street was a bookstore, and I have never been able to pass up a good bookstore. Browsing the shelves, I came across a book that particularly interested me because I had just finished *Dove*, the story of the youngest person ever to sail single-handedly around the world.

The book I found was about the *first* person to ever sail single-handedly around the world: *Sailing Alone around the World* by Joshua Slocum. It was wonderful! In 1895, Slocum had bought a derelict boat he found abandoned in a field along the New England coast. He put $553.62 into refurbishing the boat and christened it "Spray." He set sail on a three-year voyage around the world with only $1.50 in his pocket, and he couldn't swim!

In spite of these challenges, between 1895 and 1898, Slocum single-handedly circumnavigated the world. Along the way, he made money by giving lectures about his adventure. What an awesome story to read at any time of your life, but it was especially inspiring then, when I was sailing the uncharted seas of my own young life. That book was fuel in my furnace and wind in my sails. It confirmed my confidence in the value of the vagabond life I was living.

From Santa Cruz, we moved on to Monterey. After arriving, we went to a Safeway grocery store, bought some hot dogs, and proceeded to the campground. The skies were growing darker, but we found some dry wood, built a fire, cooked, ate, and set up the tent. Social life in the campground was good that night.

A middle-aged couple with a camper van invited us for tea and hot chocolate. Later, we met two young couples and had a great time, sharing thoughts and travel experiences.

Rain fell off and on, and then during the night the wind began to blow. Down went the front pole of the tent. Rather than set the pole back up, I left it down because it had been making noise as the wind whipped around the tent. But with the front of the tent down, water began to pool on its surface and soak through to our sleeping bags. While I managed to sleep through all this, probably because I was on a higher side, Jeff woke up and spent the rest of the night wet, cold, and miserable. In the morning, we showered, broke camp, and on the way out of the campground, threw the tent in a trashcan!

We spent the early part of the morning around Monterey's Fisherman's Wharf and watched the sea lions. At 10:30 a.m., we caught the bus for a beautiful ride down the coast to Big Sur. The round-trip to Big Sur was only $2.80. The bus route went through Carmel with its quaint shops and then along the coast most of the way. The rocky cliffs rose straight out of the ocean. The land was weather-beaten with cliffs divided by green ravines. The whole trip was one beautiful scene after another of pounding surf, white foam, green headlands, and huge gray rocks jutting out of the sea.

The bus driver announced that we were at our destination. We got off seemingly in the middle of nowhere. We thought, *Is this Big Sur?* We found that this spectacular stretch of coast was indeed called Big Sur. There was a small shop and an eating place that seemed to be perched high in the trees called *Nepenthe*, which, in Greek, means "no sorrow." We climbed winding stairs past the shop and up to the restaurant, which seemed like a big rambling tree house, and from its perch we had stunning views up and down the coast.

The setting of Nepenthe had an oriental ambiance with the restaurant cradled in the fingers of gnarled trees rising through the structure here and there. The restaurant was a California icon. Yes, the lunch was expensive, but the views were stunning. The bus ride had cost only $2.80 and had given us an ever-changing panorama of amazing views and now we enjoyed this amazing restaurant. The price was well worth the life experience we got in return.

Our next two stops were with friends from Big Sky. In Santa Barbara, we stayed with Cindy Smith, the girl I had nicknamed "Scout." Her apartment was only three blocks from the beach. The next day we hung out with Cindy, washed clothes, spent some at the beach and rested.

From Santa Barbara we took a late afternoon bus down the coast to Long Beach, where we stayed with Marion Fisher. As we traveled down the coast, it was a beautiful evening with palm trees silhouetted against a sunset. We passed the beach at Malibu and Pepperdine University. We also passed the Goodyear airship operations center and saw a big blimp on the ground. We finally reached Long Beach where Marion picked us up and took us back to her house.

We spent the next day and a half with Marion, seeing the local sites. We went to Hermosa Beach and skated up and down the bike-and-skate path along the beach. It was a total California scene with lots of people playing beach volleyball.

Later in the day, we toured the Queen Mary, a magnificent ocean-going grand dame from days gone by that now operated as a hotel. We took a fascinating tour, and learned all about the ship's history and the details of its structure. It is so interesting how, in God's plan, what we do in the present is always preparing us for the future. I had no way of knowing a tour like this was preparing me to think through, organize, scout out, and learn about an interesting place to go. My journal is full of interesting details of our trip. Here is a sample of my notes:

> "During WWII it was used as an armed troop transport. It took thirty tons of paint to paint her. The ship has four 40,000 horsepower turbine engines, and she travels at a speed of thirty-three miles per hour. In 1967, it cost $70,000 a day to keep her in running condition. She got thirteen feet to the gallon, and it took three million gallons to make a round-trip trans-Atlantic voyage."

This is just a sample of the notes I took. How could any graduate school have been any better in preparing me for a future in tours and travel. I was living by the seat of my pants, learning to make decisions on the fly, learning to gather information, and how to lay out an itinerary. You couldn't learn this from a book the way you could by living it. It was all here in the daily "courses" while I was living in what some people might call my "wasted years."

After two great days, Jeff and I caught the 6:45 p.m. bus for Flagstaff, Arizona. We had learned that overnight runs would put us in position to make the most of the following day. By 8:45 a.m. the next morning, we were in Flagstaff and in a totally different landscape.

Once again, because we gleaned some good intel from various sources, we bought a tour ticket that would take us to the Grand Canyon, give us a nice tour of the South Rim all the way to the Desert Outlook, and bring us back to Flagstaff at 5:00 p.m. We left at 9:10 a.m. and in two hours we were looking into the amazing spectacle that is the Grand Canyon. I wrote,

> *"It is huge and beautiful. There is a lovely change of colors starting from the bottom to the top. There are various shades of greens, reds, and browns that show the ledges and different strata of the canyon. The day was sunny and warm, and the distant parts of the canyon seem to hang under a blue haze, which I guess is caused by the sun filtering down through the atmosphere and maybe dust particles in the air."*

Once again, while I didn't know it, the future tour guide was being born in me. I wrote notes on the details I heard and the visual and spiritual impressions I absorbed. Now, as I read these notes, I still find them fascinating: *"The two nearest points of the north and south rim are four miles apart, and the farthest parts are eighteen miles apart. . . . The Canyon is about one mile deep, and the muddy Colorado River winds through it for about 227 river miles. . . . The first Europeans saw the canyon in 1540, and it has changed little since then."*

That day was a super-charged learning experience compressed into seven hours. It is amazing how much you can add to your knowledge in the space of just one day. I learned about geology, ecosystems, plants and animals, history, Native American culture, and the arts—a fantastic liberal arts education. It was said of Herman Melville that his days on the deck of a whaling ship were his Harvard and his Yale. In these wonderful years, days like these were my Harvard and Yale.

The Havasupai tribe lived in the canyon because of the river's fresh water and flat land at the spot they had chosen. John Wesley Powell, with only one arm, had led the first expedition through the canyon just after the Civil War, and he was the first to take the river route through it. Thomas Moran, who was on Powell's expedition, painted what he saw, and his paintings spread the word about this amazing place. As a result, people were eager to see it for themselves. Now I had seen it myself, and it had opened whole new rooms of exploration in my mind. There was so much to learn, so much to enjoy. One thing was for certain: Life would never be boring again.

Jeff and I were maxing out the value of our bus passes. By 9:00 p.m. that night we were back in Flagstaff and holed up in the library of Northern Arizona University, across the street from the Greyhound bus station. We read and rested until our 3:00 a.m. departure for Durango, Colorado, gateway to the incredible cliff dwellings at Mesa Verde National Park.

Our route overnight took us out of Arizona and into New Mexico, where we headed north toward the southwest corner of Colorado. We rode through varying landscapes, often with mountain ranges in the distance. Riding the bus, you saw beautiful sites—but you also saw another side of life. I wrote in my journal,

> *"Riding the bus, you see a lot of misery and heartache. You often see drunks in the bus station. In Merced, California, a woman came in the station, bleeding from the nose, followed by a man at whom she cursed and screamed. She seemed to be afraid of him. I wondered if he had beaten her. In San Francisco, we saw an old woman huddled in the alcove of an abandoned storefront. She was bent over, and we never saw her face, but we saw her several times, and I think she spent the whole day there in that same position."*

We were covering a lot of territory and seeing wonderful sites, but we had spent two straight nights on the bus and needed to get some rest. When we reached Durango, a lady at the bus station told us about a hostel that would cost us seven dollars each. We got a room with two beds and blankets, but no sheets, so we slept in our sleeping bags. Downstairs, we had access to a kitchen and a living room with books. It's amazing what you can get for a few bucks if you're willing to step outside the normal expectations.

To get to Mesa Verde, we rented a car for forty dollars. The hour-and-a-half drive to the park wound through mountains and mesas. The Cliff Palace, the largest and most photographed cliff dwelling, was closed until the summer, but we did see a wonderful cliff dwelling called Spruce Tree House. Once again, everything was so interesting that I took lots of notes.

> *"The Pueblo Indians supposedly came to this area about 1600 years ago, or about 400 AD. At first, they lived on top of the mesas but later they moved down into the sides of the cliffs where the elements had eroded a cavern into the side. Their reason for moving into the side from the top was probably to attain more protection from the weather. They lived in these dwellings only about 75 to 100 years and then left, probably because of a drought; they may also have exhausted the resources of the area and worn out the soil. There are about 600 dwellings in the park area ranging from a one-room storage dwelling to the largest, the Cliff Palace, with 217 rooms.*

> *The Indians were both farmers and hunters. They mainly grew corn, beans, and squash.*
>
> *Amazingly enough, the cliff dwellings weren't discovered until 1888, when Richard Wetherill, a local rancher, found them while he was looking for stray cattle. When Wetherill saw the Spruce Tree House, he gave it that name because it had a large spruce tree in front of it. The tree reached to the top of the mesa, and Wetherill said that the only way to get down to the dwelling on the side of the cliff was to climb down the tree."*

That night, at the youth hostel, I lay awake for a good while thinking about where I would spend the coming summer. I felt that I had seen plenty of the continental US, and I felt like returning to some place in the Northeast to further my interest in sailing. I could return to Maine, or I could go someplace new like Nantucket, Martha's Vineyard, or Cape Cod.

After Mesa Verde, we would head back south to Albuquerque, New Mexico, and then east to Texas and on to the Southeast. Our passes gave us the ability to use either Trailways or Greyhound. In Albuquerque, we got our third Ameri-Pass booklet, a ticket system that featured unlimited travel for a certain time. We were wearing them out!

We now went on a dead run across the brown and dusty expanses of New Mexico and West Texas. A day later at 5:00 a.m. we arrived in Dallas. I had now gone full circle and was returning on the same route I had taken the previous December when I went to Montana.

In Dallas, we had a three-hour layover. That was plenty of time to make a personal and very important pilgrimage. I caught a taxi to Dealey Plaza where President Kennedy had been assassinated. I had been in the third grade on that Friday when we all heard the news. The spiritual and emotional trauma of that day, and the way television so intensified those emotions, shocked and awakened my sensitivity in a big way.

I wrote in my journal about going to Dealey Plaza,

> *"It was just a spur of the moment thing, but I think the time there this morning will be remembered as the most special time so far. When I got there the sun was beginning to come up in the east behind the city's tall buildings. The air was crisp and the park-like area lay in an early morning silence. Being 5:45 a.m., I had the place all to myself and this, combined with the setting, the silence, the beauty, and the influence John Kennedy has had on my life, made this a very special time. It was through my readings of JFK's life that the Lord first introduced me to spiritual romance and beauty. Walking around this area in front of the Texas Book Depository, the grassy knoll, and above the triple underpass, was an experience of beauty and romance, and seemed to hold a timeless air."*

This moment was deepened and intensified not only by how it had affected me in the third grade but also by concepts about beauty and romance that I had discovered in reading *A Severe Mercy* at Big Sky. Again, the present is always preparing us for the future. The rest of my journal's commentary on that Dealey Plaza experience was made possible by what I had learned in reading *A Severe Mercy*. In the following passage, beauty is defined for me as a deep spiritual quality mingled with truth and eternal meaning. Timelessness is experienced when we have a moment in this world when we experience something of the eternal, spiritual world and have the time to take it all in. I wrote,

> *"This is the essence of joy; when we have a meaningful encounter of beauty accompanied by a sense of timelessness. Meaningful encounters of beauty don't come often and, so often, when they do, they are not accompanied with a sense of timelessness, rather we are rushed and hurried for one reason or another, and we don't have time to savor the encounter."*

And so, this setting in Dealey Plaza, which to another person might have been just a bunch of buildings, was, for me, an encounter with beauty in a deep, eternal, spiritual sense. We can never say what others may enjoy, for we each encounter beauty differently as a result of what is meaningful in our lives.

In the end, the deep spiritual connection of those moments in Dealey Plaza connecting a little boy in the third grade on November 22, 1963 with an older man on April 13, 1980, made it a meaningful moment that fed my spirit.

At 8:00 a.m., we left Dallas and continued east. Suddenly, after so much brown in Arizona, New Mexico, and West Texas, the whole landscape on each side of the bus seemed to miraculously go from brown to a luxuriant and lush green. I have never, before or since then, so appreciated the luxuriant green beauty of the south and the east as I did that day. Springtime in the Deep South was bursting into new life.

At this point, our plans changed. Marion developed health problems and couldn't join me for our tour of the east coast. Then Jeff and I scrubbed our plans to see New Orleans and went to Natchez, Mississippi, to see the magnificent ante-bellum mansions.

Jeff and I stayed a night in Natchez and saw two mansions, Rosalie and Dunleith. The next day, Jeff and I rode the stretch of road to Jackson, Mississippi. There we split up and took different buses. Jeff was heading to West Virginia and hopefully law school. I headed east to Tuscaloosa where I would spend a night with my friends Debbie and Pete Cavan.

It was good to be back with friends who were practically family, and it was restful to not have to focus on where I would go and what busses I would take.

> God, but the South is beautiful this time of year. This beauty is amplified by the fact that I just came through the brown deserts of the Southwest. . . . I am sitting on the steps of the Amelia Gayle Gorgas Library at the University of Alabama. I've been strolling around the campus. It is absolutely gorgeous. The day is warm and sunny. . . . The birds are singing. The pink and white dogwoods are in bloom. . . . Nearby, at a sorority house, I hear the hiss of a sprinkler watering the manicured lawn. Girls are sunbathing on a second story balcony with radios blaring and curtains fluttering in the breeze. The streets are buzzing with students strolling to and from classes.

After my stay in Tuscaloosa, I headed east again. On Wednesday, April 16, 1980, I crossed the Georgia state line at 5:30 p.m. and arrived at the Atlanta bus station at 7:00 p.m. Doug was waiting for me, and I spent a few days in Atlanta before heading home with him on Friday. My long journey home from Montana was over.

The annual four-ball golf tournament was going on in Thomaston on Saturday and Sunday. I enjoyed watching Daddy and his best friend, Bethel Ingram, play and saw lots of people I knew. On Saturday, I called Bar Harbor to confirm returning for the summer. I had chosen Bar Harbor again because it offered the best job, salary, and living quarters, a meaningful summer, a chance to pursue my interest in sailing, and, as I wrote, "because I'd rather go there than any other place I know of."

I still had some days left on my Ameri-Pass and so, at 9:30 p.m. on Sunday night, I caught the bus from Thomaston to briefly visit Charleston, South Carolina, where my Palm Beach friends Alan and Anne Cochet had moved.

Charleston was as pretty as I had imagined. Pink and yellow houses set sideways to the street with one stretch of houses appropriately called Rainbow Row. There were palm trees, hanging baskets of ferns which swayed in the breeze, balconies and wraparound porches, and open windows with curtains fluttering.

On Wednesday morning I left Charleston for what would have been a wonderful opportunity. I had been corresponding with Sheldon Vanauken, the author of *A Severe Mercy*, and he had agreed to let me sit in on some of his classes at Lynchburg College. As I headed to Lynchburg, Virginia, the route was convoluted and required an overnight layover in Richmond. Somewhere along the way—tired of long days of riding, tired of overnight layovers, and not having enough money left for a hotel—I gave up on the plan. And so, I headed back to Atlanta and home. Every traveler has his or her limits.

I continued to correspond with Sheldon Vanauken and visited him later at his tiny home in Lynchburg. But, in the rearview mirror of my life, I wish I had seen Professor Vanauken in his teaching element and had spent that time with him. What a rich experience that would have been.

I have a saying, "Travel has created for me a vast spiritual reservoir from which I drink on a daily basis." Sometimes in life you have to be intentional, proactive, and creative to make certain opportunities happen. Sometimes you have to go the extra mile to get an experience that adds richness and depth to your spiritual reservoir. Though I missed this last one, I have had more than my share of rich and wonderful experiences that have filled my life to the brim.

And so, after twenty-eight days, my great trans-America bus voyage ended. I closed my journal with this amazing statistic, "My travel by bus, since leaving Montana has been around 6,143 miles. That is twice the length of the United States."

9

BAR HARBOR REVISITED

1980

In May of 1980, I drove to Bar Harbor by myself. During my resort years, the only place to which I took the bus was Big Sky of Montana because of distance and weather. I either drove or rode with others to all the other places I worked. Since I was alone on my return to Bar Harbor, I could chart my own course and make stops that held a personal interest to me.

AN INTERESTING STOP IN LEXINGTON, VIRGINIA

On this second trip to Maine, I chose a different route. I decided to go north up the Shenandoah Valley in western Virginia. The Shenandoah was full of Civil War sites, and my mind was full of memories from a biography I had read about Stonewall Jackson. I stopped for the night in Lexington, Virginia, home to Washington and Lee University and Virginia Military Institute.

I arrived in Lexington in the middle of the afternoon. Rather than immediately look for a hotel, I drove over to the campus. This proved to be a seemingly random, but fortunate decision.

As I drove in, I saw a big old white wooden house with the sign that said "Overnight Guests." I noted that and then set off to explore the two campuses.

The Washington and Lee campus was beautiful in the late afternoon. Part of its charm was its small, elegant, and quiet feel. The heart of the campus was a long row of stately buildings made of red brick set facing a beautiful green lawn. The deep red of the buildings was punctuated with dark green shutters and beautiful white columns. It was the picture perfect of an academic sanctuary.

Originally, the school had been called Washington College after George Washington. After the Civil War, Robert E. Lee became president of the College, so it was eventually called Washington and Lee. Across the green lawn, facing the row of buildings, was the Lee Chapel which contained the tomb of Robert E. Lee. Inside, I saw Lee's tomb and outside, beside the chapel, was the grave of Traveler, Lee's horse. After taking time to bathe in the beautiful quiet setting of the campus, I walked next door to the campus of Virginia Military Institute where Stonewall Jackson had taught before the Civil War.

VMI had a huge parade ground surrounded by fortress-like buildings made of cream-colored concrete with crenelated rooftops. I found a museum that was still open. Inside I saw the rain slicker with a bullet hole in the shoulder that Stonewall Jackson had been wearing at the Battle of Chancellorsville when his own men accidently shot him. The museum also featured the stuffed body of "Little Sorrel," Jackson's beloved horse.

As I headed back to my car, the sign in the yard of that white house piqued my curiosity. The house looked interesting and the location was perfect. I knocked on the front door and an elderly lady came to the door. I asked about a room for the night. She said she had a room available for four dollars. Wow! The room was nice and gave you the feeling that you were staying with your grandmother. What a find! I had expected to pay thirty dollars at a generic hotel, and here I was, right on campus, in a neat old home with lots of atmosphere, for only four dollars!

My room was at the end of the second floor and was full of interesting old furniture. The bed had huge, fluted posts and a headboard with inlaid wood. A little wooden nightstand held a porcelain lamp and a stack of old magazines. The room had a sink and the shower was downstairs. I had hit the accommodations jackpot! As it turned out, a retired schoolteacher named Ruth Rees owned the house and another teacher helped Ms. Rees run the place.

The next morning, I found that I could eat a big breakfast in the cafeteria at W&L for only two dollars. In the end, I had comfortable, atmospheric accommodations and a huge breakfast for only six dollars! Many years later, I went through Lexington again. Remarkably, the old house was still renting rooms—and the price had only gone up to $6.

THE GROTON SCHOOL

My next stop was Groton, Massachusetts, on the outskirts of Boston. I wanted to see The Groton School, which Franklin Roosevelt had attended as a small boy and where he had been shaped by the great headmaster Endicott Peabody. At first, I tried sleeping in the car, but, after spending two hours in a vain attempt to find a comfortable position, I gave in and found a hotel room for $31—a lot for me in 1980 dollars.

My visit here was like a rich spiritual pilgrimage. Once again, I intentionally chose experiences that would add to my spiritual reservoir. Spiritual experiences like this are best done alone. If I had been with someone else, my mental and spiritual focus would have been distracted. Far from being selfish, moments like these are times of taking in so that later you have something deep and rich to share with others. Being alone, I could take my time, let the experience soak in deeply, and become a part of who I was becoming. All these intentional experiences go into your spiritual reservoir like investments and act together like compounding interest building on each other preparing you for a future for which you were designed.

As I drove onto the campus that beautiful spring day, I saw students playing baseball. The founder of the school, Endicott Peabody, had emphasized the importance of sports in developing character and teaching the life lessons of cooperation, competition, and the price to be paid to reach a goal. I found a parking place and went into a gold-domed building which housed classrooms and what looked like the headmaster's office. I took a few minutes to look at pictures and take it all in. This experience was like walking into the pages of history. Then I saw a door to what I figured was a secretary's office. I went in and told her my reason for coming and about all I had read about the school, its great headmaster, Endicott Peabody, and how it shaped the character of Franklin Roosevelt. She ushered me in to see the headmaster. I entered a great office with huge windows letting in the sunlight of the brilliant spring day. The headmaster, William Polk, looked to be in his late 30s or early 40s. He was short, with thinning hair and, as seemed appropriate for a headmaster at a great school, he was smoking a pipe. As we talked, he suggested a few books I might read to round out my understanding of the school and Endicott Peabody. He corrected my pronunciation of the name Peabody, not by telling me, but by the way he pronounced it in a sentence.

The last half of the name was pronounced "ba-DEE." So, phonetically, it was Endicott "Peebahdee."At his suggestion, I bought and eventually read *Peabody of Groton* by Frank Ashburn. That book proved to be very inspiring and led me to an interest in reading about the headmasters of other great schools. That interest eventually gave me a host of vicarious mentors who would challenge me academically and exhort me to be all I could be.

The headmaster said he had declared the day a holiday for the students. Once a quarter, the headmaster would declare a surprise holiday. This was great for the students and great for me too, because he basically gave me the freedom to enjoy the grounds, the classrooms, the school chapel, and wherever I pleased. One room held pictures and autographs of all the presidents of the United States. Another was filled with over a hundred old wooden desks. I imagined the scenes those desks had witnessed through the years. Engraved on the walls around the room were the names of former Grotonians. All around the room, whether on little stands or in niches in the walls, were busts of famous people like Homer and George Washington. Imagine how an atmosphere like this would encourage you to live up to the high examples and aspirations of great people throughout history. This room was by far the most impressive of the classrooms I saw, both in size and atmosphere.

The school buildings were of stately red brick architecture and laid out around a perfectly manicured central green with outlying fields behind the main buildings for baseball, soccer, tennis courts, and a gymnasium. As I walked the campus, students were throwing Frisbees, reading, or lying in the sun. The library had pictures of life at the school in former days. There were also framed quotations exhorting the ideals of the school: "Be practical as well as generous in your ideals." "Keep your eyes on the stars and your feet on the ground." "Right is right and wrong is wrong, and it is a sign of weakness and not generosity to confuse them." "In the long run, it is the doer of deeds and not the critic who counts." In the library I saw a few pictures of Quentin Roosevelt, the youngest son of Theodore Roosevelt, who had attended Groton. As a pilot in World War I, he had been shot down and killed. One of the pictures showed him in his airplane, accompanied by a letter of praise for his bravery in the war. With so great a host of inspiring alumni, with such beautiful architecture, and with such a rich atmosphere, how could you not aspire to be your best? That was certainly the effect on me.

My morning at Groton was a rich deposit into my spiritual reservoir, and when I review my notes from that time, it is almost like going there again. It is so important to feed your spirit on the things you find meaningful in life. You have to be intentional about it; these kinds of experiences don't just happen. Over time, they compound one on the other and create a deep and rich spiritual foundation for the future. When you make time for those experiences, God blesses you with unexpected things that make the moments even richer. I can recount so many times in my life when I took the time to make something happen and came away blessed beyond anything I could have imagined. My day at the Groton School was certainly one of those days.

LIFE AGAIN IN BAR HARBOR

Next on my journey, I stopped at Gordon-Conwell Theological Seminary to visit Doug Engstrom, my friend and spiritual mentor from Bar Harbor the year before. Driving up the coast, I stopped at L. L. Bean in Freeport and the beautiful harbor town of Camden. When I got to Camden, the sun was setting, creating a beautiful harbor scene. Six schooners rested in the harbor, and, in the yellow light of sunset, it was all so beautiful, quiet, and picturesque.

I finally got to Bar Harbor about 9:30 p.m. After putting my stuff in my attic room, I went to Geddy's pub before calling it a day. I was back in this wonderful setting in my old bed overlooking the harbor and the islands. What a blessing! How fortunate could a person be? I got out my journal, and wrote, "Well, I'm here again. Lying in my bed. It is 12:30 a.m."

The next day, on the bedroom walls, I put up archival photos of Theodore and Franklin Roosevelt and John Kennedy. I also put up a print of Winslow Homer's "Breezing Up" and a print of a "View of Hyde Park." As always, I had plenty of books. The highlight of my living space was the double casement windows with their view of the harbor and islands. I was now set for another great season on the beautiful Maine coast.

That summer, my work life started off so much more smoothly because I already knew the system. The old trunk-line switchboard had been replaced, and the new procedures were easy to learn. I quickly settled into my old lifestyle of working, reading, exercising, spending time with friends, and taking hikes in the national park. I wrote: "I live like a king here! Free room, free food, $160 a week, and a room with a beautiful view of the bay! All I have to do is open my window to hear the lapping of the tide on the rocks below. Everywhere the scenery is beautiful. I can sit, as I did today, on the hotel balcony, and read or write with an incredible view of the bay and the islands."

Sometimes on my days off, I would explore Maine's beautiful, ragged coast as I had the previous year. Sometimes I went with a friend and other times by myself. One of my favorite places was Camden, Maine. One day I wandered around the town, spending time in the beautiful, old public library with its huge windows and great paintings. In the 1800s, ships were built in all the bays and coves along the coast of Maine, and a painting in the library depicted a great ship under construction, showing the huge exposed wooden ribs of its great hull.

I wandered in and out of the interesting shops and then out to the grassy knoll overlooking the harbor. Camden's harbor is so perfect that it seems as if an artist had sculpted it. And, as God is the ultimate artist, it was. It is always full of schooners and yachts, and the view of that harbor has never failed to cast its spell on me.

South of Camden, outside Boothbay Harbor, I visited two classic, old wooden inns, and it seemed that I had slipped through a time warp. One inn, not yet open for the season, was the Spruce Point Inn and the other was the Neewagen Inn, situated on a rocky point with lots of spruce and fir trees framing the white wooden buildings and their green trim. It seemed like the essence of a classic long-ago Maine.

My plan of spending more time sailing never happened, and I don't remember why. Maybe because it was expensive and required me to drive to Southwest Harbor or Manset, on the other side of the island. That interest just seemed to fade, and I spent my time in other ways.

READING ADVENTURES

I read *Peabody of Groton* and really enjoyed it. As always, my reading acted as a living agent in shaping who I was. The Holy Spirit was behind the scenes, sculpting me, challenging me, and exhorting me to be all God had created me to be. In reading about Endicott Peabody, I also met people who inspired and shaped him. Here are some of the ideas I put down in my journal. The same ideas and principles apply at any stage of life, whether we are working with students, co-workers, or clients.

> Two headmasters may have influenced Peabody though he never studied under them. They were Thomas Arnold and Edward Thring. Arnold was a Christian and saw Christ not only as his redeemer, but also as his master and friend. Arnold, as a headmaster, tried to be master, friend, and co-worker of sorts with his students. As he preached to them in chapel, he exhorted them warmly, with feeling, as a co-laborer in the fight against evil. He felt that Christianity was an integral part of education, because education must be based on truth and the perspective truth can give. Arnold had a tremendous personality and this more than anything is what won the hearts of his students.
>
> Edward Thring was a Christian also, and he believed in the importance of the individual. He believed education should expose a student to a wide range of subjects as well as the arts and sports. Thring felt that education was responsible for developing the whole person, the character of the student as well as the mind.
>
> With Peabody, feeling was more potent than thought. Peabody got a law degree and also prepared for the Episcopal ministry at Cambridge Theological Seminary. *In deciding on his future work, he considered the family brokerage firm, but the overriding question in his mind was this: given*

> *his character, his abilities, his background, and his inclinations, where could he be of most use?*[1]

As I read these notes decades later, I am so grateful that, through the years, Christ led me through a maze of open and shut doors, over bridges of transition, sometimes blocked by failure, and at other times propelled on by opportunity and success, to a place where I could be of most use, and to an endeavor that brought all my strengths and gifts, interests, and passions to their fullest fruition. As I sit here now, I am thankful that God knew me better than I knew myself and that His dreams for me were so much better than the ones I had for myself. This is why I said in the introduction that I see my journey as one of epic grandeur, because it is a journey that has been, is, and will be in the future linked with my eternal Creator.

Peabody's words so inspired me:

> *"Cambridge was anxious to blend the most earnest piety with the most active intelligence and so to cultivate a deep, enthusiastic and reasonable faith. . . . Cambridge teachers were men of deep learning . . . encouraging the students to feel free to express their thoughts however mistaken they might seem, eager to lead them to that which had revealed itself to them as truth. [One teacher, Dr. Steenstra, was] never "nervously orthodox," i.e., he never feared that "something would happen to the truth".*[2]

I think that books, especially autobiography and biography, are living agents that God uses to sculpt, build up, and encourage us in our life's journey. I never knew Endicott Peabody, Thomas Arnold, or Edward Thring, but their words have mentored me just as if I had known them. And what is more, in a biography or autobiography, you have their undivided and undistracted attention.

Linda Carter, my co-worker and friend from the year before, was teaching in Orono, Maine, and was coming down on some weekends. We would go into the park for walks and then go dancing at Geddy's or Il Giardinos. If it was raining, we would look around the interesting shops in Bar Harbor or in the little village of Northeast Harbor. I also attended a Bible study once a week at the College of the Atlantic that Jody Smith had started.

One night, when there was a full moon, Bruce Parker and I drove to the top of Cadillac Mountain. The reflection of the moon struck the water and made a golden road all the way to the horizon. Below, in the darkness, you could see the clustered lights of the various villages around the island, as well as the single blinking light of Egg Rock Light out on its rocky island. All around were the dark shadows of mountains, and in the distance on the horizon was the shadowy form of the Schoodic Peninsula to the north.

By my bed, next to my picture of Theodore Roosevelt, I placed a quote of his that I felt I was living out: "We loved a great many things—birds and trees and books, and all things beautiful, horses and rifles and children, hard work and the joy of life."

Years later, I visited Jody Smith when she was living in Connecticut, and she had a quote by Ernest Hemingway sitting in her kitchen window that I think greatly compliments the Theodore Roosevelt quote.

"To stay in places . . . and to leave
To trust . . . and to distrust

To no longer believe . . . and to believe again
To care about fish, the different winds, the
changes in the seasons
To see what happens
To be out in boats . . . to sit in a saddle
To watch the snow come . . . to watch it go
To hear rain on a tent . . .
To know where I can find what I want . . ."

These two quotes show a sensitivity to the sacredness of our passing moments. The Bible says that all things work together for good in the life of the believer. Looking back, I can see how the early trauma of my young years caused me to turn inward and jump-started a sensitivity to the sacred nature of our passing moments. I am so thankful for how God had used both the good and the difficult in my life to give me the tools to experience the deep richness and vibrancy of life.

On Friday, May 30, in my journal, I wrote a three-page discussion of how, when my travel days were over, I would teach history in my hometown. This was one of the first times I wrote seriously about what I would do beyond travel. I felt that my travels were preparing me for a life in education and, given my interests, desires, and talents, everything was pointing to a career in teaching. With my love of biography, I would teach historic events by studying important people in those events. I felt that students would get caught up in the fascinating details of a person's life and, by extension, learn all about the historic event in which the person was a central figure. I could also see how discussions of my travels would expand the horizons of those in my small rural town. Finally, I could also see having Bible studies and sharing with the students a vision for how Christ could help them reach their full potential.

DEEP-IMPACT READING

That summer of 1980, I read *Wanderer* by Sterling Hayden, who had been an actor with a lucrative career in Hollywood. *Wanderer* is Hayden's account of how and why he chucked his acting career and sailed off to Tahiti. He had taken the road less traveled, and his words resonated with me. I wrote in my journal on June 14, 1980, "It is now 8:28 p.m., dusk. . . . My window is open and the lamp is on, the room lies in a shambles of undiscipline—a sandwich in wax paper, books everywhere, a bottle of coke almost empty, clothes, desk drawer ajar, and Sterling Hayden staring at me from behind that hand of his holding a lit cigarette." With his eyes squinted and leveled at me, these are some of the words from *Wanderer* that resonated with me:

> *"To be truly challenging, a voyage, like a life, must rest on a firm foundation of financial unrest. . . . Voyaging belongs to seamen, and to the wanderers of the world who cannot, or will not, fit in.*
>
> *Little has been said or written about the ways a man may blast himself free. . . . "I've always wanted to sail to the South Seas, but I can't afford it." What these men can't afford is not to go. They are enmeshed in the cancerous discipline of "security." And in the worship of security, we fling our lives beneath the wheels of routine—and before we know it our lives are gone.*

> *What does a man need—really need? A few pounds of food each day, heat and shelter, six feet to lie down in, and some form of working activity that will yield a sense of accomplishment. That's all—in the material sense. And we know it. But we are brainwashed by our economic system until we end up in a tomb beneath a pyramid of time payments, mortgages, preposterous gadgetry, playthings that divert our attention from the sheer idiocy of the charade.*
>
> *The years thunder by. The dreams of youth grow dim where they lie caked in dust on the shelves of patience. Before we know it, the tomb is sealed.*
>
> *Where, then, lies the answer? In choice. Which shall it be: bankruptcy of purse or bankruptcy of life"?*[3]

This was heady stuff to be reading in the midst of my own voyage. I had chosen the road less traveled, and in the end, it had made all the difference in my life's journey.

But my life is not your life, and Sterling Hayden's life is not your life. You have a life that is precious. Live your life; don't live my life or Sterling Hayden's life or anyone else's life. As Marilyn Monroe said, *"Trying to be someone else is a terrible waste of who you are."* Work out your own journey. As the Bible says, you are to work out your salvation in fear and trembling. Follow your heart, your desires, your vision. Maybe that is to sail to the South Seas, but it very well may be to be a mother, a doctor, a schoolteacher, a helper, a lawyer, or a technician. Whatever it is and wherever it is, find it on your own and go after it. Live it with all your heart. Consider the advice of others, but don't live someone else's life.

Listen to Eugene Peterson's words in his book, *Run with the Horses*, *"What a waste it would be to take these short, precious, eternity-charged years that we are given and squander them in cocktail chatter, when we can be, like Jeremiah, vehemently human and passionate with God."*

I was right there with Sterling Hayden. While he was sailing to the South Seas and Tahiti, I was exploring what Thoreau alluded to in *Walden* as the uncharted interior of my own being. Hear Thoreau as he exhorts us from the pages of *Walden*,

> *"Direct your eye right inward, and you'll find*
> *a thousand regions in your mind*
> *Yet undiscovered. Travel them..."*

> *"What does Africa—what does the West stand for? Is not our own interior white on the chart? Black though it may prove, like the coast, when discovered. . . . Be rather . . . the Lewis and Clarke . . . of your own streams and oceans . . . be a Columbus to whole new continents and worlds within you, opening new channels, not of trade, but of thought."*
>
> *What was the meaning of that South-Sea Exploring Expedition, with all its parade and expense, but an indirect recognition of the fact, that there are continents and seas in the moral world, to which every man is an isthmus or an inlet, yet unexplored by him, but that it is easier to sail many thousand miles through cold and storm*

> *and cannibals, in a government ship, with five hundred men and boys to assist one, than it is to explore the private sea, the Atlantic and Pacific of one's being alone."*[4]

That summer night in 1980, I was sitting in my attic retreat on the coast of Maine, but in my mind, I was exploring and mapping the uncharted seas and the rock-bound coast of my own life and mind. And I have to tell you…it was a thrilling journey!!!

In *Walden*, Thoreau had expressed perfectly what I was trying to work out in those journals,

> *"I went to the woods because I wished to live deliberately, to front only the essential facts of life, and see if I could not learn what it had to teach, and not, when I came to die, discover that I had not lived. I did not wish to live what was not life, living is so dear. . . . I wanted to live deep and suck out all the marrow of life, to live so sturdily and Spartan-like as to put to rout all that was not life, to cut a broad swath and shave close, to drive life in a corner, and reduce it to its lowest terms, and, if it proved to be mean, why then to get the whole and genuine meanness of it, and publish its meanness to the world; or if it were sublime, to know it by experience, and be able to give a true account of it."*[5]

I now realize how important and life-changing these years were for me; how the future was being built on the spiritual/philosophical foundation I was laying down in those years. How important it was for me at that time to: (1) travel alone, (2) keep a detailed journal working out my thoughts about life and myself, and (3) analyze all that was happening from a Christian perspective so that I saw life in a clear and *complete perspective and not half-seen or half-hidden.*

Colossians 1:15–16 says that Christ "is the image of the invisible God. . . . For by him were all things created . . . all things were created by him, and for him." In John 14:6, Jesus says, "I am the way, the truth, and the life."

Looking back, I now see that, in those years, the *Lord and I* were continually building a spiritual/psychological house that was so firm, so sound, and so eternal, that it is essentially the house that we live in today, virtually unchanged. The fundamental truths we were laying down would carry *us* through the voyage of the coming years, through the fair skies, sunny days, and beautiful sunsets, and also through the heavy seas, the storms, and the darkness of the unexpected and sudden typhoon in the middle of an uncharted ocean. I am thankful that, on this voyage, I am never alone, and furthermore, that I am first mate, and that He is the master at the helm.

IMPORTANT BOOKS I READ DURING MY SECOND SUMMER AND FALL IN BAR HARBOR

Peabody of Groton, Frank Asburn
Wanderer, Sterling Hayden
Walden, Henry David Thoreau

By now, in my travels, the spiritual/psychological house was pretty much completed. This second "semester" in Bar Harbor and all the places I would work going forward would reinforce and fine-tune all the major themes and life-lessons I had already learned.

---

1. Frank Davis Ashburn, *Peabody of Groton*, (New York: Coward McCann, Inc, 1944), 67.

2. Ashburn, *Peabody*, 40.

3. Hayden, Sterling. Wanderer (Essex, Conn.: Lyons Press Maritime Classics, 2018).

4. Henry David Thoreau, Walden, (Boston: Houghton Mifflin, 1854).

10

BIG SKY REVISITED

1980–1981

As I worked in resorts around the country, Doug became convinced that spending a few years doing the same would add to the value of his life. As a result, he quit his banking job, went on a backpacking trip to Europe, and then went with me to Big Sky of Montana for the winter and summer seasons of 1981. To get there, we used the reliable services of Greyhound bus lines, which had served me so faithfully in the past.

My experiences during this period were different because Doug and I were together. His companionship lessened the intensity of being on my own. We enjoyed the gift of sharing this western adventure together. We made a close friend in Taylor Middleton from Georgiana, Alabama, and the three of us lived together in a condo. Karen McCredie from Woodstock, Vermont, joined us for a great ski resort experience in the winter and a pseudo dude-ranch experience in the summer. This was my first time to experience the wonderful beauty and atmosphere of summer in the West.

It was nice to have a more social season in life—as if God said, "Okay, you have put in the time and hard work, and together we have built the psychological and spiritual house for your future. Now I am giving you a time to kick back, take a break from your journals, and enjoy Doug and your friends in this wonderful setting."

Don't get me wrong, I had had a wonderful time over these years, but my last two resort destinations of Big Sky and Nantucket were pure pleasure and relaxation.

HIGH ADVENTURE IN COLORADO ANSWERS AN IMPORTANT QUESTION FOR ME

In mid-summer I took two weeks off from my job at Big Sky and drove to Colorado for a Christian, outward-bound-type experience called Christian High Adventure. We spent two weeks learning hiking, camping, and outdoor skills in the Uncompahgre National Forest south of Montrose, Colorado. There may be a forest somewhere around there, but we were in the high mountains, often above the tree-line. We carried sixty-pound packs and learned rock-climbing, rappelling, and compass skills. The experience did not have the high psychological demands that other programs have, but it had an added Christian side with Bible studies and discussions.

This camping and hiking trek answered a big question for me. While it had a great component of adventure, it showed me that the real passion of my life was in the fascinating voyage and trek of the mind and spirit.

In life, it is very important to know who you are and who you're not. There is only so much time, and it is vital to focus your time and talent in the area of your expertise and passion. This time I spent learning who I was *not* was just as important as the time I spent learning who I *was*. I learned, as Thoreau said in *Walden*, that the outward journey is a mental picture of the inward journey of the mind. And I learned that the true source of passion for me was found in charting and exploring the *terra incognita* of the spirit and mind.

ROAD TRIP HOME IN A QUESTIONABLE DODGE DART

In between the winter and summer season at Big Sky, five of us took a great, long road trip back to our homes in the South. Joining Doug, Taylor and me, were Stuart Howard from Salisbury, North Carolina and John Dameron from Memphis, Tennessee. We piled into Stuart Howard's questionable Dodge Dart, which had a horseshoe wired to the front grill. With our setting out on such an ambitious voyage in such a questionable road-ship, I guess we thought we needed all the luck we could get. The engine was leaking oil so badly that we bought oil by the case, and when we pulled into a gas station, we would tell them to "fill the oil and check the gas." We had a great trip heading south through Salt Lake City and then through the glorious National Parks of Zion and the Grand Canyon.

Eventually we got home, spent time with our families, and then headed back to Montana in that same Dodge Dart. In life, you have to know the limitations of both yourself and what you put your trust in. We made it all the way back to the Little Big Horn Battlefield just south of Billings, Montana, when the motor-mount broke on the engine. The Dart had given us her best, and she was willing to finish the drill, but she needed help.

It was at night, and Stuart used a coat hanger to secure the engine enough to limp it into a mechanic's garage. The next day, the mechanic did what he could do, no doubt some welding was involved, and we finally limped the Dart back up the mountain to Big Sky.

That last summer for me was great, as I had never spent a summer in the American West. I would have missed a whole side to the West if I had only worked the winters. We had a great group of friends, the weather was wonderful, and it was incredible to see the gorgeous American West with its greens and browns washed in the soft sunlight of summer, as opposed to the white blanket of winter snow.

We took side trips to Jackson Hole and Idaho. Doug and I took the Idaho trip together, and we paid our respects at the grave of Ernest Hemingway in Ketchum. Hemingway, his writing and his passion for diving deep into the passing moments of life, had been a mentor to both of us.

11

SHIFTING GEARS

During my years of resort work, as I mentioned, the vision of a future in teaching had begun to crystalize in my mind. In May of 1978, I had graduated from the University of Georgia with a degree in history, and then during my resort years, after reading *A Severe Mercy*, I fell in love with literature. In 1981, during my second stay at Big Sky of Montana, I began feeling very clearly that resort work, the great graduate school of my life, had served its purpose.

I have come to see through experience that one of the tools in God's big toolbox is intuition. I was so excited and fulfilled about how God had used resort work to shape me, but I came to a very clear understanding that this season of my life had served its purpose and was winding down. I then began to see a future in which I would go back to Georgia, get a second degree in literature, as well as a teaching certificate, and teach high school English or history.

In the fall of 1981, I returned to Georgia to begin my degree in English. I took two classes, had great teachers, and did very well. Nevertheless, I decided to return home and finish my literature degree and get my teaching certificate through Tift College, which had classes in Thomaston. This all worked out, and in the spring of 1982, I did my student teaching at my old high school, R. E. Lee Institute, under Ruth Presley who, though she was tiny, maintained great discipline in her classes. My student teaching experience was very good, but because she exercised such good discipline, I had no clue about the discipline hurricane that would await me when I taught classes on my own.

NANTUCKET

During that fall of 1981, Doug, Taylor Middleton, and I all applied for jobs on Nantucket Island off the coast of Massachusetts. With our resumes filled with an extensive list of resorts and jobs, we were confident we would all get job offers. Time passed, Christmas came and went, and still we heard nothing.

One morning in January or February of 1982, I was living at home in Thomaston, and finishing course work for my English degree. While I was exercising, I realized none of us had heard from Nantucket. I said a quick prayer about it and continued my push-ups and sit-ups. Within five minutes, the phone rang. I picked it up and heard: "Russ, this is George Wingenfeld on Nantucket. I just got back from vacation, and I am starting to go through a stack of job requests. Yours is on top, and I see you have a recommendation from the president of the Grand Hotel Mackinac. I can offer you a front desk job at the Harbor House."

We talked about salary and housing, and as we were finishing our conversation, another thought came to ask about Doug and Taylor. Thank the Lord, he put it in my mind just like everything else about this miraculous answer to prayer. I said, "Mr. Wingenfeld, If you like my resume, and need two other people who have similar resumes and qualifications, look through that stack on your desk, and consider Doug Head, who is my brother, and Taylor Middleton, who is my friend."

After a few moments he found their resumes and offered them jobs on my recommendation. *Bam!* Outside my prayer of salvation, that is, to this day the most amazing, immediate, and stunningly obvious answer to prayer in my life. The resumes had been mailed months earlier. Then on some "random" day in January or February, I just happened to say a prayer while a man about a thousand miles away was sitting down to look through a stack of resumes, and mine just happened to be on top. If you think that is just coincidence, then you are striving with every fiber in your being to deny the obvious.

So, after I completed my student teaching with Ruth Pressley at R. E. Lee, I spent one final "semester" of "graduate school" on Nantucket. As it turned out, it was an extended semester that went through the summer and the fall of 1982.

Not only did we get jobs on Nantucket, but we all three were hired as front desk clerks and were given the best room in an employee dorm complex. It was a huge room with its own bathroom. The rest of the rooms had a common bathroom, similar to a college dorm.

While I did my student teaching in the spring, Doug and Taylor went up in May. By the time I got there in June, they had the whole island scouted out, as well as all the pretty women, and that allowed me to walk right into an effortless and wonderful summer and fall. Unfortunately, so much was going on that I didn't keep a journal.

Nantucket is the best-preserved, still-inhabited, historic whaling village in the world. The beautiful boat basin hosts gorgeous boats of all sizes, and great shops and interesting boutiques are everywhere, along with a wide variety of good restaurants.

And to complete the picture, Nantucket has the best, unspoiled beaches in New England. I worked at the Harbor House Hotel, and Doug and Taylor worked at the White Elephant Hotel. We all worked as front desk clerks and became good friends with Peter Eastment, the desk clerk at the Breakers.

We worked five days a week and had plenty of time to go to the many great beaches because, even on the days we worked, we had a good part of the day off. It was the perfect place to finish this important part of my life. Great friends, great social life, great beaches, quaint villages, interesting shops, and wonderful restaurants!! I couldn't have wished for more!!

God even blessed me by extending this time into the fall, almost to Thanksgiving. In August, out of personal interest, I took a second job at Glidden's Island Seafood, a third-generation fish market. Since fishing was such a part of coastal and island life, I just wanted to know the ins and outs of the fish business. When the hotels closed in October, and Doug and Taylor left, I stayed on, rented a room in a local residence, and worked the scallop season at the fish market. The fishermen would bring in huge buckets of big, white, glistening sea scallops that looked like giant marshmallows.

In late October and November, the island grew quiet amidst a long, beautiful Indian summer. It was sunny and cool, but not cold. As I walked the cobbled streets of the Old Town, the gentle breeze and turning leaves gave me a psychological feeling that was both sacred and intimate—the essence of fall. It was a wonderful way to end the great graduate school of my life.

In the spring of 1983, I accepted an offer to teach tenth grade English at Pike County High School, in nearby Zebulon, Georgia. My grandfather had been a doctor in Zebulon, and my grandmother, Adele, still lived there. I had one summer left before I would embark on that career in teaching high school English and/or history. That summer I would fulfill a dream that had begun taking shape many years before . . . a trip to Africa.

AN AFRICAN ADVENTURE

Traveling to Africa in 1983 would be my first overseas trip, and it was to be not only a romantic dream of a trip but also a supercharged boost in my confidence that the Lord and I were working out the pages of a great and adventurous life.

Africa had always held for me the mystique that it holds for so many people. I remembered the day, years before, in Camden, Maine, when my eyes moved from cover to cover past the many miscellaneous volumes in Lillian Berliawsky's ABC bookstore. As I saw the magic combination of Theodore Roosevelt and *African Game Trails*, I felt as excited as if I'd found a lost treasure.

The following weeks, I pored over those pages and pictures, absorbing the experiences and impressions Roosevelt had recorded on his year-long expedition to East Africa in 1909. Through its pages, I became acquainted with Philip Percival, the great hunting guide who accompanied Roosevelt and later hunted with Ernest Hemingway on his safaris in 1933 and 1954. Hemingway was to immortalize Percival in his novel *Green Hills of Africa*. Indeed, Hemingway himself did a great deal to further my interest in East Africa. I found *Green Hills of Africa* fascinating and went on to read "The Snows of Kilimanjaro" and "The Short Happy Life of Francis McComber."

Then there were the powerful photographs and history of East Africa in Peter Beard's epic work, *The End of the Game*. From Beard's book I was led to Izak Dinesen's classic *Out of Africa*. All these impressions of beauty, wonder, and adventure I absorbed in more than a passing way. I could so relate to Denys Finch Hatton's reaction to his experience in Africa:

> *"Denys had watched and followed the ways of the African Highlands, and better than any other white man, he had known their soil and seasons, the vegetation and the wild animals, the winds and the smells. He had observed the changes of the weather in them, their people, clouds, the stars at night. Here in the hills, I had seen him only a short time ago, standing bareheaded in the afternoon sun, gazing out over the land, and lifting his field-glasses to find out everything about it. He had taken in the country, and in his eyes and his mind it had been changed, marked by his own individuality, and made a part of him."*[1]

In the same, Africa had become a part of me, and I hoped that one day, I would go there and feed my spirit. So, after securing a teaching job for the fall, I decided to go. I decided to spend two weeks in Kenya exploring the cities and game parks and one week in Tanzania climbing Mt. Kilimanjaro. July 14 found me with plane ticket in hand, my final destination: Kenya, East Africa.

In the planning of the trip, my travel agent did a good job with the week-long climb of Mt. Kilimanjaro, but we could not agree on the two weeks in Kenya. He kept wanting to put me in high-end hotels, and I finally told him I would figure out the first two weeks when I got there. I am sure he felt this would result in a major logistical apocalypse. My thinking was that because English was spoken in Kenya, I felt confident that, after years of living by the seat of my pants, I could figure things out. That may have been a bit naïve. My past travels had been in the United States; this would be Africa. A third factor may have been that I had a lot of experience in trusting God to send His angel before me to prepare the way.

My exploration of Kenya started on the long plane ride. I flew to New York and then to the west coast of Africa. The plane skipped around the west to Dakar, Senegal; Monrovia, Liberia; and Lagos, Nigeria, before going on to Nairobi, Kenya. When we landed in Senegal, we were told we were half way to Nairobi. It amazed me that after crossing an entire ocean, I had only come half way.

As He had in my past, God did indeed send His angel before me to prepare the way. On the plane ride, I met a man who worked for the Rockwell Corporation in Arkansas. When he heard I had no place booked in Nairobi, he offered to let me ride in his taxi to the hotel where he was staying to see if they had rooms available. I only needed one night, as I was flying on the next morning to the coastal town of Mombasa. When we landed, we passed through security checkpoints manned by military personnel wielding weapons. This was long before terrorism, and so the sight of armed military or paramilitary guards felt a bit unnerving.

We caught a taxi and rode through the darkness to his hotel. Fortunately, a room was available for me to sleep off my twenty-four-hour transit from Atlanta to Nairobi.

The next morning, I overslept and missed my flight to Mombasa. This was so out of character for me, but I guess I was incredibly exhausted from my first long, trans-Atlantic flight, as well as from the kaleidoscope of sights and sounds along the way. Thankfully, I was easily able to book another flight. One memory of that morning was seeing a line of ladies, maybe eight or ten, lined up with handmade brooms made of bundled twigs, sweeping off the runway.

Mombasa is the primary seaport for Kenya. The old harbor there was where Roosevelt and Hemingway began their African adventures. I stayed at the Manor Hotel in the center of town. I am not sure how I wound up there, but once again God was silently working out the details of what would be a wonderful trip.

The Manor was a well-preserved holdover from the colonial days, and it continued many of the old ways within its wonderful historical ambiance. There was early morning tea at 6:30 a.m. and afternoon tea from 4:00 to 5:30 p.m. Tea was always served with a plate of small cakes or cookies. Lunch and dinner were five-course affairs, served by silent, graceful waiters.

Structurally, the Manor was open to sea breezes that came off the Indian Ocean. Drinks and tea were served in an open-air, palm-shaded courtyard, and a similar courtyard hosted a dining area. Open breezeways connected the different sections of the hotel, and even in the main indoor dining room, windows were flung open day and night to let the sights and sounds of the courtyard and town engage the diner.

At the Manor, I paid thirty dollars for a wonderfully appointed room with French doors and a beautiful armoire. The room was two tiered, with an air conditioner to stifle the equatorial heat and a mosquito net that was let down from the ceiling at night to surround the entire bed.

Despite the quaintness of the hotel, I was eager to explore the fascinating old city. Everywhere I found Western-style businesses along sidewalks lined with makeshift sheds where artisans sold inexpensive goods or wooden carvings. I went to the old Arab section of town with its harbor and Portuguese fort. For centuries the Arab traders had come to East Africa from India and the Middle East to buy and sell. They would arrive in December in boats called *dhows*, driven on the wings of the monsoon winds, bringing dates, salt, and carpets. Months later they would return to their homes with sisal, limes, coffee, ivory and exotic animal skins.

In the old town, I explored a maze of dusty, narrow winding streets and alleys. On one stretch I walked a seemingly deserted avenue, but then I realized an evanescent trail of Arab and Indian children were following me. They walked at a distance, stopped when I stopped, and sometimes asked for shillings. One Indian girl, playing with her brothers in a dusty side street, came over to me, looked up with a grimy face and beautiful chocolate eyes, and uttered in the most exquisite English, "One shilling?" The children seemed unconcerned whether they got a shilling or not. The begging seemed more of a game or a conditioned response to a white face.

Another interesting landmark on the fringes of the Arab quarter was Fort Jesus. Built by the Portuguese in 1593, the massive fort sat on a bluff giving it a commanding view of the harbor. It is amazing that two small countries like Portugal and the Netherlands were at one time masters of the trading world. With its crumbling walls and the endless play of light in the equatorial sun, the fort was a great place for photography.

After two days in the heat of Mombasa, I headed for the cooler highlands and Nairobi. Mombasa and Nairobi were connected by a historic railway, which offered an interesting and inexpensive way to get to Nairobi. Fourteen dollars provided an overnight passage and a fold-down cot in a second-class compartment.

Completed in 1901, the Kenya railway was integral in the development of East Africa. It was called the "lunatic line" when it was built because of all the formidable challenges that had to be overcome in order for it to reach Nairobi and its final terminus on the shores of Lake Victoria, deep in the heart of the continent.

At Vo, the Indian workers refused to continue working because two marauding lions had killed not only a number of workers, but also some of the hunters who were sent to kill them. Because of the pair's unusual behavior, the workers felt that the lions were demon possessed. Professional hunters eventually killed the two "Man-eaters of Tsavo." Today the two lions are in the Field Museum of Natural History in Chicago.

One pleasure of travel is the variety of people you meet. On the overnight train, I had a wonderful conversation with a young cook in the dining car. His real name was James Kramba, but he referred to himself as James Bond. Needless to say, he was an avid 007 fan, and he was also very interested in the United States.

James was very proud of his ability to speak English, and he invited me to share some *ugali*, a native dish made of maize. I asked him to teach me some Swahili, a type of universal language in East Africa, and he assumed the task with a proud smile. James lit a cigarette and began to question me on the Swahili names for a knife and fork. When he saw that I didn't know, he puffed his cigarette and smiled as if amazed that a supposedly educated man from the West could not come up with the most basic Swahili terms. After enjoying his exalted position, he condescended with a smile, took another puff of his cigarette, and gave me the answers.

One particularly nice memory of the train ride was that of standing in the open loading door near the kitchen and staring out into the African night. James seemed proud that someone from such a rich and powerful country as the United States could take pleasure in the beauty of his country. There was something mesmerizing about staring into the moonlit landscape of shadows, and grasping the fact that, in this moment, I was just not *thinking* of Africa; this was that place called Africa. As the shadows of Acacia trees flashed by and we raced through the night, I realized that the light from the kitchen threw my shadow onto the landscape. Then I remembered the words of Izak Dinesen in *Out of Africa*,

> *"If I know a song of Africa . . . of the giraffe, and the African new moon lying on her back, the ploughs in the fields, and the sweaty faces of the coffee-pickers, does Africa know a song of me? Would the air over the plain quiver with a color that I had on, or the children invent a game in which my name was or the full moon throw a shadow over the gravel of the drive that was like me, or would the eagles of Ngong look out for me?"*[2]

Likewise, I thought it remarkable that my shadow would make its mark on these Kenyan plains, if only for a fleeting moment, as our train raced through the night.

In Nairobi, I stayed at a youth hostel and arranged to go on a safari to the game parks. Based on a tip someone on the train had given me, I found an outfit that gave a nice six-day, tented, camping safari to the lake region and the Masai Mara. This left me few days before that safari, and I found a three-day safari covering several nearby areas including Amboseli National Park in the shadow of Mt. Kilimanjaro. Plans developed quickly, and the next day I was headed south to Amboseli National Park and my first views of big game.

Ernest Hemingway spent several weeks hunting in Amboseli in 1954. So, it seemed appropriate that I had my first, and many of my best, views of big game in Amboseli. I got closer to elephant there than any other park.

On that shorter safari, we stayed in hotels. At one amazing place, we stayed in round bedroom pods built on pylons and set around a salt lick. The pylons gave the wildlife a much freer sense of movement through the grounds than they would have had with buildings on ground level.

The salt lick was lit at night when elephant and other animals came to it. Once a mother elephant stopped about twenty yards from the salt lick and hid her calf in a clump of bushes. The mother then cautiously approached the salt-lick, waving her trunk in the air to discern the scent of danger. When she felt the coast was clear, she gave some signal and the calf ran to the mother and grabbed the mother's tail with its little trunk in the same way a child would grab its mother's hand.

The longer tour was a tented safari with a company called Gametrackers and included everything that was needed for $40.00 per day. Camping in tents at night with a big campfire fulfilled all my dreams of what a safari would be like. We traveled in Land Rover vehicles specially made for eight or so people with hatches in the roof so you could stand and take pictures. We saw lots of lions, water buffalo, giraffe, zebra, elephant, warthogs, impala, cheetah, wildebeests, hippo, and other plains animals. The only big game animal we never saw was a leopard.

Camping in the African landscape brings to life the whole feel of the land and the wildlife. The atmosphere heightens a person's sensitivities. When night falls over the camp, a person's imagination begins to play, and all the romance of Africa awakens. At the campfire, everyone sits on camp stools, faces lit in the amber glow of the flames. On the fringes of the circle, you are aware of the triangular shadows of the tents, and farther beyond, a different light, that of the pale African moon, sheds its glow over the landscape of thorn trees. Inevitably, the sounds of hyena and other animals float into camp, and you become aware that you're on a domesticated island in a sea of wildness. A tented camp is essential to set this stage, and it creates a truly magical atmosphere.

In the lake region in the north, we went to Lakes Baringo, Begoria, and Nukuru. Along the shores of these lakes, we saw millions of flamingos. It is truly an amazing sight as you look out at a sea of pink. Also, in the Masai Mara, we visited the famed Masai tribes. All these experiences over my two weeks combined to give me a memory that was all I had hoped it would be.

I spent my final week in Tanzania climbing Mt. Kilimanjaro. I stayed with eleven Germans at a base lodge run by a German lady named Erica Lany. Mt. Kilimanjaro, at 19,340 feet, is the highest mountain on the African continent, and it has the distinction of being an eternally snow-capped mountain, situated virtually on the equator. One fascinating thing about the climb is the successive exposure to diverse eco-systems. On consecutive days you climb through rain forests, giant heather, desert, and finally snow.

Because of the thinness of the air as you ascend the slopes, the climb is a demanding study in personal discipline and patience. You must always walk at about one third of your normal walking pace; to walk any faster would seriously jeopardize your chances of making it to the summit. A young woman passed me, complaining that a slow pace tired her as much as a fast pace. Despite my warnings, she briskly continued. Later she passed me—headed back down. She had succumbed to the cumulative effects of low oxygen and high altitude.

Mt. Kilimanjaro is an extinct volcano. On the final ascent, eleven of our party of twelve made it to Gilman's Point on the crater rim, amidst the snows of Kilimanjaro. Feeling as if we were using the last ounces of our energy, we collapsed, gasping for air, and were nursed by our guides who, because of acclimatization, apparently felt little of our pain and exhaustion.

My African adventure proved to be all I had hoped it would be. Now, once again, I was heading into a future in which I had my vision and dream and God had His…

A TRAVEL AGENCY

God can keep a lot of ideas and intentions in the air of your life at the same time. He said "I am the Alpha and the Omega," the beginning and the end. A lot was happening in 1983 that would open doors for a future for me that only God could see. That year I finished my second degree, did my student teaching, got hired for a teaching job in the fall, traveled to Africa, and finally entered a partnership that would open a travel agency and be the base for my future career in travel.

Early that summer, before I started teaching, God was preparing a future for me that I had no idea about. For a while, Doug and I had talked to a close friend, Steve Short, about a side business that all three of us could do together. We thought about a pizza and sandwich place on the square in Thomaston. But we also talked about a travel business of some sort. I had used a travel agency in nearby Griffin, Georgia, to help plan my Africa trip, and in my interactions with them, it occurred to me that this kind of business would work well with my love of travel.

One night during the summer of 1983, before I went to Africa, Doug and I visited Pete and Debbie Cavan at her parent's home in Thomaston. Debbie's mother worked with the Chamber of Commerce, and as we all stood around talking, Debbie's mother, Elsie Williams, asked what Doug and I were doing. We explained that Doug was working at a local bank, and I was going to teach.

We also mentioned that we were thinking about a sideline business with Steve Short to start either a pizza/sandwich shop or a travel agency.

Mrs. Williams said that earlier in the week, a woman named Lauren Armistead had been in the office talking about wanting to start a travel agency in Thomaston. Lauren happened to work for Thomas Travel in Griffin, the agency I had used for my Africa trip. Mrs. Williams said Lauren had the experience, but she was looking for local partners. This was all the right timing, because there were other bigwigs in Thomaston who might have had more money and a bigger presence. The opportune timing of this again shows me that God orchestrates our lives in far more detail than we might think. We immediately called Lauren.

Once we talked with Lauren, things fell together quickly and smoothly. We met over a dinner in Griffin. We all felt comfortable with each other. Lauren had travel experience and met all the qualifications to start a travel agency. Thomas Travel, where she worked, had the major corporate accounts in Thomaston, and she already had a great working relationship with the sales teams at Thomaston Mills, BF Goodrich, Federal Paperboard, and The Theo Bean publishing company. Steve, Doug, and I were well known and well liked in Thomaston, and we knew pretty much all the men with whom Lauren would be working. Furthermore, we would not have to risk much money for the start-up. We would each put in about $2500 and could stay in our jobs. Lauren would take the biggest risk by giving up her job, but she felt sure that, based on the sales she was doing, it was as sure a deal as a person could hope for. That night at our first and only meeting, we decided to start the travel agency.

Many people who didn't have Lauren's perspective of seeing firsthand the travel potential in Thomaston felt Thomaston couldn't support a travel agency. Others felt that four equal partners, and three of those being friends, was a formula for disaster, but our business relationships worked well. Steve Short and Doug were both in the banking and loan-finance business, so they knew how to set up the business side of things. At that point I had little to offer, but in time I would become the one who would carry the agency into the future. So after I returned from Africa, and on the day after Labor Day 1983, we opened for business. Our office was small but adequate, located in the Hotel Upson right in downtown Thomaston, and the rent was $150.00 per month, utilities included.

MY ONE YEAR OF TEACHING
AUGUST 1983 – JUNE 1984

My vision for the future had me teaching high school with a side interest in the travel agency. And so, in the fall of 1983, I began a year of teaching English at Pike County High School. If I had any sense at all, I would have spent a few weeks that summer with the course textbooks preparing for the start of the year. But that never occurred to me. Failure to prepare, left me behind from the beginning. Each day I went home exhausted and then struggled to create lessons for the next day.

I look back on that year as a way God would direct me along my way to the future. I am glad the Lord was in control of my life because He led me through a series of open and shut doors, bridges and detours to a Garden of Eden job that fulfills all my quirky talents and passions, strengths and weaknesses.

Along anyone's journey in life, there are times when you can see a good way down the road, and there are other times when it is so foggy and dark that, in spite of the headlights, you can only see fifteen or twenty feet ahead of you. In either case, you should be true to the bit of road you see, and wherever you find yourself, make the best of where you are, give your best effort, and get the most out of it.

My one year of teaching tenth grade English was rough. Pike County was a good system with a good administration and students. I was the problem. Because I didn't prepare any material ahead of time, I was barely staying a step ahead of the students.

I also didn't know how to maintain discipline. For my daddy, discipline seemed effortless. I loved him and respected him. He set a great example. He was strong where he needed to be strong and soft where he needed to be soft. I felt that, if I was passionate about my subject, showed the students that I loved them, and showed the direct application of the things in a story or poem to their lives, discipline would not be a problem. After all, the emotions and feelings and ideas in literature and poetry were just like the ones the students had, and, as we studied a poem or story, they could find themselves and define their identities through literature and poetry. History and literature had helped me define who I was, and I would help them make this connection as well.

I had not counted on the fact that, in the tenth grade at a rural public school, the students were more interested in the good-looking boy or girl across the aisle or in working at their uncle's shop. Also, the authors and poets whose works we studied had written their stories and poems from the depths of their life experiences with a mature mind to interpret that experience. In the tenth grade, students don't have much life experience, and their minds aren't developed enough to make a lot of what they do experience. So, while I was passionate and enthusiastic about what we studied, they were a bit bored and were more entertained by my passion and enthusiasm than by the story or poem we were reading.

It was a very long year. I would wake up anxious about the day, go to the bathroom, dry heave a few times, and head to work. I would dry heave five days a week and then take the weekend off. I only stopped dry heaving when I decided I would not go back the next year. I was offered a contract in the spring, but I had had enough physically and emotionally.

I have a metaphor for first year teaching. It came to me one day in a rush of anxiety-fueled inspiration. It goes like this: First-year teaching is like suddenly finding oneself at the helm of a ship that you don't know how to sail, on an unknown sea, with an unknown destination, and an unsympathetic and mutinous crew. All that matters is that you survive. The ship can be lost, the cargo lost, even the crew lost. But you must survive so that someday in the future you might be able to get the ship through, some cargo through, and hopefully some of the crew through.

Along your life's journey God can use the physical, the mental, and the spiritual to open and shut doors and to build bridges. In that year of classroom teaching, God allowed my experience to break me mentally and emotionally. He shut the door of conventional teaching but built a bridge to a different kind of teaching. In the future, I would create and lead tours to Western Europe and North America. I would teach to a willing audience on location, incorporating all my love of biography, history, art, organization, and design. I would build some of my first tours out of the places I had worked during my resort work: the Maine Coast and Southern New England.

From beginning to end, God knew me better that I knew myself. He knew me not only as the person I was, but the person I would become. He would give me the best of all worlds based on the individual He had made me to be and the individual I was becoming.

---

1. Isak Dinesen, *Out of Africa*, (Indianapolis: Indiana University), 1965.

2. Isak Dinesen, *Out of Africa*, 81

12

MY LIFE IN TRAVEL

I finished the year at Pike County High in June of 1984 and began to work full time at The Travel Connection. When I look in the rearview mirror of my life, I see that, all through the years, God had been preparing me for a life in travel. It began with my mother's interest in travel and our planning tours we never got to take. My love of biography led me to getting a history major. My interest in biography led me, the boy who was reluctant to leave home, to break the bonds of hesitancy with a passion to see the places I had read about. My resort years took me to the places where I would lead tours in the future, and living by the seat of my pants taught me to be creative and innovative in changing circumstances. It seems that God used every piece of my past. No part of the journey was wasted. God is an efficient sculptor and guide.

For the first ten years The Travel Connection was a regular travel agency with daily business split between 80 percent corporate and 20 percent leisure travel. In those days travel agents gave a free service because they were paid 9 to 13 percent on what they booked, whether it was air, cars, hotels, cruises, or package tours. This was a great deal for the airlines because they had us book 80 percent of their tickets and saved money by not having to pay employee salaries and benefits.

The corporate side of our business was the economic engine with our booking air, hotels, and rental cars for the sales teams at Thomaston Mills, BF Goodrich, Federal Paperboard, and The Theo Bean Publishing Company. On the leisure side, we did cruises, package vacations, and independent vacation itineraries.

Corporate travel paid the agency bills, and leisure travel added financial dessert to the corporate main course. The people of Thomaston and the surrounding areas really supported us, and we were profitable from the beginning. In God's bigger picture, we were also building capital to make a smooth venture into the group tour side of the travel industry that only He could see in our future.

I would sometimes sell leisure package tours created by major tour companies. Whenever I sold a tour that went to places where I had been or worked, I looked at where they went and what they did. Every time I thought, *If I were designing this tour, I would do it differently*. But the fullness of time had not come.

Now God was leading me very efficiently and logically into the heart and soul of who I was and what I was called to do. The travel agency years break down into such a well-designed and logical game plan. I am not smart enough to have come up with this plan. In many ways, I was just along for a thrilling and wonderful ride. I was driving the car, but in every meaningful way, I was following God's directions on a journey that He had created me for. Although I couldn't always see the big plan, He did, and it was a plan to bring me into my fullest fruition and realization—to be used by Him to bless others with experiences that they might not otherwise have had.

During the 1980s I led a few tours, but God was busy preparing me in other ways. Not only were we building capital, but I took my first personal trips to Europe, and I began to learn how to build itineraries. My first trips were by myself or with friends, and we moved about on trains, subways, and local transportation. Just as He had done in my resort years, God was having me travel, helping me learn places and modes of transportation by making mistakes and learning through what I encountered. Again, I see that there was no waste in those years. I was learning in the best possible school. I was not letting someone else do it for me, nor was I learning it from a book. I was a student in the school of actual experience.

God was preparing me so that when I would lead my first tours, I would know where I was going and what I was doing. God used those ten travel agency years in every possible way, both financially and experientially so that when 1993 came, I would be ready.

MY FIRST REAL TOUR

I always had a desire to take people to resort areas where I had worked. Because I lived in a small town, people knew me and had faith in me. They first trusted me because they loved my father, but through the years I earned their trust in my own right.

The first thing God did was to allow me to get restless with booking regular travel. In the late '80s, I was having a hard time maintaining interest in regular travel, and I had always thought about designing a tour of my own. But how was I to do it? It seemed more complicated than it really was—sort of like trying to write a term paper and not knowing where to begin. Sometimes in life, as with a term paper, you just have to begin the journey, and then along the way, many things that seemed a mystery will become self-evident.

People knew I had traveled a lot, both in resorts and backpacking around Europe. In the winter of 1993, the parents of three high school seniors, approached me about taking their sons backpacking in Europe for spring break. The time was right, and I was ready because of my own backpacking vacations in the '80s. I was also ready because during all that impromptu bus travel, I had gained wisdom and confidence in dealing with unforeseen problems that would invariably come up during a trip. I took the boys, and, on that trip, we used trains to relocate overnight to make the most of each day. We went to Belgium, Paris, Venice, Florence, Tuscany, Rome, and Switzerland. It all worked out, and we had a great time. As a result of that trip, word got around, and for the next couple of years, I did spring break trips for students to Europe.

Later that year, in the summer of 1993, I was planning a personal sailing vacation on a Windjammer Schooner along the coast of Maine. I had never done a sailing trip, and I wanted to see what one would be like. Meanwhile, I happened to see a tour itinerary of New England in a brochure by one of the best-known tour companies in the US. It touted a tour of Maine, New Hampshire, and Vermont. The itinerary showed a tour starting in Boston, making one stop in Kennebunkport, Maine, and then leaving for New Hampshire and Vermont.

When I saw that, I was disgusted. From having worked on the Maine Coast for two summers and falls, I thought of all the magnificent places the tour would miss. They would miss Pemaquid Point Lighthouse with its rocky shores, Camden with its picturesque harbor, Bar Harbor, and Acadia National Park just to name a few. The tour told people it was going to Maine, and technically it did, but for the sake of checking off more places in a short amount of time, all they chose to see was Kennebunkport.

That was the straw that broke the camel's back. I thought, *I am going to design a real tour of New England that sees the best of Maine, New Hampshire and Vermont.* I was so determined to lead a tour that I thought, *I am already going to spend money on a vacation to Maine. I will just cancel that sailing trip and put the money into a tour.* I would consider it an investment in how to create a tour. I was willing to lose money just to make it happen.

God had been preparing me through a mixture of desire, vision, and frustration, and finally, it was the fullness of time. Two ladies in my town, Libby Ingram and Ann Hunter, had said they wished I would do a tour to the places I had worked at in New England. Here was my chance!!! I decided to cancel that personal sailing vacation, and I called Libby and Ann and asked if they would like to go with me to Maine, New Hampshire, and Vermont to see the fall foliage. They said "Yes!!" and so I designed a "Fall Foliage" tour to Maine, New Hampshire, and Vermont!

Word got around our small town that I was taking a few people on a tour to New England, and before we knew it, we had ten people in two seven-passenger vans. Tommy Hankinson, who had planned to go with me on the sailing trip, canceled his trip and went along to New England to drive the second van.

I told the participants that I had never led a tour and that we would consider it to be an adventure. They seemed to think that made it even better and more exciting. We did the tour, they loved it, and when we got home, they wanted to know if I would take them to New York at Christmas.

We went to New York in December and had a great time. After New York, they wanted to know where we could go in 1994. So we went to southern New England, visiting Boston, Newport, Rhode Island, Cape Cod, Nantucket, and Martha's Vineyard. At the same time, others in town had heard about the New England Fall Foliage trip and wanted me to do that in the fall of 1994. Both trips were great successes. In the coming years, people would keep asking for new itineraries. And just like that, a tour company had been born, and as the years passed, the tour snowball got bigger and bigger!!

God always had a plan, and His plan was to use experience and changing life dynamics to get the most out of me. Jesus said, "I am come that you might have life and have it more abundantly" (John 10:10). God's plans are bigger and better than ours, God's dreams are bigger and better than ours. We think we have life, and then God takes us to a level beyond what we imagine.

God uses all things, both good and bad, to achieve His ends. As it turned out, the '90s brought a perfect storm for travel agencies, particularly in places like Thomaston. During the 1990s, the airlines had price wars, and the customer lost perspective on what it truly cost to run an airline. When the dust cleared, the consumer had won, and the airlines had priced themselves into unprofitability. They began to look for places to save cash. They couldn't lower pilot salaries, because they might strike. But thanks to the increasing popularity of the personal computer, they saw a place where they could save money: People began to book their own travel, so the airlines developed websites and encouraged the public to buy their tickets over the computer. At the same time, they began to take away our commissions.

First commissions went from 10 percent to 8 percent, then to 5 percent, and finally to 0. Where travel agents had been able to offer a free service, making their commissions on air, now they had to charge a fee. This worked against travel agents because most of the public preferred the option of buying their own tickets and saving the booking fee.

Then came more trouble. The Thomaston corporations, which were our financial bread and butter, began to go bankrupt due to foreign competition or, as in the case of the Theo Bean publishing company, were bought out by bigger companies with their own travel agencies. So, by the end of the '90s, our corporate business, which had been 80 percent of our bottom line, dwindled to nothing.

And what about the leisure side? Consumers were also doing more of their own travel arrangements. By the end of the '90s, the perfect storm wreaked havoc on the travel industry in general and on Thomaston in particular. With commissions dwindling, the advent of the personal computer, and local corporate bankruptcies and buyouts, the financial pie was reduced to just a sliver.

But there was one God-sent saving grace. My tour groups were getting more popular. I had led three tours in 1993, and that began a snowball of increasing interest. Each following year, I did more tours until 1999, when I led thirteen tours. As the years passed, the tour business became more and more profitable and the regular travel business became less and less profitable. And, best of all, I was doing something I truly loved. Also, scouting, creating, advertising, and leading tours led me to use all my curious combination of skills and talents that God had developed in me through the years. In my way of thinking, God had led me back to the working equivalent of the Garden of Eden.

Again, what seemed to be bad actually worked in my favor. One thing that further propelled the growth on the tour side was the continual expansion of my client pool. We could never have successfully started the travel agency anywhere but Thomaston, but we could not have lasted past the '90s without the tours. In turn, the tours could not have lasted without our growing client base. In this regard, God was working on this even though we didn't know it, and as always happened in my case, He was using the things I love. Over the years, God arranged for me to meet and collaborate with a number of key people, who would help me exponentially expand my client pool. Here are a few key people to whom I will be forever grateful for helping me expand and grow my client pool.

PAT HANKINS

In 1994, I audited an art course at my old alma mater, Gordon Junior College. Pat Hankins taught the course, and we became good friends. Before the class was over, we planned a week-long art trip to Tuscany in Italy. I would do the technical side, and she would do the art side and pitch the tour to her students and friends. That trip was a great success and led to yearly trips bringing in a wider pool of travelers. Pat introduced me to more people in Barnesville, in Griffin, and across her wide network of friends, students, and art lovers. This friendship with Pat was very important in substantially expanding my client pool. God was growing my business in a very organic and natural way. God's miracles are all around us, hiding in plain sight, in the passing moments of our life. The processes which God uses to lead us in life are often so practical and logical.

TOM SOMMA

In the spring of 2000, I was scouting out Washington, DC, and decided to visit the National Gallery of Art. As I entered, I saw a guy getting ready to lead a group of college students. My timing, or I should say, God's timing, was perfect. This would be another watershed moment in the growth of my tours.

I thought, *I will just hang on the periphery of this group and see if this guy's commentary is any good.*

I am an eternal student, always eager to learn something new. I thought he might be a guide for the museum, and, if he proved to be good, I could use him if I brought a group to the National Gallery. Also, a guided tour is often the best way to learn the highlights of a museum.

I fell in with this tour, and the guide didn't seem to mind that I was tagging along. For the next hour, I listened to an incredibly amazing commentary on the paintings he selected. The theme of the tour was the Ashcan School of Art, but when the tour was over, I felt as if I had just had a spiritual meal. I had learned about art, but I had also learned about life and about myself.

After the tour, I introduced myself and told him what I felt about his commentary. I gave him my card and, on the spot, asked him who he was and what he did. Tom Somma was a wonder in an art museum. He was a Ph.D. and the curator of the art museum at Mary Washington College in Fredericksburg, Virginia. He also taught enrichment classes in sculpture and art to the guides at the Library of Congress and the U.S. Capitol. And, he was an adjunct professor at Georgetown University. This was all wonderful, but he had sold me with what I had heard on the tour.

I asked if he would help me with a tour to Paris in the coming fall. His part would be to lead the tours in the Louvre, the Musee D'Orsay, and the Rodin Museum. Also, I said the Paris trip would be a test run, and if we were compatible, we could team up and lead tours for the people he taught. This was, without question, a God-arranged moment. From that point forward, every time Tom Somma led me or my groups in an art museum, I felt the same exciting feelings I had during that first tour in Washington.

That fall Tom went with me to Paris and did what I would come to see as his usual, amazing job. We then decided to team up and pitch tours to his "students," some of whom were students at Mary Washington College, but others who were guides at the Library of Congress, the U.S. Capitol, the Smithsonian, and other museums throughout northern Virginia.

Our first tour with his groups would be to Paris. I felt a little intimidated as the tour date approached. What would these scholars think of me? Tom would lead the tours in the art museums, and I would design the tour and lead the historical walks and commentary to balance out the tour. I wondered if my level of learning and commentary could satisfy the intellectual level of these knowledgeable guides and students.

Fortunately, I realized my level of learning was what it was, but one gift God had given me was in the things I chose to point out and the things I found fascinating. I thought, *Don't try to fake it, just be yourself, be authentic. Point out the things that you find interesting, and talk about them.*

On any given trip, I generally start off with a light and easy orientation walk to show the people the area where they will be staying—the restaurants and stores—and teach a little history to ease into the stay. This time, as we took our walk, I pointed out the Parisian gift for artistic display in shop windows. I took them through indoor shopping arcades and pointed out mosaic tile designs on the floor. I taught them to see the French gift for aesthetic beauty that lay all around them that they otherwise might not notice because of their focus on museum art.

I walked them through the gardens of the Palais Royal with its fabulous history and dramatic architecture. I trusted my instincts and simply shared the Paris I found fascinating. You can imagine my feelings of joy and the satisfaction I felt when I overheard Tom's wife tell him, "Honey, we have been to Paris, but we haven't seen it like this."

Yes! I now knew I was up to the challenge. What had won the day was that I had chosen to be who God had created me to be using the intuition, gifts and talents He had given me. This life lesson would serve me well in the years to come, not only in travel, but in all other areas of my life.

The working relationship Tom and I had in designing and leading tours was amazing. We complemented each other perfectly, and we never had a cross moment. One key was Tom's genuineness and his love of sharing, traits I shared and valued. Quite often, Ph.Ds. are territorial and jealously guard their intellectual domain. Tom was never that way. We were united in our passion, and others got caught up in our joy of art, history, architecture, and life itself. We made a great team.

Through Tom, my client base expanded. On that tour to Paris, there was a wonderful lady named Hazel O'Toole, who worked at the Gari Melchers Home and Studio in Fredericksburg, Virginia. Hazel loved the Paris tour and loved my style. She thought I would be good to help lead tours at the Gari Melchers Home and Studio. Hazel introduced me to Joanna Catron and Betsy Labar at Gari Melchers, and before we knew it, we were off and running with tours for Gari Melchers.

Between Tom, Hazel, Joanna, and Betsy, my client base would spread throughout the Northern Virginia and the Washington, DC, area. In the coming years, I led many tours for both the guides at the Library of Congress and the Gari Melchers Home and Studio. These tours were not only a financial blessing, but the rich friendships I developed have been a great blessing in my life that has continued through the years.

Sadly, about four years into our working relationship, Tom Somma was diagnosed with pancreatic cancer. For the next couple of years, as Tom fought the cancer, there were tours he could not go on. Tom's magical commentary and sweet spirit were sorely missed, but I was able to get some very good local guides by using the recommendations in the Rick Steves guidebooks.

Tom died in 2009. Our friendship was made in heaven. We loved and respected each other, and we created some wonderful moments for our clients. To this day, I am still blessed by Tom's legacy as I continue to lead the groups we started together.

WALLI BEALL

Another real help to me in expanding my client base was Walli Beall. Walli was from Tallahassee, Florida, and was a very important person at Goodwood Historic Home, a beautiful antebellum home in downtown Tallahassee. Walli's friend, Betty Joyce Hand, invited her to be her roommate on my "Week on the Maine Coast" tour. Walli loved everything about the tour, and when it was over, she asked me to work with her on building home-and-garden tours for the patrons and friends of Goodwood Historic Home. That, too, was a working marriage made in heaven. It led to many tours and expanded my client base throughout northern Florida.

PEGI VAUGHN

Pegi Vaughn led a travel program for Monroe Academy in Forsyth, Georgia. We began doing tours together in 1999, and, over the years, took students and parents to both Western Europe and North America. These tours, and the network of people they brought in, were another tributary feeding into an ever-increasing client pool. Through the years, Pegi has not only helped me build my business, but she has become a devoted friend and spiritual help-mate.

As I have always said, I don't feel I could have built my group travel business anywhere but my hometown of Thomaston. The people were willing to trust me based on their love and trust for my daddy. In the years to come, I would earn their trust in my own right, but I could not have lasted for the long run of what is now 299 tours to Western Europe and North America without those friends outside Thomaston who have helped me! Pat, Tom, Joanna, Betsy, Hazel, Walli, and Pegi not only helped me expand my business, but they also became good friends and opened my life to a vast array of people who have blessed me in so many ways.

ANOTHER BIG GOD-MOVE IN SHAPING MY BUSINESS AND ME

Again, what seemed to be bad actually worked in my favor. God was on the move shaping me, using events, and accomplishing His will. As we moved into the new millennium, the financial meat on the traditional travel side of my business, for all the reasons I have mentioned, got less and less, but the money on the group side was getting better and better. Then I believe God began to give me a vision for the future.

Throughout the first years of the new millennium, I began to feel more of a passion for the group tours, and I began to wonder what we could do if we devoted ourselves totally to groups. God is so practical as well as spiritual. He began to work on me on the emotional side as well.

As the traditional side of our business declined, God gave me a vision and wave of intention that would not go away. The vision consistently seemed to say, *"I have created you as a unique person, and I have brought you on a unique path. I have given you a curious set of gifts and talents, and now I want you to stop diluting your talent. Quit trying to be all things to all people. Take the step to do purely what you love. Take this business home, and become a tour-only business and do only your tours. This is what all that has come before was leading to. It is the fullness of time, take this last step in the evolution of your business, and I will show you what I can do both in you and your business!"*

This feeling would not go away. It hovered in my mind for a few years, but we are people of habit, and we seek security. It was hard to quit the traditional side of the business of doing cruises, airfares, package trips, and other travel. To walk away from it seemed to be walking away from money on the table as well as the people who still wanted to work through a travel agent. But not only were the returns on that side steadily declining, I was also losing all enthusiasm for that side of the business.

Finally, I could not shake that recurring wave of intention. And then I asked myself a question: "Ten years from now, if you don't take this step to focus and load your talent in a tour-only business, how will you feel? Will you look back, having diluted your talent in a dwindling part of the business you have lost interest in, and wonder what might have been?"

At this time, I was still faintly hanging on to the tattered, frayed ends of the security that seemed to be offered by the traditional side of our business, and then God stepped in with His big and creative toolbox to help me take the final leap.

Around 2005, I was in New York, on one of my December holiday trips. I was eating at a great restaurant called the Union Square Café. I'd enjoyed a wonderful meal, and I went to pay my bill at the counter. As the staff processed my payment, I saw a cookbook for sale containing popular recipes from the restaurant. I can never keep myself from at least taking a peek in a book. So, I opened it, and God spoke to me as clearly as if it were Scripture. I saw these words: *"A profound wine is usually produced when a winemaker is courageous enough to cut back his vines, sacrificing a large grape production and potentially valuable crop in favor of a smaller harvest with fewer, better nourished, and more intensely flavored grapes."*

Those words exploded in my mind! The choice of words like "profound," "courageous," and "intensely flavored" pierced my psyche. Those words painted a visual image like nothing else could have. I passionately wanted my life to be "profound," and not just average or mediocre. To make that final move, I had to be "courageous." For me that meant walking away from an established business with a broader spectrum of travel and cutting back to only do my tours, which was where my intense passion lay. Yes, I would be leaving money on the table, but, with each year the financial meat on that bone was less and less. In reality, I would trade the false security offered by the tattered ends of the old business in return for a "better nourished, more intensely" flavored life. I bought that book and walked out thinking, *if you say no to this, you are saying no to everything you are and everything you believe.*

So, I returned home and began laying plans to change the course of my life and my business. I would wind the traditional travel side down, take the business home, and for better or worse, for richer or poorer, become a tour-only business, doing mostly tours of my design.

In the coming years, everything in that metaphor of the vineyard would come true. Wine is a living thing, and the results of that move have not only given me a richer life but have also given it to me more intensely and more abundantly. In the culmination and confirmation of life lessons that God had been teaching me through the years, God used my business to bless me financially and experientially. He also blessed others with life experiences they might not have had otherwise, and He used everything along the way to bring my identity and spiritual nature to its fullest realization and expression. When all that comes together in life, you get the wonderful by-products of joy, beauty, meaning, and fulfillment. What more can you ask for in life?

I could not have had this much success without all the great travelers who went on my tours. The friendships I have had with them have enriched my life in so many ways. Also, I could not have had success without a great staff through the years. Chief among those has been Linda Best. She came into my office in 1996 and, from the start, treated the business as if it were her own, and she treated our clients as if they were friends and family. She did so many things I did not know how to do, and she set me free to do what I love and what I do best.

God and all the wonderful people He brought into my life, have helped me in each moment along the way to move knowingly and unknowingly in the direction of His dreams for me. In it all, He enriched me with wonderful relationships with my clients and my business associates, always and ever moving me into the direction of joy, contentment, and fulfillment. All along, as Psalm 139 says, He knew me better than I knew myself, and his dreams for me were so much better than my dreams for myself. For all this, I am so thankful and grateful.

I have had, and continue to have, a wonderful life. When I came home from Palm Beach in the spring of 1979, I told my father that if I died that night, I would have lived a full life. I continue to feel the same feeling with each day that passes. God is Faithful. God is Good. And He continues to send His angel before me, preparing the way for a future that only He can see.

13

SPECIAL GIFTS OF GOD

I have written this chapter to discuss unique, special gifts of God that I believe he designed specifically for me. Before I list these, I would like to talk about the general gifts He has given me, without which I would be lost in the deepest and purest sense of the word.

Each of us would do well to meditate on and thank God for the many blessings He has given to us. They are indeed too numerous to count. I will be brief about these because I have previously described them in detail.

When I look back on my life, it is hard to begin to thank God for all His blessings and gifts. First, I was truly blessed to be born to my parents and to be born here in the United States. These were both important gifts that would shape my journey.

Another blessing of eternal value is that God came into the landscape of my life and found me when I wasn't really looking for Him. Over time, He literally revealed Himself to me. He opened my eyes and ears to see and understand the great gift He was offering me with salvation through the death of His Son. That salvation brought with it forgiveness, peace, joy, meaning, and a relationship with my Creator. Every day I live in the wonder and beauty of this life in Him, and these spiritual treasures cannot be lost by financial misfortunes or by any personal or world calamity.

Another blessing is that of the indwelling Holy Spirit, which is the incredible experience of the God of all creation living within me. Think a little bit on what that actually means!!! Through the Holy Spirit, I, like any believer, am indwelt by God and get to live in the incredibly rich majesty of His presence amidst the common, passing moments of life…and this incredible gift is offered to us all, free for the accepting!!! In Revelation 3:20, Jesus said, *"Behold, I stand at the door and knock, It any man hear my voice, and opens the door, I will come into him and sup with him and He with me..."* Dear reader, if you have never opened that door and let Jesus into your life, I urge you to do it now. It is the purpose for which you were created!!

The contemplation of this prospect is for me inexhaustible in its glory and beauty. However much I meditate on it, I only seem to scratch the surface of what this actually means in real time. It seems the best thing is just to praise Him in the wonder of that which we so feebly understand. This reality supercharges the consciousness of our common, passing moments. God has truly pulled back the veil for me and shown me a glimpse of the depths of what Jean-Pierre de Caussade wrote in *Abandonment to Divine Providence*, "There is nothing trivial about our passing moments, as they enclose the whole kingdom of holiness and [they are] the food on which angels feed."

Another blessing is that God led me through a series of open doors and shut doors to a job that suits me perfectly, allows me to indulge my passions and interests, and brings my being to its highest possible fruition. I revel in all the parts of creating and leading tours as well as enjoying the people I meet through my tours.

These are the greatest gifts of God, but there are also special gifts I believe God has given me, because He knows me intimately and apparently wanted to give me special gifts just for the joy of it. In the following pages, I would just like to tell of a few of these gifts He has given me.

SPECIAL "GOD WINK" GIFTS OF GOD

I believe that God sometimes gives us special gifts designed to bless us specifically according to our personality and interests. I also believe that when we are proactive and intentional in pursuing our identity, dreams, and passions, God blesses us with these unexpected gifts. I have seen this happen over and over in my life. Some might describe the following experiences in this essay as "God Wink moments."

MEETING ANDREW WYETH

In the mid-1990s, I went to Maine by myself to spiritually soak in that ragged coastline, landscape, and culture on which I love to feed my spirit. I firmly believe that what I get out of times like these adds depth to my passion of a place, and that comes out later when I take a group there.

I was spending most of my time on that trip on Monhegan Island, a stunning place. Because of its beauty and quaintness, Monhegan has a large artists' colony. One day I went to the mainland to visit the Farnsworth Art Museum, which had an exhibit on a certain theme by Andrew Wyeth. Over the years, God has taught me a lot about life through Andrew Wyeth's art. The Farnsworth Museum in Rockland, Maine, and the Brandywine River Museum in Chadds Ford, Pennsylvania, are, in many ways, shrines to the art legacy of the Wyeth family.

On this day, I enjoyed the art exhibit and then headed back toward the coast to the small village of Port Clyde where I would catch a late afternoon ferry back to Monhegan Island. Just before Port Clyde is another harbor village called Tenants Harbor. At that time, it had a fish and lobster market right on the docks. They also served lobster, shellfish, and other items. You bought your food inside the market and then ate it on picnic tables on the docks. It was a gorgeous day, and I decided to stop at this market, which was called Land's End. I went full-on Maine and got a lobster and a small, netted bag of mussels. They served it on a tray with a drink and warm drawn butter. How much better could life get—a beautiful day on the coast of Maine after I had just enjoyed the paintings of Andrew Wyeth, and now I was diving into a plate of lobster and mussels with a quaint harbor before me.

For me, this is about as good as a day on this earth can get. But God was about to give me a spiritual gift to make it even better, just because He could, and just because He knew me and loved me and wanted to bless me.

As I ate at a picnic table, I looked around. It was a bit early to have dinner, so almost no one was there, only a couple of guys talking at one of the tables. One had curly hair and was wearing what I thought was a fishmongers rubber apron. I had worked in a fish market on Nantucket and worn a similar apron to protect my clothes from the grit, grime, and slime of a fish market. The other guy was unmistakable—he was Andrew Wyeth! The two talked and, as I was finishing, Wyeth walked the other guy to the end of the dock and saw him off on a boat. The other guy, I would later realize, was his son, Jamie, also a great painter, and the fishmonger's smock was more likely a painter's smock.

Here was probably my one chance in life to meet Andrew Wyeth, and I was going to take it. I cleared my table, threw away the trash, and went out to the small parking lot to wait for him. I approached him and told him how his art had informed my life in many ways. He asked if I was an artist, and I said no, but that I had what the great art teacher Robert Henri would have described as "the art spirit." Andrew Wyeth would have known all about Henri and have read his book on art, and so I felt that even though I wasn't a painter, he saw me as a kindred spirit. Before we parted, he allowed me to take a photo of him. What a thrill… what a blessing!

I have been very deliberate and intentional in my life to feed my spirit on the things it loves, but added moments like these are a pure gift of God. What are the odds that our paths would meet? On that day, I absolutely believe God wanted to bless me with that gift.

OLSON FARM

Back in the 1980s, when I was just getting familiar with the work of Andrew Wyeth, Doug and I and some friends were on the coast of Maine near Cushing, where Wyeth had painted at the Olson Farm. For years he had immortalized the daily drama lived out in the lives of Christina Olson and her brother, Alvaro.

On this particular day, I had a book of the paintings that Wyeth had done at the Olson Farm, and we were roaming the countryside, looking for the unmistakable farmhouse. The Olson House is a museum today, but, back then, the movie producer Joseph Levine privately owned it.

We made a lot of mistakes that afternoon. There was no such thing as GPS, so we were driving down country roads and asking around. Late in the day, we finally found it. It was so amazing, and all the more so because we had this iconic house and landscape all to ourselves. Because of its situation on a rural peninsula and because of its architectural style, the house has an incredibly strong personality.

When we got there, we soaked in the atmosphere of the old farmhouse, the out buildings, and the beautiful views of land and sea. It was just like in the paintings, the massive house of weathered grey clapboard, with its vast spiritual presence, looking out over this wonderful rural landscape. Although no one was there, there was a palpable presence of the spirits of the people who had lived there, and the things that had happened there. It is hard to describe, but like other special, eternal moments, it was like drinking from the sacred fountain of life. We were thankful to be there.

Next to the big farmhouse, stood a small house with a pen of bloodhounds behind it. As the sun was going down, a man suddenly drove up in an old truck. He asked us what we were doing, and we told him and showed him the book of paintings of the farm. As we talked, we asked him if any Olsons still lived in the area. He said yes. We asked him if he was an Olson, and he said, yes, he was Fred Olson, Christina's nephew. The bloodhounds were his, and he used them to track escaped convicts from the nearby Maine State Prison in Thomaston, Maine.

By now, he saw that we were really interested, and he said he was the caretaker for Mr. Levine, and he had all the keys to the house and the out buildings. He asked if we would like him to show us around. For the next hour, we followed Fred Olson and walked through the sacred world of the spirits of the Wyeths and the Olsons. Some of the pictures in the book could only be fully appreciated when we went into the house and into the out buildings. When it was over, we felt as if we'd had a deep spiritual meal. Do I think that opportunity was a coincidence? Absolutely not. God's handprints were all over that experience.

KUERNER FARM

Given what happened in the 1980s at Olson's Farm, it is amazing that I had an almost identical "coincidence" about twenty-five years later at Andrew Wyeth's other painting locale, the Kuerner Farm in Chadds Ford, Pennsylvania.

Around 2012, I went to Philadelphia to scout out a home-and-garden trip for Goodwood Historic Home in Tallahassee, Florida. I had already taken Goodwood to Philadelphia on a prior trip, so the focus of this return trip was to do new things. I was also scouting homes and gardens in the countryside south of Philadelphia and added the Wyeth sites and the Brandywine River Museum in Chadds Ford.

On that trip, I was scouting so many Dupont homes south of Philadelphia that I decided to stay down there for a few nights to avoid the extra commute from the city with its rush-hour traffic. I got up early one morning, and went to Chadds Ford just to soak in the atmosphere as I had done at the Olson Farm in Maine.

When I got there that beautiful, sunny morning, I parked the car and walked the rural road in front of the farm to just feed my spirit on the place, the view, and the moment. There were the railroad tracks where Andrew's father, the great illustrator, N. C. Wyeth, had been hit by a train and killed. There were the beautiful rolling hills of the Kuerner Farm, with the old barn and farmhouse in the dew and stillness of early morning. At that time, the farm was not a museum, but was still a private property, in the hands of the Kuerner family.

I got back in my car and drove just beyond the farm to the ruins of Mother Archie's Church. During Andrew Wyeth's youth, the church had been the center of a small community of African Americans known locally as "Little Africa." Wyeth had painted the church and befriended many of the locals who were subjects in lots of his paintings.

I was reveling, as I had done in Maine many years before, in the world of Wyeth. There was the hill where Wyeth had loved to sit under the pine trees with a bird's eye view across the rural kingdom of Karl Kuerner. When his father had been killed, Andrew painted himself as a young boy running down that hill, as if to get way from the trauma of the tragedy and the loss of the imposing presence of his father.

As I was in the midst of all these thoughts and images, a truck pulled up. It was virtually a replay of what had happened at the Olson Farm many years ago in Maine. The man in the truck asked me what I was doing. I told him that I was a Wyeth fan, and that I was just communing with the spirit of the place and soaking in the atmosphere where so many of his paintings had been done and where he and his subjects had lived. Then I asked him if any Kuerners still lived in the area. He said yes, and I asked him if he was a Kuerner, and he said yes. He was a Karl J. Kuerner, the grandson of Karl Kuerner, the subject of so many of Wyeth's paintings. I pointed to the hill near us with three pine trees high on the crest, and asked him if that was where Andrew liked to go and sit and look down on the Kuerner Farm. He said yes and that he owned the place and that if I would get my car and follow him up a little dirt road that he pointed to, I could park up at his house and walk out and sit under those trees. This may mean nothing to most people, but for me, in that moment, it was as if I had been invited into a very sacred spiritual experience.

I drove up the road, and by the time I got there, Karl was inside his house. I went in, and he asked me if I would like some breakfast. I said no, that I had already eaten, but he offered me a glass of orange juice, and we sat and talked a while. He told me that he was a painter in his own right, and that he had been taught by Andrew's sister, Henriette. He showed me a book of his works, which were in the same spirit of Andrew Wyeth and were exhibited in the nearby Brandywine River Museum, which was a shrine to the Wyeths and other artists whose works they inspired.

We had a wonderful talk, and then he invited me to sit under the pine trees and enjoy the magnificent view of the Kuerner farm below. Again, this may seem like a trivial invitation to most, but it was as if I had been invited into a secret world where you received deep riches and treasures simply by being there.

I drank from the fountain of that experience for a good while, and then I returned to the house. During our earlier talk, Karl also offered me a second incredible invitation. Though the farm below and the barn were not open to the public, he had the keys. A helper would be arriving shortly to take me down and let me look around the farm and go in the barn. As I wandered the grounds and through the barn, I saw the views that Andrew Wyeth had captured through the years. Just as in Maine at the Olson Farm, by the time I left, I felt I had been fed a rich spiritual meal that would continue to feed my mind and spirit through the years.

EDWARD HOPPER'S STUDIO IN NEW YORK

Ever since my amazing visit to the Little White House when I was in high school, I have been convinced of the spiritually transformative effects of being in places where history happened. Since that time, I have sought out places that are important to me. These places are always tied to the lives of people who have played a significant part in the evolution of who I am. These sites may involve art, architecture, war, or landscape, but they are almost always tied to some important person, living or dead, who played a transformative part in my life.

Since 1993 I have taken groups to New York during the December holidays. One year I decided to go to Greenwich Village in my free time and see if I could find the brownstone art studio of Edward Hopper. I am drawn to the art of Edward Hopper, and have been a long-time fan of his work. During his life, he lived in a brownstone apartment facing Washington Square in Greenwich Village, and he also lived on Cape Cod, high up on the dunes at Truro.

So, one day I had some spare time in the late afternoon, and I headed down to Washington Square to see if I could find Hopper's studio apartment. Although I had an address, sometimes numbers change and buildings evolve in their look. I had the location narrowed down to the northeast side of the square, but I couldn't find a historic plaque, and I was not satisfied that I could find the exact location.

On the door of one of the brownstones, a sign indicated an office of New York University, so I thought they might know. Even though it was almost in the exact location of where Hopper's studio should have been, they were unsure.

Having no luck looking around the front of the brown stone row, I walked around behind the buildings and found a carriage lane that ran along an alley on the backside of the buildings. As I walked down the lane, I continued to look at the rooftops to see if I could see anything that might give me a clue. And there it was, a big glass skylight on the rooftop. Light is a key element for any artist, and Hopper would have wanted a skylight on the rooftop to let light into his studio. No other apartment had one, and it was right about where Hopper's studio would have put it.

As I stood there happy and convinced that I had found the location, God had a greater gift for me. Just because He loves me.

At that moment a woman walked up from out of nowhere. (Was she the biblical angel unawares?) I asked her if she lived in these apartments, and she said she did. I then pointed up to the skylight and asked if she knew if that might be where Edward Hopper's studio might have been. She said yes it was and that she lived there, and would I like to come up and see it?

Again, I was thrilled to be able to see Hopper's studio, but I also was knocked over by God's love and His showering me with this blessing. Here I was, in the studio of Edward Hopper, one of the major American painters of the twentieth century. As with all these types of experiences, I felt I was in a sacred space, having a rich spiritual meal. I stood where he would have stood, looking out at the city as he would have done.

Was this sheer chance or coincidence? I am convinced of God's intimate love for me, and I am also convinced that, in that late afternoon in New York, He wanted to bless me with a wonderful gift for which I am eternally grateful. As I have said, the layering of these types of experiences over the years has formed within me a vast spiritual reservoir from which I drink on a daily basis.

MEETING GEORGE PLIMPTON AND HONORIA MURPHY

In January 1985, I was working at the travel agency and read an article about a Hemingway festival and conference in Key West. I had never been to Key West, and I was a huge fan of Ernest Hemingway, who had lived there. The article mentioned that George Plimpton and Patrick Hemingway would be speakers, and this got my attention. Before I knew it, I was booking an airline ticket and a room in Key West and preparing questions for the speakers at the conference.

I was eager to meet author George Plimpton. He had written a number of books about his experiences in a number of professional sports. Two of his best-known books were *The Bogey Man*, about playing in the Bing Crosby Pro-Am, and *Paper Lion*, about his playing with the Detroit Lions. I had read *The Bogey Man* and really enjoyed its humor and insight into the world of professional golf.

Plimpton had also helped found *The Paris Review*, and had interviewed Ernest Hemingway. Because of this, he would give the keynote address at the conference. In preparation for the conference, I read Plimpton's interview with Hemingway, and by the time I left, I was fully armed with knowledge and questions.

I planned to fly to Miami and drive a rental car to Key West. When I landed in Miami, I suddenly decided I didn't want to take the long drive to Key West, so I checked on the price of a flight. The round-trip prices were quite reasonable, so I bought a ticket, cancelled the car, and went to the gate to await the flight.

As I sat at the gate, reading material to prepare for the conference, the area filled with people. In a few minutes there was an announcement for a flight that was not mine, and everyone in the room left. I was left in the quiet of that empty waiting room.

As soon as everyone else was gone, who do you suppose came into the room? George Plimpton himself. He sat near me, and full of excitement, I engaged him in conversation and found that we were taking the same flight to Key West. I was able to ask him the all the questions I had prepared. When we boarded the small plane for Key West, there was only one passenger besides us. We had a great conversation going over, and he gave me a ride into town with his chauffeur, who met him at the airport.

These are experiences that I took the time to make happen, but God infused them with a far greater spiritual richness than I could have ever hoped for. I am firmly convinced that the layering of these types of experiences have a cumulative effect in adding spiritual depth to our intellectual, spiritual, and emotional evolution. I also believe that such experiences have an unseen effect on my life with others as well as my presentation of a place when I give a tour, even if I never use that particular experience.

Hemingway talked about this effect in his book about the bullfight, *Death in the Afternoon.*

> *"There are some things in life which cannot be learned quickly and time, which is all we have, must be paid heavily for their acquiring. They are the very simplest things and because it takes a man's life to know them the little new each man gets from life is very costly and the only heritage he has to leave. . . . If a writer of prose knows enough about what he is writing about he may omit things that he knows and the reader, if the writer is writing truly enough, will have the feeling of those things as strongly as though the writer had stated them. The dignity of movement of an ice-berg is due to only one-eighth of it being above water."*[1]

God uses the compounding interest of the things and moments we have chosen to invest in, and these investments pay unseen dividends to us and to those around us in ways we may never know. The lesson to be learned is, live life to the fullest, pursue life, and God, and your interests with a ravenous passion and hunger, be intentional, make things happen, and leave it to God as to how He uses it in your life and the lives of others.

I love life. I love to laugh and tell a funny joke, but I also realize that we only find the colors of life, and the depths of joy and meaning, when we take life seriously. In the richness of this thought, I would like you to consider this quote by C. S. Lewis from *The Weight of Glory: "We must play. But our merriment must be of that kind (and it is, in fact, the merriest kind) which exists between people who have, from the outset, taken each other seriously."*

At that Hemingway conference, I met many interesting people. One person I met was Honoria Murphy, daughter of Gerald and Sara Murphy, who had been significant historical mentors in my life. I write about their influence on me in another section of this book. I had fascinating talks with Honoria, and as a result of this, I later spent an afternoon with her at her home in East Hampton, New York. Both at the conference and later at her home on Long Island, it was amazing to sit and hear her reminisce about her memories of Ernest Hemingway, Pablo Picasso, and all the fascinating artists and writers who shared the orbit of her mother and father's life.

Honoria told me a wonderful story about Ernest Hemingway in answer to a question I had asked her about the public macho image which Hemingway cultivated versus the private reality of a more sensitive writer. Once the Murphys and the Hemingways had spent a vacation together at a dude ranch in Montana. One morning, Ernest asked Honoria if she would like to go fishing. Honoria was just a little girl of maybe five or six, and Ernest called her "daughter." She loved spending time with` him and so she excitedly said, "yes!"

They gathered the fishing gear, got a canoe, and paddled out on the lake. It wasn't long before Ernest, being the consummate fisherman, pulled in the first catch. When he brought it to the boat, Honoria started making it evident that she didn't like being around flopping and flapping things like icky fish. Ernest patted her gently on the leg and said, "Now, daughter, we don't act like that when we fish. Let me show you about this fish."

And then he proceeded to lay out the fish, perhaps on the flat of the paddle, and give her a fascinating lesson on the life and anatomy of that fish. She said he made her so comfortable and the lesson was so fascinating that she totally lost her icky feelings about fish!

Visiting her at her home on Long Island was in itself another wonderful gift of God. She said, "I want to show you something I think you will be interested in," and she brought out old family scrapbooks from the 1920s. As we paged through the scrapbook, it was like walking through the lives of people I had only read about. Here was a picture of her and her family with Ernest Hemingway; here she was with Pablo Picasso; there was a picture on the beach with Rudolph Valentino. She talked about when she and her brothers had a drawing contest, and Pablo Picasso was the judge!

We had a wonderful, few hours together that day. I had made the effort and been proactive, Honoria had given me the gift of an afternoon, and God had delivered the magic!

THE GIFT OF A BOOK

Years ago, I was watching the PBS Ken Burns series about the history of the National Parks. One figure who jumped off the screen and grabbed my imagination was Stephen Mather. In 1916, Stephen Mather became the first director of the National Park Service. Part of what grabbed me was that he was a driving force of nature who had such a passion for our National Parks that, in his tenure, he created virtually all the significant features that today enhance our National Park experience.

It was his idea to have scenic highways, scenic pullouts, and hotels in the parks. He petitioned the wealthy to give land and money for new parks. He helped turn the park ranger from a military custodian into a naturalist who could inform and guide the visitor. But what grabbed me most about Stephen Mather was that he did all this in spite of a lifelong battle with depression and mental illness. That, to me, is a true hero—someone who does great things in spite of the challenges that life may bring.

While watching the PBS special, I became so fascinated with Mather that I determined to learn as much about him as I could. God thrust Mather into my life and basically said, "This man is a mentor I have provided for you. Get to work and spend some time with him!"

As a result, I searched Amazon for biographies about him. I was surprised to find only one biography, *Steve Mather of the National Parks* by Robert Shankland. All the copies on Amazon cost about $60, but I had to have it and so I bought it. Little did I know God was directing me to the right source and would soon amaze me far beyond my expectations.

The book arrived while I was on a trip. When I got home, I excitedly opened the package. I was astonished to find that C. M. Goethe had owned the book. Mr. Goethe was a personal friend of Stephen Mather and had played an important part in developing the National Parks.

In the first years of the National Park System, Stephen Mather knew that he had to do everything he could to attract people to the parks. In 1919, someone wrote Mather that they had attended a naturalist show at Lake Tahoe put on by two teachers.

The idea so impressed Mather that he asked the two to take their naturalist show to Yosemite for the summer of 1920. They told Mather that they were amenable to the idea but that they were bankrolled by C. M. Goethe in Sacramento, who would have to agree. Mather contacted Goethe, who gave them the green light and the two teachers put on the first naturalist show in the National Park system in 1920. This evolved into the park ranger becoming a naturalist who led informative talks and walks. Before that, rangers had basically been just custodians who policed the park.

One magical thing about the book I got was that Mr. Goethe had filled it with fifty or more letters, news items, and notes that covered important moments in the history of the national parks. There were letters from numerous park directors, a personal note and inscription in the front of the book from the author, Robert Shankland, a personal invitation to the opening of Everglades National Park, and much, much more.

I found a letter from Stewart Udall, Secretary of the Interior, and two letters from Horace Albright, the second director of the National Park Service and Mather's right-hand man when Mather was director. Horace Albright skillfully ran the park service when Mather entered a sanitarium to fight his battles with depression and mental illness. Albright had also dreamed of a greater Yellowstone Park and worked tirelessly with John D Rockefeller Jr. to make that dream into the reality that became Grand Teton National Park.

I kept looking and hoping for a letter from Stephen Mather himself. Finally, I found not just a letter from Mather, but what I consider a significantly historic letter. It was dated March 30, 1920, and was from Stephen Mather to Mr. Goethe. This letter is significant because it was on the eve of the first naturalist programs in the National Parks, and, in it, Mather thanks Goethe for a $150.00 check to help promote the "nature study work in Yosemite."

He ended the letter with, "I also have the copies of the articles which are to run [in the newspapers] during the next month or two. I certainly think those who have any interest at all in the out-of-doors will be headed toward Yosemite Valley this summer."

Here was the first director of the National Parks corresponding with the source of the naturalist programs on the eve of the first programs we now take for granted! And it is personally signed by Stephen T. Mather himself!

SPENDING THE NIGHT AT THE HOME OF C. S. LEWIS

Over the years, I have come to love and get a lot of spiritual encouragement and insight from the works of C. S. Lewis. Lewis died on November 22, 1963, within an hour of the assassination of President John Kennedy.

A number of years ago, I met Lewis scholar, Will Vaus, and together we decided to do a "Life of C. S. Lewis Tour." To prepare for the tour, Will and I went to Northern Ireland and England and scouted all the sites the tour would include. Will had written a number of wonderful books about C.S. Lewis and made a lot of contacts through his years of research.

On our scouting trip, we covered a great many sites that played a prominent part in Lewis's life. We also met many interesting Lewis scholars. One of the greatest gifts was meeting and spending time with Walter Hooper who had been Lewis's personal secretary during the last year before Lewis died. Since Lewis's death, Walter has skillfully managed Lewis's literary estate, keeping his books in publication and his name in the forefront of modern Christian literature and apologetics. Lewis felt that, within ten years of his death, he would be forgotten. Walter's skillful stewardship and management of the Lewis literary estate has made sure that the works of C. S. Lewis live on to vitally challenge and shape contemporary Christian thought.

One of the unique blessings from that scouting trip was that Will used his contacts to arrange a stay of three nights in the Kilns, the home of C. S. Lewis. Will knew David Beckmann, the onsite warden who oversaw tours for visitors as well as visiting scholars who stayed there while doing research. When we were given rooms, God blessed me with the incredibly sacred privilege of spending three nights in the room where Lewis spent his last days and in which he died on November 22, 1963.

Wow! Imagine me, the little boy from Thomaston, Georgia, the boy who began making Bs in the second grade, but also the boy God blessed with a romantic imagination getting to spend the night in that room! A lot of people cringe, asking me if I was creeped out by staying in that room. My immediate answer is that I found it incredibly exciting and a sacred privilege to stay in that room. I always think, "How could I be creeped out to stay in a room where the great Lewis died and which was his launching pad for heaven?"

---

1. Ernest Hemingway, *Death in the Afternoon*, (New York: Scribner, 1978).

14

FUNNY STORIES FROM MY LIFE

I'VE GOT FIRE!

Sometimes in life there can be a very short journey from unbelief to belief.

When Doug and I were little, every Thursday night we went to Nanny and Mister's house for dinner. They were my mother's parents. We'd all have a great meal prepared by their maid, Evangeline Stinson, who we loved and called "Auntie." Then, after dinner, the children were free to leave the table and go to the den and watch TV, while the older people talked at the table.

Sometimes, Doug and I would get bored with TV and then we might "get to work!" Once, we took all the weights out of Nanny's beautiful grandfather clock. But, on this particular occasion, Doug and I were just playing and making a lot of noise. Apparently, the noise level rose to the point where Daddy walked up to the front of the house and peeked into the den. We saw his full figure, standing in the doorway, and He said, "Boys, if y'all don't straighten up, I am going to whip the fire out of y'all."

This was a saying he'd used before. We knew exactly what he meant but, for some reason, Doug obviously felt that tonight was his night to shine, and, before he knew it, the words were out of his mouth. "Daddy, I don't have any fire in me."

Sometimes people say things on impulse, which, they may not have said if they had taken the time to give the issue more consideration. But the words were out there, hanging in the air between Doug's mouth and Daddy's ears. If Doug could have reached out and clawed those words back, he would no doubt have done so, but it was too late.

My eyes got big as saucers, and I felt for my brother as things began to transpire rapidly. Doug's boastful declaration had set the wheels of justice in motion and now I could only sit back and let this be a "teaching moment." Daddy took off his belt, doubling it up in one hand while grabbing Doug's hand with the other. Doug sought to escape, but locked in to Daddy's hand, he could only run in a circle the radius of which was the length of daddy's arm. And so they began to turn in a circle like a crazed carnival carousel. Doug would take three steps, the belt would be applied to his rear end, and he would leap into the air and cry out, "I've got fire!"

Step, step, step, *whack*, "I've got fire!"

Step, step, step, *whack*, "I've got fire!"

I stood at a distance, transfixed, taking in this display of justice with a medley of mixed emotions, feeling everything from fear and empathy to an adrenaline-fueled sense of wonder.

In later years when I thought back on this episode, it occurred to me that rarely does life give one such a clear demonstration of the very short journey it can sometimes take to go from unbelief to belief.

DOUG AND RUSS RECREATE THE "OLE APACHE WHEEL"

When Doug and I were little, the main Christmas tree of choice was a common cedar tree, which people used to find along a country road and cut down. If someone was selling trees, they usually sold cedar and an occasional spruce. Nowadays there are many more choices, but in the 1960s, your choice in a small southern town was pretty much limited to a cedar tree.

Back then, lights on the trees were bigger and multi-colored. Because of the size and early technology of the lights, they got a lot hotter. The Christmas balls back then were bigger than they are now and more fragile, being made of thin metal or glass. You also draped silver tinsel on the boughs so it looked like icicles hanging off the limbs.

Because of the heat of the lights and the dryness of the trees, there was always a threat of fire, so people usually waited until the week before Christmas to put up their tree. The tree stand had a bowl for water, but by Christmas, the tree would be brittle and turning brown. One Christmas we used boards as part of the tree stand and nailed the boards to the living room floor.

Back in the '60s, the most popular TV series at night usually either involved westerns or army shows. There was *Gunsmoke, The Rifleman, Wagon Train, The Gallant Men*, and *Combat*, just to name a few. As a result of these shows, little boys tended to have a cowboy hat, guns and holsters, and boots. You might also have a plastic army helmet and a toy rifle.

One Christmas, Doug and I had an outfit that included a pair of double holsters, dart guns, cowboy hats, and stick ponies. The stick ponies had a plastic head with a little bridle, so you could straddle the stick, hold onto the bridle, and pretend you were riding the horse.

Doug and I learned from the westerns that when the Indians attacked the circled wagons of a wagon train, they would use a tactical technique called the Apache Wheel. The Indians would ride in a circle and attack just one side of the circled wagons. When they circled close to the wagons, they would fire their arrows or rifles, and when the circle took them away from the wagons, they would reload. This technique gave the effect of continuous fire in the same way you would get with a Gatling gun, or later, a machine gun.

One morning Doug and I got bored, and we decided to attack our Christmas tree, using the Apache Wheel strategy. Daddy and Momma were gone, and Mattie, our maid, was busy in the kitchen. We saddled up our stick ponies, put on our holsters with our loaded dart pistols, and proceeded to lay siege on the defenseless tree with its big delicate Christmas balls.

At first, our shots were a little off, but pretty soon, we got zeroed in and our shots began to hit their marks. *Pow-Pow*! There went one Christmas ball, half hanging from the tree with the rest of it in pieces on the floor. *Pow-pow*! We were getting the hang of it now and feeling the adrenaline rush and satisfaction of hitting our marks. *Pow-pow*! "This is fun!" Within ten minutes a shining metallic halo of shattered metal covered the floor beneath the tree, and what was left of the rest of the balls dangled above, holding on for dear life from their little hooks.

About that time the adrenaline rush drained away and was replaced by a dull sense of foreboding. It dawned on us that maybe this hadn't been such a good idea; that there was a sheriff in town, and he would come home for lunch at high noon. All the fun wilted away, and we began to wonder what the consequences of our morning's shooting spree might be. We decided to unsaddle our ponies, head to the kitchen, have a sarsaparilla (Coke), and wait for the sheriff. With a sense of impending doom, the minutes seemed like hours.

I don't recall what happened. I'm sure we got a "whipping," as we called it. My daddy was such a great hand at meting out the appropriate amount of justice. I have always believed in the efficacy of whippings because my daddy did it so well. With him, punishment and justice came quickly, in an appropriate amount, and we never got a whipping we didn't deserve.

After the whipping, daddy would leave us to lick our wounds, but he would always return a short time later and tell us how he loved us and that he didn't enjoy whipping us, but that he had to do it to teach us the boundaries.

Daddy was loving and just and kind. Because he whipped us early and only when we deserved it, we learned where the boundaries were. It made life so much easier for us all, and in the end, we got very few whippings. I have seen so many families where, due to lack of discipline and boundaries, or a misguided sense of love and justice, parents and children alike live in an undisciplined and hellish disorder. Daddy's wonderful sense of love and justice made for a predictable, loving order.

Later in my life, on the spiritual side, Daddy's love and justice would be a great benefit to me. He was of such great character that he made it very easy for me to believe in a loving, just, and kind heavenly Father.

ESCAPED CONVICTS IN THE NEIGHBORHOOD

When Doug and I were little, it seemed that we lived in the neighborhood of choice for escaped convicts. A jail-break map must have floated around the prison, and that map must have indicated that the first stop on the way to freedom was our neighborhood. The county jail was outside of town, and a number of times we would come home and be told that we had to stay inside because an escaped convict could be in our neighborhood. That is enough to strike fear in most little children. Fighting to hold down a tingle of terror, we imagined that if we so much as ventured out onto our terrace, we were taking our life into our own hands.

While we never saw a convict, and one was never caught in our neighborhood, my great aunt, who lived a few blocks away, found an abandoned convict uniform in the woods behind her house.

This fear played on our minds in other ways too. My sister, Susan, had a nice playhouse in the back yard. It had a little porch, a cot, and some furniture inside. One night, the Edenfield twins, and Doug, and I wanted to sleep in that playhouse. We begged until finally our parents gave us permission.

As long as it was light outside everything was fine, but once it got dark, well then that was another story. With four little boys in a small playhouse, it was hard to fall asleep so naturally we started telling stories. Eventually the topic of convicts came up. Just for fun, someone said, "Have you heard that there is an escape convict loose in the neighborhood?" This was followed by a moment of dead silence. Once those words floated through the darkness and settled into the imagination of those four little boys, our night of camping in the playhouse was pretty much over.

Very quickly we, who only an hour or two earlier had begged to sleep in the playhouse, were now praying we could run the forty yards from the playhouse to the back door of our house without landing in the clutches of an evil man-killer. Our imagination was now ramped up to a fever pitch as we cracked open the door of the playhouse. Paralyzed with fear, we stood there trying to get up enough nerve to make a break for it. Suddenly, we bolted and raced across the back yard, up the steps, across the terrace, and frantically banged for dear life on the back door.

Bam-bam-bam! "For the love of God, while there is still time, before we are all taken hostage, someone please, please open this back door!"

It was dark, but not late enough for our parents to be asleep and soon salvation arrived, just in the nick of time!

SEPARATING TWO EGGS

John and Jim Edenfield, the twins next door, had a mother who was a great cook and caterer. Everyone wanted Catherine Edenfield to cater their wedding reception or special event. I am a bread lover, and she made rolls that would melt in your mouth.

One day, when we grew tired of all our usual activity options, we decided to try cooking. Mrs. Edenfield's kitchen was always well stocked with whatever you might need to cook a meal, so we wound up in their kitchen. We got a few pointers from our maid, Mattie, and no doubt Mrs. Catherine and the Edenfield's maid, Cleone. It was summer, and we made a blackberry pie with piecrust made from scratch. It turned out great, so we moved on to cupcakes.

We were told to consult the simple recipe given in the most popular southern cookbook of the time, *Southern Cooking*, by Mrs. S. R. Dull. Mrs. Dull was a writer for the *Atlanta Journal*. She wrote articles on southern cooking and toured the state, giving cooking lectures and demonstrations. She had lectured in Thomaston, so almost every serious kitchen in our neighborhood had a copy of Mrs. Dull's cookbook.

As we waded into the cupcake preparation, we hit a few snags. First, when we put the batter into the electric mixer, we turned it on high. Batter splattered all over the kitchen. Rather than lower the speed, we draped a towel over the mixer and "Let 'er rip!" We then used a spoon or knife to scrape the batter from the towel back into the mixer. Problem solved!

The next obstacle raised its ugly head when we realized that recipes held cryptic meanings understood only by the initiated culinary illuminati. This became apparent when we got to the part where the recipe said, "separate two eggs."

Well, this seemed pretty straightforward. No need to consult higher authorities. So, we got two eggs, cracked them, and added them to the contents in the mixer, carefully placing one egg in on one side of the mixer and one egg in on the other side. We were so meticulous in our preparation that we fully expected to follow our blueberry pie victory with what was certain to be a second culinary triumph.

For some reason, our cupcakes didn't turn out like Mattie's. What could possibly be the problem? We went for a consultation and learned the true mystical secrets of what was meant by "separating two eggs." We were told that each egg has a yellow yolk and clear white inside, and we were supposed to separate not the eggs, but the yolks and the whites. If that's what they wanted, why didn't the recipe say so?

The complications of making cupcakes pretty much ended our foray into the world of cooking. I thought, *If there are secret meanings to something as simple as cupcakes, then how much more complicated must the road ahead be when we would attempt to venture into biscuits, cornbread, and fried chicken?*

This is when I decided that a person could either be someone who cooked or someone who appreciated good cooking. Then and there, I decided to go with the seemingly selfless virtue of enjoying good cooking and complimenting and cheering on those fought their way to the heights of gastronomic stardom after years of negotiating the complicated minefields of recipes with all their intricate meanings.

AUNT BETTY

My Aunt Betty was my daddy's sister, but their personalities couldn't have been more different. She was beautiful, exciting, and when she smiled—which she did often—her face lit up the room. She was a force of nature whose passing moments personified the term "living large." I can't think of her without smiling. A feeling of celebrity swirled around Aunt Betty, and when you were with her, you were in for an exciting—and sometimes roller coaster—ride. You couldn't help but love her. She lived and acted as if she were royalty. You didn't so much see Aunt Betty as much as you experienced her. She was a self-propelled whirlwind of personality who was better observed rather than challenged.

My grandfather, Doc, was a much-beloved country doctor in the small town of Zebulon, Georgia. He was very good at what he did, and he had a great personality. Doc and my grandmother, Adele, had two children, Douglas Lamar Head, who was my father, and Elizabeth Head, who we called Aunt Betty.

Daddy grew up simple, like his father. Daddy loved to hunt and fish. Doc raised bird dogs, and early on Daddy came to love hunting. Daddy also grew up to love golf and his medical practice. Daddy, like his father before him, was blessed with a winning personality, had the common touch, and was loved by his community. Beside these qualities, as a father, he was loving, just, and kind.

Aunt Betty was a different piece of work altogether. Doc had a sister, our great aunt, whom we called "Lutie." Lutie had a plan to teach school for twenty-six years, and she did just that. She never married, and she lived in a house directly across the street from Doc and Adele. Lutie was very strict, prim, and proper.

I imagine she was a good teacher, but I would think she ruled her classes with strictness and an intimidating presence which ensured order and discipline.

I think Lutie had big plans for Aunt Betty, and those plans involved getting her out of the little town of Zebulon. Lutie convinced Doc to send Aunt Betty to a boarding school in Atlanta called Washington Seminary. This is where I suppose she came to feel and act like royalty. Don't get me wrong, people loved Aunt Betty. But when she entered a room, her persona dominated the atmosphere.

Aunt Betty loved tracing her genealogy, and of course she traced it right back to some blue blood families in early Virginia. Once she was explaining this to my brother, Doug, and while he was trying to get it all straight, he said, "So Aunt Betty, are you saying that we married into Thomas Jefferson's family?"

"Oh no," Aunt Betty corrected him, punctuating her comment with a pointed finger for emphasis. "Thomas Jefferson married into *your* family."

Aunt Betty was the original drama queen. No moment or event in her life was less than epic, and she exuded an atmosphere of excitement where you felt that you were in a movie. She was a part of the high society of Savannah, and she was a member of the prestigious Oglethorpe Club.

No part of her life was without drama. I once called her during the summer, and during our conversation, I asked her if it was hot in Savannah. In her dramatic voice, she replied, "Is it hot? Why, it's hotter than the hinges of hell!"

Aunt Betty married Willis Richardson, who was voted the handsomest man at the University of Georgia. Uncle Dick was a "drama king." His life was epic as well. He played on The University of Georgia's National Championship team that went to the Rose Bowl in 1942. While there, Uncle Dick had a number of dates with the actress Betty Grable, complete with photo ops and an offer of a career in Hollywood. After college, Uncle Dick got a law degree and spent time in the FBI before settling down in Savannah, where he practiced law for many years. As you might imagine, being drama kings and queens, Aunt Betty and Uncle Dick's long marriage was both eventful and turbulent. Imagine two self-generating whirlwinds vying for the alpha dominance in a small space.

Aunt Betty and Uncle Dick had two sons, Scott and Bill. While Bill sought a quiet, simple life, Scott married into probably the wealthiest family in Savannah. John D. Carswell controlled an insurance empire that included Savannah, Hilton Head, and the account of the C & S Bank of Georgia. As you might imagine, John D. Carswell, being king of his empire, had quite an ego, and eventually, that was bound to get, as the British would say, "sorted out" sooner or later by Aunt Betty.

After the marriage of Scott Richardson and Margaret Carswell was announced in Savannah society, a round of parties began. Right off the bat, Aunt Betty's relationship with John D. Carswell got sorted out. On this particular night, King John was apparently giving out his usual round of commands, when he made the mistake of giving an order to Aunt Betty.

I can imagine the reading on a blood pressure cuff if she had been wearing one. Aunt Betty moved in to close the point of attack, and, with her finger pointed and eyes glaring, she delivered the verbal *coup de gras*, "Now you listen to me, John D. Carswell, I am not of your tribe! I am of the Head tribe, and you don't give me orders."

Aunt Betty told me that her response had indeed clarified their relationship, and they got on very well from then on.

Aunt Betty loved art and history, and like me, she was a lifelong student. She was a great guide for historic Savannah, and with her big personality, everyone loved her. She brought the fascinating history of old Savannah to life. She loved to travel and did so extensively in North America and Europe. In the latter part of her life, she took a few trips with me.

Aunt Betty was such a force of nature that, within a group, she was a lot to handle. One on one, we had great times. But with all her drama and her Queen Elizabeth persona, she really needed a valet, a personal assistant, and a staff.

Aunt Betty once joined me on a tour to the American Southwest. We visited Sedona, the Grand Canyon, and Lake Powell, rafted the Colorado River, saw the cliff dwellings at Canyon de Chelly, saw the dramatic rock formations of Monument Valley, and much more. Things started well, but for Aunt Betty, they started to go south when we got to Monument Valley.

In Monument Valley we stayed at Goulding's Lodge, where many of the John Ford westerns were filmed. John Wayne had starred in many of these, and staying at the Lodge added atmosphere to the stay. The location was stunning, and the tour was off to a great start.

Our plan in Monument valley was to take a tour of the valley, led by the local Navajo Indians, and then have a steak cookout in the evening. We toured the valley in open-air trucks. The first part of the tour went well, but suddenly a sustained dust storm blew up. By the time we were heading back, we had seen some great sites, but we looked like a group of weather-beaten Bedouins who had just crossed the Sahara. And Aunt Betty wasn't exactly looking like the Queen of the Nile.

I knew right away what would turn things around for her—she loved her five o'clock drink. But then I realized there was a big problem. We were on the Navajo reservation. There was no easy way to break the inconvenient truth, so I just laid it out. "Aunt Betty, it occurs to me that right about now you would like a drink, but we are on the Navajo reservation, and they neither serve nor sell alcohol."

Her eyes got as big as saucers, and indignation filled her face, "You're kidding. People in Savannah wouldn't stand for it."

To make matters worse, our cookout had to be cancelled due to the continuing dust storm. That evening when we were seated in a restaurant, Aunt Betty was still trying to process the fact that they didn't sell alcohol on the reservation. When the young Navajo waitress approached our table, Aunt Betty leveled her eyes and said, "Don't y'all sell fire water here?"

The waitress replied that they did not, and Aunt Betty was left to suffer through her meal without her desired libations.

The next morning, as I thought about the days ahead, I realized that for the next two days, we would go from Monument Valley to Canyon de Chelly, where we would explore its magnificent Canyon with Native American cliff dwellings and petroglyphs. It would be wonderful, but everything was on the Navajo reservation where the sale of alcohol was strictly forbidden. Poor Aunt Betty. What to do? Then I remembered that our hotel in Sedona had given me a complimentary bottle of wine. It was still in my backpack unopened. Eureka! Problem solved!

Aunt Betty beamed when she heard I had a bottle of wine. When we got to Canyon de Chelly, I took her the wine, and we arranged to meet for dinner in the hotel dining room. I felt good about coming up with the bottle of wine, and when we met for dinner, I expected to hear a cheery report. But it was not to be, for the wine was not to her liking. When Queen Elizabeth arrived, she said, "You can come get that wine. It's not the kind I drink."

I think Aunt Betty was beginning to feel some of the sacrifice and privation experienced by the early pioneers when they set out to settle the American West!

And so, we soldiered on. Ever onward. Our last night was in Flagstaff, Arizona. I felt I was home free with Aunt Betty. Right? Well, not exactly.

Our hotel was in the center of town. It was a weekend, and a festival was going on downtown. We were in the middle of the excitement, and we were well positioned to take advantage of the celebration. Nevertheless, when we checked in, I felt a sense of foreboding when the desk clerk informed me that a band in the bar would play until after midnight. She mentioned that they had earplugs at the front desk if anyone needed them.

After checking in, Aunt Betty informed me that she was having some digestive problems, and that she needed me to procure the suitable meds as soon as possible. I went to the front desk and got directions to the nearest drug store, which was a half-mile away. I was ready for a long walk to decompress, so I put my things in my room and set out for the pharmacy. Along the way, I was able to get a good idea where all the night's festivities would be, but the farther I went from the hotel, the more things felt like the Wild West. Most of the small businesses had bars on the windows. I thought, *Just keep your eyes forward and your head down. Look like you live here.*

Eventually, I found the pharmacy, got the meds, and returned through enemy lines to the town center. Back at the hotel, I delivered the meds to Aunt Betty, only to find that she did not like the room she was staying in. I called the front desk and they transferred her to the only room left, a two-bedroom suite.

This was the last night of the trip. Everyone on the tour enjoyed being in the middle of the celebration, and people ate wherever they wanted. Aunt Betty went out with me and a few others, and we had a good meal, enjoyed the festivities, and then returned to the hotel for a good night's sleep. The next morning, we would head to the Phoenix airport for our flight home.

Thankfully, our group's block of rooms was far away from the bar, so the band noise was not a problem. But Aunt Betty had asked to be moved, and where do you suppose her new room was? On the second floor directly above the bar and the band!

Around 11:30, I was about to turn the lights out. Another tour was almost in the books. I was home free!! And then the phone rang. "Mr. Head, this is the front desk. Your Aunt is here and would like to speak to you."

"Russ," Aunt Betty said, " I don't understand this hotel. My room is directly over the bar, where approximately 2000 young people are apparently having the time of their life. As a result, I won't sleep a wink tonight. How far is the airport?"

I replied, "Too far to go there tonight; meet me at your room."

I figured that while I probably couldn't solve the problem, I could at least give an appearance of making a good faith effort. We met in the room, and I couldn't hear the band. Either the party was over, or the band was taking a break. The room had two air conditioning units, and I turned them on to muffle any noise, just in case the party wasn't over.

As I bid Aunt Betty good night, and just as I was about to head out, she said, "I have no idea who is staying in that other room." I said, "Aunt Betty, this is a two-bed room suite, and it is all yours." And with that, I headed back to my room, hoping that that that was all the fun we would have for the night.

The next morning, we drove to the Phoenix airport and checked in. Now I was home free. Well, not exactly. When I got to the gate, there was Aunt Betty cussing mad and looking through her pocketbook.

"What's wrong, Aunt Betty?"

"I can't find my damn boarding pass!"

Aunt Betty was so flustered that I asked to look through her pocketbook. You have to know something about Aunt Betty's pocketbook. Uncle Dick referred to it as "the black hole of Calcutta." He said that things went into that purse that never again saw the light of day. I looked through the purse and found lots of paper and other travel documents, but I couldn't find the boarding pass.

I was about to have another boarding pass printed when Aunt Betty decided to take her purse to the bathroom so she could lay things out on the counter and take one last look. And she did just that. Except she didn't set the pocketbook on the counter; she set it in the sink so she would have more counter space to spread things out. That, in turn, activated the motion sensor on the sink faucet. Now the pocketbook was filling with water, with Aunt Betty probably eliciting verbal requests for help from a higher power.

Eventually the boarding pass was found, and we had a nice flight home. Two days later, Aunt Betty called me, and I expected her to list a number of things for me to correct on my next tour. But no, she called to say that it had been a wonderful trip, and she looked forward to traveling with me again in the future!

A FUNNY STORY THAT IS PART TRUTH AND A GOOD PART FICTION

During my high school years, Doug and I played on the golf team. In our senior year, the team went to Newnan, Georgia, to play in the region championship. During the post-play tally of the scores, Darryl Jones, our tour escort, discovered that Johnny Wells, a player on our team, had signed an incorrect scorecard for a score lower that what he had actually made. It was an honest mistake, and we weren't in the hunt for the regional title anyway. As a result, according to the rules of golf, Johnny was disqualified. In memory of that event, and purely for humor, I later wrote the following, hugely embellished account as if it were a newspaper article. Almost everything in the account is fiction. About the only thing that is true in the whole story is that Johnny got disqualified as a result of Darryl pointing out the mistake on the scorecard.

"TRAGEDY STRIKES LOCAL GOLF TEAM AT REGIONAL MEET"

The R. E. Lee golf team left Thomaston Thursday morning with high hopes for a good finish to what had been a difficult season. The local golfers had started the year with a string of seven losses, but had rebounded in the last three matches with two wins and a tie. So, in spite of the cold and rain, the team departed for their region tournament with a renewed sense of hope. Throughout the day the courageous team fought hard over a cold and rain-soaked course. When senior captain, Doug Head, holed a sand shot for a bogey on the first hole, everyone seemed to sense that this would be a very special day.

Good news found its way back to the clubhouse throughout the day. After he returned from a two-hour lunch at Sprayberry's Bar-B-Que, team escort, Darryl Jones said he arrived back at the course, confident that the team was doing well. Reports from the morning's round had told of a bogey here, a double there, and then a par. Jones would later admit that the cold and rain had prevented him for venturing out to see firsthand what was going on, but as one player and then another trudged up the final fairway and the scores were posted, suddenly the impossible seemed possible.

When the final scores were tallied, the team had, beyond belief, come in second and, with that second-place finish, gained a much-coveted invitation to the state tournament in Bainbridge.

Then tragedy struck!

School officials later tried to reconstruct what school principal Kenneth Moore called the "trail to tragedy." As the team was awaiting the awards presentation, amidst much backslapping, Jones says he casually began to add the score of Johnny Wells, a promising junior, who had finished strong with double-bogey, bogey, bogey.

Jones, though no golfer himself, and ignorant of the rules, suddenly realized that Well's score had been wrongly calculated and was actually one stroke higher than shown. Jones remembered thinking, *No matter, we still won second place by two shots over local favorite Bradshaw High.*

Jones said that when he called attention to the mistake to Harvie Ward, Bradshaw's coach who was recording the scores, Ward seemed to smile and get a curious glimmer in his eyes. Then Ward, after confirming the mistake, drew a long line through Wells' score and wrote a huge "DQ" over Wells' name. When asked what "DQ" meant, Ward replied with a big grin, "Disqualified."

Jones was thunderstruck! When it was realized that this not only disqualified Wells, but also meant the team would now have to rely on the score of team alternate Nate Brown, a sober silence filled the ranks as Brown's score was tallied. When the final total was added, Bradshaw edged the Lee linksters by one stroke. A dejected team co-captain, Russ Head, was heard to mutter, "Thanks Coach. Way to go."

The school has recently opened an investigation into possible charges of supervisory negligence. The charges focus on just how much time Jones spent at the course. When asked to give a timeline of his actions that day, Jones estimated that he had spent about two hours at Sprayberry's Bar-B-Que, a popular local eating establishment. When employees at Sprayberry's were questioned, a different story began to emerge. Woodrow Dawkins, curb attendant whose career has spanned twenty-seven years, said he remembered Jones very well.

Dawkins said that Jones arrived shortly after opening time at 10:00 a.m. Jones had a cup of coffee, read the paper, and made small talk. At approximately 11:00 a.m., Jones moved from the counter to a booth and ordered the Sprayberry Bar-B-Que Extravaganza, a veritable "tour of the menu on a plate," which the menu recommended for two people. Jones managed to "complete the tour" unassisted, paid with a school check, and at about 12:00 noon, moved to the arcade section of the restaurant.

Dawkins remembered that Jones put down a $50.00 bill on the counter and asked for five rolls of quarters. He then spent the next two hours in the arcade issuing a boastful challenge to all comers. Dawkins clearly remembered that Jones left the restaurant at closing time which was 2:30 p.m.

"Yeah," Dawkins recalled, "He said he would help us close up, and that he had brought some students over to the golf course and was in no hurry to get back in the rain and cold. Golf pro Jack Sweeney says he didn't recall seeing Jones in the pro shop until the scores were being recorded at 4:00 p.m. At this time, it is uncertain where Jones was from 2:30 to 4:00 p.m. A pair of new "gold toe" socks, and a dress shirt which was still in its package which were found under the front seat of the van lead authorities to believe that at least some of the time unaccounted for had been spent at a local Belk's department store.

Head golf coach, Burns Pruett, was not able to attend the meet and had secured the services of assistant football coach, Darryl Jones, to drive the team van to the match. When questioned later, Pruett was adamant that, before leaving, he had given specific instructions to Jones to "keep your mouth shut and just drive the van." Apparently giddy with joy at realizing his charges had come in second in the meet, Jones forgot his promise to Pruett not to involve himself in the finer points of the game's rules. Jones would later admit that it was the first time he had set foot on a golf course.

Coach Burns Pruett issued a statement saying that he hoped this tragedy "could somehow act as a cautionary tale about the fickleness of earthly achievements."

Pruett put it quite poetically when he looked misty-eyed at a dog-eared and muddy disqualification notice and said, "For one brief, shining moment, life seemed to be presenting these young men with the crowning achievement of their young careers and then fate raised its ugly head."

The tragedy was particularly devastating for the two seniors for whom there will be no tomorrow. Phone calls to the Jones residence went unanswered Thursday night. A family spokesman said that Jones was inconsolable.

ON LEARNING THE PROPER USE OF A TOILET PLUNGER

One of the places I worked after college was Big Sky of Montana. Big Sky was started by Conoco Oil Company, and a group of people including the famed sixties newscaster Chet Huntley. Big Sky is in southwestern Montana south of Boseman and north of West Yellowstone.

I did various jobs at Big Sky, and, for a while, I kept the lobby and lobby bathrooms clean and answered various room needs and requests called into the front desk. One day Room 222 called in with a stopped-up toilet, and I was sent to check out the problem.

One thing worth noting is that I have a weak stomach and a serious gag reflex with a direct line to my sense of smell. Though I had graduated from college and was about twenty-five years old, believe it or not, I had never become acquainted with the proper use of a toilet plunger.

I went to the room and knocked on the door. A man opened the door, turned around, walked back, and sat with his wife and daughter at the foot of the more distant of the room's two queen beds… the bed further from the bathroom. He said nothing but simply pointed. With what was about to take place, I cannot for the life of me understand why that family of three decided to stay. One of the three was responsible for the contents in the toilet. Maybe they had a twisted sense that they were in for a few minutes of once-in-a-lifetime entertainment.

I walked into the bathroom, and found myself immediately overwhelmed by an incredibly powerful and foul odor. Before I passed the lintel of the bathroom door, a gut-wrenching and uncontrollable gagging started.

Ugguh! Ugguh! Ugguh!

I viewed the contents and heard a voice ask if I was all right. I assessed the situation and fought my way back, as if I were in a house fire, toward the bathroom door. With a guttural retching, I made it known that I was okay.

Upon emerging from the bathroom into the light of day, I looked at the nice family and told them that I had to go get a plunger to deal with the "situation" behind me. As I opened the door and left the room, the family did not move from their position at the foot of the bed.

I went to the front desk and asked if they had a toilet plunger. They thought there might be one in a box of various items that had been found in a spring sweep under the gondola lines of the ski runs. I followed someone to a nearby storage room and there we found the box. The box was filled with ski goggles, poles and gloves that had been dropped from the ski lifts over the winter. Yes, there was a plunger in among the other things, but suddenly, it occurred to me that the best way to deal with this situation was a bit of humor. Among the other things I saw was a pair of nice ski goggles. I grabbed those, put them on, and, plunger in hand, headed back to Room 222.

I knocked on the door. The man opened it, and I, with goggles in place, held up the plunger and told him that if I could not dislodge the contents with the plunger, I would have to go in and manually dislodge the lethal contents. The man, upon hearing this, did an about face, and returned to sit with his family at the foot of the bed. I guess, having sat through round one, they figured they might as well sit through round two.

When I walked into the bathroom, I again began retching while fighting my way back to ground zero. To allay at least some of the foul smell, I looked up toward the ceiling, directing my nose up and away from the source, all the while grasping the plunger with both hands and pumping with the vigorous will of a madman.

Mind you, I had never used a plunger before. I didn't know that when the blockage was released you would know when the contents swirled out. So, even though nothing happened after a considerable amount of time, I decided it was time to give 'er a try!! You can imagine my panic when I turned the handle, flushed the toilet, and thereby triggered a rising tsunami of toilet paper and refuse. In this manner I successfully ramped up what had been a code-two-clogged toilet situation to a full-on-code-red wet-vac situation. My mind gets a little foggy at this point, but I am sure this required moving the family to another room. When I emerged from the bathroom to tell them the news, there they were, still sitting there on the foot of the bed as if they had been nailed to it.

What can we learn from this situation? There is a job for every person and a person for every job and that this is what you get when you send an improperly trained lobby guy to do the job of a certified plumber. They say you learn something new every day, and this was the day I learned how to use a toilet plunger!

WHEN YOU GOTTA GO, YOU GOTTA GO

In the 1980s our local country club was in full swing. On Wednesday nights during the summer, the pool stayed open until 9 p.m., and some people would go swimming and then cook out using the grills situated around the pool.

One Wednesday night I did this with friends. We had a nice time, and we were getting ready to leave, when suddenly I felt the call of nature. I went to the pool bathroom. It was grungy, with a small open stall that offered no privacy. The flooring was green Astroturf, and the toilet looked as if it had seen better days.

I decided to pass and walked up to the clubhouse. Unfortunately, I discovered that the main clubhouse was locked and closed for the night.

I had a decision to make. *Do I use the grungy pool toilet, or do I drive home?* I decided to drive home. After all, the situation didn't seem particularly urgent, and the drive was only a few miles. I said my goodbyes, and headed home on this ill-fated mission.

I wasn't more than a half-mile from the club before the situation quickly progressed from a routine, code green, manageable situation, to an urgent, blinking, code-red situation. The die was cast, and there was no turning back, so I pressed the pedal to the floorboard and began to hear alarm bells going off in my head. I began to pray, "Sweet Jesus, take the wheel and see me through!"

About a mile from home, I was fighting off a rising panic while trying to hold back the call of nature. In situations like this, one must "get a grip." I knew now that I had to remain calm and think through every detail of my situation, leaving nothing to chance. I drew upon my golf experience tried to envision what success might look like.

I assessed my street options and had no choice but to continue north on South Center Street at a high rate of speed. As I wheeled left onto Roquemore Street with the tires screaming, I realized the probability of success was deteriorating at an alarming rate. I slammed on the breaks at the stop sign at South Church, glanced quickly to the right, and floored it!

Now the flashing red lights in my head had made the final change from blinking yellow to full on red. This activated the voice in my head similar to the auto-recording a pilot hears when he is too low except my voice was saying, "Arrival required now! Arrival required now!"

But I still had a quarter mile to go as the car lunged onto Hill Street and barreled down and then up the long hill. All alarms in my head were now screaming at a maximum pitch.

As I approached the final right turn onto Bland Avenue, I tried to remain calm and went through my checklist to prepare for arrival. My driveway was not paved, and I decided that the jiggle-jaggle of a bumpy dirt and gravel landing were more than the O-rings could take, so I decided on a smoother street-side touchdown. I wheeled right onto Bland, went full-throttle for the last fifty yards, and came to a screeching halt. I flung the door open, and without bothering to close it, walked stiff-legged like a tin man as fast as I could across the yard, while frantically fumbling for the house key.

At that point, the situation was so delicate that even the slightest improper move could end in utter disaster. I gingerly stiff-legged myself up four steps and safely made it to the back porch.

The sounds in my head were deafening as I frantically went through the key choices for the French doors on the back porch. The key identified, I only had to insert it into the keyhole, but due to the extreme demands of the emergency, my hand-eye-motor skills were shutting down. I saw and heard the *rata-tat-tat* of the key dancing around the keyhole, but I couldn't focus. Finally, the key found the hole, and I jerked it to the right. And then, as they say in the movies, something went terribly wrong.

I only needed to negotiate thirty feet across the kitchen and into the bathroom. But as I turned the key to the right, things seemed to fall into a dream-like state. I had no sense of hearing and only a faint view through the French doors into the kitchen. As I felt the key turn and the lock give way within, I simultaneously felt the complete unlocking of the very bowels of hell!

The payload compartment had given way. And where, only seconds before, there had been noise, panic, and chaos, there was now only quiet and a warm sense of peace and calm. It was over now. No more sense of urgency. The deed was done. Victory lay only a few feet away, but it was not to be.

Dusk was falling outside, and night was coming on. There was nothing to be done now but to begin the clean-up operation and to contemplate in the days to come the supreme effort I had given and the victory that might have been.

A SCHOOL OF MY OWN AND A BRIEF LIFE OF SIR JOSEPH WICKHAM

Early in my tour career, I took a small group to Paris. I was leading the group in the Louvre when two museum guards approached me. They informed me that I could not lead a group of the size I had—fourteen—and they escorted me toward the front door.

It was early in my tour career, and I had no idea that I had to have permission to lead a group. It was embarrassing, and my mind was racing to find a way to solve the problem. I asked them what was the maximum size that a person could lead a group without permission. They said eight. So, I quickly asked if, for this one time, I could break the group into two groups, one of eight and one of six. I said I would work with each group separately, but never together. This solved the problem, but caused me to have to juggle between groups while we were there.

I later stopped by the museum office and asked more about how I could lead a larger group. They said I would either have to have a local professional guide or that I could lead a group if I was a teacher with a school group. This got me to thinking. *I am a teacher.*

While I had been a teacher and had a teacher's certificate, that really wasn't the point. I love teaching. I was born a teacher. I didn't need any certificate to validate what I naturally was by birth.

And furthermore, what is a school? If I was a teacher, then the people with me were my students, and my school was not one of bricks and mortar, but rather one of a spiritual nature, giving an education in the spirit of Harvard, Yale, Oxford, and Cambridge.

So, I decided to found my own school. I thought of the great and ancient universities and boys' schools of England. I tried to think of an English-sounding name, so I came up with the Wickham Institute for Advanced Studies. I rather fancied the term "senior fellow," and since I was advancing in age, and I was a man, I felt that gave me the two defining requirements to be a "senior fellow."

I thus proclaimed myself a senior fellow at the Wickham Institute for Advanced Studies. I had a faculty ID made up and decided to write the following short life of the school's "honorary founder." While Sir Joseph Wickham is an entirely fictitious character, the following biography is laced with actual historic events in a Forrest Gumpish sort of way.

A second connection that tied my school to real history was my incorporation in the story of the Irish "hedge schools." The beginnings of the hedge schools date back to the seventeenth century Ireland. It was a time when the ruling Anglicans in Ireland forbade Catholics to be taught by Catholic teachers. The fear was that the catholic schoolmasters would teach their students what the protestants felt was all sorts of superstition, idolatry, and evil customs—and in truth, loyalty to Rome. So the Catholics developed what came to be known as the Irish hedge school. In his book *The Hedge Schools of Ireland*, P. J. Dowling, wrote,

> *"Because the law forbade the schoolmaster to teach, he was compelled to give instruction secretly: because the householder was penalized for harboring the schoolmaster, he had perforce to teach, and that only when the weather permitted, out of doors. He therefore, selected,*

> *in some remote spot, the sunny side of a hedge or bank which effectively hid him and his pupils from the eye of the chance passer-by, and there he sat upon a stone as he taught his little school, while his scholars lay stretched upon the green sward about him. One pupil was usually placed at a point of vantage to give warning of the approach of strangers; and if the latter were suspected of being law-officers or informers, the class was quickly disbanded for the day—only to meet again on the morrow in some place still more sheltered and remote."*[1]

Because I felt I had to create my own school as a result of the oppressive museum laws, I was forced to live by my wits and accomplish my ends in a secretive manner, much like the old hedge schools of Ireland. I loved this romantic association and promptly considered myself a modern hedge school.

And so, I now give to you a short biography of our school's beloved honorary founder.

A BRIEF LIFE OF SIR JOSEPH WICKHAM

Sir Joseph Wickham was born in 1842. He was the only son of John Wickham, a Cotswold quarryman, and Joanna Wickham, who served as the village laundress. The village in which he was born now goes by the name of Upper Slaughter but was then called Cheatham-on-Stow.

As a young boy, Wickham was taught at home by his mother who had a passion for learning instilled in her by her Irish grandfather. Joanna Wickham gave her young son readings and assignments to do while she boiled the village laundry in a large iron cauldron. From his mother, the young boy got his lifelong love of literature and poetry. His father sparked his son's interest in history and adventure. At night, after supper, old John Wickham, though tired from a long day at the quarry, would light his pipe, pull up a chair before the fire, and tell the young boy all manner of tales involving history, war, travel, adventure, and stories of the lives of the great explorers of the past.

These engrossing tales, told by a master storyteller in the warm glow of the family hearth, set the course of the boy's life. Wickham idolized his father and, to the end of his life, recalled the wonderful romance of these stories and their influence on him. He wistfully remembered lying on the floor late at night in the warm glow of the flickering fire, with the smell of his father's pipe floating on the air, listening and agonizing in a vain attempt to stay awake to hear the end of his father's last and most enthralling tale.

This homeschooled atmosphere proved to be an excellent early education. His mother had decided on this course of study for the boy's education because both her grandparents on her mother's side had a similar education in the old hedge schools of Ireland. She had also had a dream during her pregnancy that convinced her that this child would be special and that she should give him a great amount of intellectual freedom early on to fire his quicksilver intellect. This dream proved prophetic as later studies showed that the methods prevalent in English primary schools of the time would have stifled the precocious mind of the young boy.

At the age of nine, the boy began to fish with a local ghillie who was the private guide to the king when he came to his country house in the nearby village of Broughton-on-Water. It was through this connection that the young Wickham became friends with the King's son, and thereby gained admission to Eton and then Oxford. The boy's brilliant mind and his effortless skill at cricket won him the king's grant that paid for the priceless higher education his family could never have afforded.

At Oxford Wickham excelled in literature and the sciences, which were later to serve him so well on his countless expeditions. On weekends he fulfilled a custodial job at the Royal Geographical Society in London. He would take the train into the city and was given quarters in a small room made available to senior fellows during the week but vacant on weekends. At night with a candle burning, he roamed the darkened halls of the RGS, looking with fascination through the many private exhibits open only to members. He pored over the actual handwritten journals of David Livingstone and Gordon of Khartoum.

During these weekends the boy met and cultivated a long friendship with Sir Richard Burton and John Hanning Speke, both of whom had sought so tirelessly to find the headwaters of the Nile. Wickham was with Speke on the ill-fated hunting expedition in Dorset when Speke tripped over his own rifle and shot himself stone dead. Such a pity. This happened on the very eve of the great Nile debates between Speke and Burton. Newspapers ran stories of how Wickham ran the ten kilometers to Chauncey Station in a vain attempt to summon a doctor. Today, the annual 10K "Chauncey Challenge" covers the same ground and commemorates the young man's admirable but unsuccessful effort. The "Challenge," as it is known to locals, annually garners more donations for the Royal Geographical Society than even the Prince's Ball at Studley Priory.

This all started Wickham's lifelong devotion to the RGS and his many explorations under their flag. His detailed journals are in the RGS library in London and rare copies have been rumored to be in certain private collections in Georgia in the United States and in Albany, Australia.

Everyone is familiar with his disappearance at age fifty-nine in the summer of 1901 on what was to be his last Antarctic expedition. He was last seen leaving the Ross Ice Shelf headed for Queen Maud Land where he hoped to establish a birding station for monitoring the flight patterns of the rare arctic tern.

Sir Joseph was a lifelong bachelor and died without heirs. In his will he left his entire estate as grant money for starting the now-famous Wickham Institute for Advanced Studies. The Institute is founded on the same old Irish hedge school principles that proved so valuable to Wickham in his early years. The teaching methods of the institute, spelled out so carefully in the will, are now admired and copied by renowned schools all over the world. Sir Joseph would be proud. And we, the beneficiaries of his kindness, are truly grateful.

TWO POSSUMS AND A BIBLICAL LEGION OF FLEAS

In the late 1980s, I lived in a small, two-bedroom, one-bath house at 104 Bland Avenue in Thomaston. The whole house was about 850 square feet. I like to read before I go to bed, so one night I was lying on my sofa, reading. Around 11:30 p.m., I decided to go to bed. I turned out the lights and walked in the dark back to my bedroom.

As I walked by the foot of the bed, I brushed what I thought were the covers on the floor. I turned on the light beside my bed and then saw a sizable, hairy animal standing on his hind feet, baring his teeth, and hissing. In an instant, I launched flat-footed from the floor to suddenly standing on my bed, looking into the face of an animal maybe just shy of a foot tall.

My heart and mind were both racing. Chaos descended over any kind of rational judgment. My first thought was to try to identify the animal. After all, it now seemed obvious that what I brushed on the floor was this living, hissing, furry demon. My mind raced to the direst possible prospects of what this animal might be: a wharf rat. A giant wharf rat! And a rabid one at that!! That explained its unusual behavior of holding one position and not moving around. A giant, rabid, wharf rat!

My next thought was to figure out what to do. The apparent wharf rat continued to stand erect at the foot of my bed, not yielding any territory, hissing and holding up its two front paws like a boxer challenging me to a fight. "This is my territory," he seemed to say, "and I ain't giving it up without a fight." I looked at him, and to the open door I had just come through. My mind was a jumble of adrenaline-fueled fear. And then a plan developed. I could jump off the bed and through the door, run to the kitchen and get a broom and a paper sack, then sweep the rat into the sack, and take him outside.

Now if this had really been a rabid wharf rat, the plan would have been incredibly dangerous. My unfortunate state of hysteria was responsible for both my misidentification of the animal as well as my dangerous plan. How could this be a wharf rat when we are nowhere near the sea? And if this were a rabid rat, he would have torn that paper bag—and then me—into pieces. I obviously wasn't thinking clearly.

I jumped off the bed, ran through the door, and into the kitchen. I quickly found a paper bag and a broom and returned to my bedroom. And he was gone!

I slowly and quietly searched the room. For those who are old enough to remember, imagine Inspector Clouseau searching his house for his servant Kato, who was ready to pounce from who knew where. He could be anywhere. And then I looked in a space between an armoire and the wall, and there he was, backed against the wall, still on his hind feet, still hissing, somewhat listless yet ready to fight. In my mind, I thought the rabies would explain the listless behavior. Right! Now to execute the capture.

I cautiously moved toward the rabid animal to get him into the paper bag. I half expected him to make a break for it, but he let me sweep him into the bag. This is when, if he had been rabid, he would have torn me and the bag apart. But no, he seemed to be okay with being swept into the bag and being transported through the house and into the midnight darkness of the back yard.

I hesitate to tell you what I then did, but I must be honest. I dumped him out on the ground, and then—this is sad to say—while still in a state of adrenaline-fueled hysteria, I found a large stone nearby and gave him what could only be described as a biblical stoning. Yes, I am ashamed, but please consider the state of shock I was in at the moment. On one hand, he was just being a wharf rat doing what wharf rats do. I was acting irrationally, fueled by the shock of fear and rage.

The next morning, I was in the back yard looking at the dead quarry, when I saw my neighbor, Jim Fletcher, in his back yard. I asked Jim to come over and look at the rat I had killed. He came over, quickly identified it, and said, "That isn't a rat, it's a possum, and where there's one possum there is usually another one."

A night or two later, I was again lying on my sofa, reading, when I felt a tickling sensation on my arm. I saw a spec-sized thing on my arm, and when I tried to pin it down, it hopped to the side. It was a flea, and I had no idea what I was in for.

The next night there were more fleas, and the next even more. Jim said there must be a host somewhere in my house, a dead animal, or maybe a dead cousin of the possum I had stoned a few nights earlier. Then the house began to smell, and I honed in on the strongest area of stench. I pulled out the baseboards below the kitchen cabinets, and there lay a smaller dead possum. I disposed of the dead carcass, and now falsely assumed my flea problem was solved.

But no. Now the growing flea problem turned into biblical legions. They were everywhere. I finally moved out of my house and stayed with my brother while we dealt with the fleas. I bombed my house both inside and underneath with flea bombs. I had my house professionally bombed three times. The pest control guys were amazed and had to spray down each other's suits when they came out of the house. The pros still couldn't get rid of the fleas.

You could look through my French doors on the back porch and see hundreds of fleas having a free-for-all on my kitchen floor. I half expected to see a tiny sign that said, "Nightly dance party, Russ's Place, no cover."

I had been out of my house for two months, and I began to envision having to envelop my house in a big pesticide bag. I had heard of that being done, and I desperately hoped it wouldn't come to that. What could possibly be the solution? And then, eureka! A thought came to me. *If there is such a thing as a queen bee, maybe there is such a thing as a queen flea, and, if there were such a thing, where would her throne room be?*

I determined it would be where the dead carcass of the dead possum had been. So I got a pesticide bomb and put it under the kitchen cabinets right where the dead possum had been. Somebody had told me Sevin dust would help, so I spread Sevin dust all around the kitchen. I then set off the bomb, and waited a day to check the results. When I came back, they were gone. Hallelujah! I was finally rid of the fleas and the long ordeal that had begun with a terrifying house invasion by a not-so-rabid non-wharf rat! It was finally over.

You may ask, how did the possum get into my house? Some guys had recently repaired the plumbing under my kitchen sink. When they fixed the problem, they did not properly seal the space between the piping and the hole cut in the floor under the sink. The two possums had gotten under the house in some way, squeezed through the gap left by the improperly sealed hole, and gained access into the house.

COLD CALL FROM A STOCK BROKER

In the late 1980s, Doug and I bought out Steve Short and Lauren Armistead, our other two partners in the travel agency. When we did this, we went to a lawyer and formed a corporation. In our discussions with the lawyer, just for fun, I asked if I could make myself CEO. I always liked the impressive ring of that title. The lawyer said I could if I liked, and Doug didn't seem to care, so for the fun of it, I made myself CEO of The Travel Connection.

It seems there are stockbrokers in New York or Chicago who comb the pages of Dun and Bradstreet looking for people with impressive titles to cold call to see if they can get them to invest with a total stranger. They must get a few takers or they wouldn't keep up the practice.

Not long after we incorporated, I started getting cold calls from strangers who happened to be stockbrokers and thought since I was CEO of The Travel Connection, I must have money to burn. One day I got a call from a guy who started off with the familiar line that he didn't want to sell me anything; he just wanted to establish a relationship. I replied, "Sir, to establish a relationship with me, you would need to move to my town and live for ten years. Are you prepared to do that?"

I heard the phone line go dead.

Another time, I got a call from a broker who said he had a hot tip, and he needed about $100,000. I said, "Sir, I am not remotely familiar with those kinds of figures."

He replied in disbelief that, as CEO, I must have some money to invest. In retrospect, I think my next reply was quite inspired, and pretty much put an end the broker cold calls.

I replied, "Sir, I am going to paint you a picture of my life, and if, when I am finished, you still want to talk, then we will talk business, but even as we speak, I am looking out my store window at my 1989 Volkswagen Jetta. At five o'clock today, I will walk over to that car hoping against hope that the last of four doors will still open, because, as you may know, the little mechanisms in the door handles of Jettas tend to break down and deteriorate, and I am down to my last door. If I am so lucky as to get in, then I have got to hope that it isn't raining, because the electrical circuit for the windshield wipers doesn't work right, and if the fuse is in, they go all the time. So I leave the fuse out and only insert it when it is raining. If all goes well up to that point, I will drive home to my 850-square-foot ponderosa on a street called Bland Avenue. Now do you really think you want to talk to me?

His reply was short and sweet, "Sir, you have a nice day."

And that was the end of cold calls from stockbrokers. I have always wondered if they disseminate information on a nation-wide scale to alert brokers to something that amounts to a "don't-waste-your-time" list.

DRIVING TO WORK IN REVERSE

One day, in the mid-1980s, I was driving to work. I lived a little more than a mile from where our office, and all of a sudden, my car lost power. When it came to a stop, I put it in park, and then I tried all the options on the automatic shifter. Would you believe that none of the gears worked except *R* for "reverse"? I could go in reverse!

A lot of people find it amusing that I actually drove to work in reverse. Although I was still at least a half-mile away and had a number of turns and streetlights to negotiate, it never occurred to me that anyone else would do otherwise. It was time to be at work, I had a car, and I had a means to get there even though it was in reverse. Problem solved! So, I put the car in reverse and drove to work. By the way, in case you ever find yourself driving anywhere in reverse, remember to stop far enough from a stoplight to be able to look out the back window and still see the light.

I got to work safely, and then, after work, I drove, again in reverse, through side streets along the edge of town, to the repair shop. That drive was about a mile away also. I was too busy driving to see if I was getting any funny looks, except in one case when a passing driver almost broke his neck when he whipped around to make sure he was seeing what he thought he saw.

GAS OR ELECTRIC?

I am a twin. When Doug and I were born, the egg split, and I got the side of the brain that has the aesthetic and artsy stuff like history, art, and psychology. I didn't get much of anything that had to do with numbers, instructions, mechanics, building, or math.

When I was in my early fifties, I was at an age, as a man, where you would think I would know a little about things around the house. But the problem is, I am a big believer that in this life of ours, we are given only a certain amount of time, and I want to devote as much time as possible to my passion and my calling. That involves a lot of reading and study.

I also believe some people have gifts and make their livelihood in yardwork, mechanics, appliance repair, and other fields. It takes all kinds to make this world go around, and if possible, we all need to help each other and let everyone do their part. As a result, if I can afford it, I want to lay on the couch and read and study the details of my trips, and pay others to do my yard work, auto repair, and other things that take me away from being as good as I can be at what I do. Which all brings me to the subject of a few stories.

One day a couple of guys came to check on a problem with my air conditioning unit. They came in and asked, "Is it gas or electric?"

This question hit me like a question from outer space. I did assume correctly that they meant the air conditioning unit. I was stunned like a deer in the headlights. My mind was racing as I tried to assess the question and decide how to answer in the milliseconds it would take to keep them from knowing I wasn't sure. I thought, *You are 52 years old, you are a man, you are expected to know the answer to questions like this, but the fact is you don't really know.*

As my mind raced, I was thinking that things like my stove, which has a blue flame, are gas. The logs in my fireplace have a blue flame, so they are gas. When I turn on the heat in my house, there is a deep rumble, so that is probably gas. But the air-conditioning? It didn't make a deep rumbling sound, and yet I wasn't sure that the answer was electric.

Now in my moment of truth, the answer to the air conditioning question was a 50/50 gamble. Do I roll the dice at 52 years old and hope that I am right, or do I utter the words of shame that I just didn't know? A third response crossed my mind. I could just say in a disgusted tone, "Oh, is that how this game is played? I answer all the difficult questions, and then I still pay you. Why do you think I called you?"

But all in that flash of time, I swallowed my pride and said I thought it was electric but that I really didn't know. They didn't show a look of disgust, and I guess they kept any opinion of me neatly hidden behind that service game-face that they are trained to wear.

I CAN DO THIS!

Once I had a small problem with the float in my toilet tank. I had seen those floats sold at Home Depot and thought, *I can do this*.

Why I didn't just call a plumber, go get a good book, and hit the couch, I do not know. It is one of the mysteries on the long road of learning in my life. So I decided that would be the day I would fix a plumbing problem. After all, how hard could a simple float problem be? So I went to Home Depot, bought a float, and returned home, confident I could do this.

I am convinced that there is a secret society of plumbers where they decide to place the works and guts of plumbing in places where you have to be a little Harry Houdini to even get near the site of the problem. Second, this secret society decided a long time ago to conspire with a toolmakers' society to make odd and special tools that must be used to fix a problem without creating greater problems.

So, I arrived back at home, float in hand, and equipped with what few tools I possessed that I thought could be pressed into duty to get the job done: pliers, a screwdriver, and an adjustable wrench. Mind you, not the kind of wrench that a secret tool society would make for this job, but the common kind in which the bottom jaw adjusts wider or narrower. My mission was probably already doomed at this point. I should have known better.

Another group of people who seemed to have aligned themselves in an unholy trinity with the plumbers and the toolmakers are the chiropractors. Once I assessed the problem, I tried to turn off the water, but that required getting on the floor and torquing my head and neck in an attempt to get at the metal thingy to turn the water off. For this, I chose the wrench and tried to turn the piece, only to find it was seized up. I tried a little harder, and now my neck and head position began to come into considerable discomfort. My blood pressure rose, and the mano-a-mano I had going on with the inanimate piece of metal now became a matter of personal honor. Was I in danger of losing my man card? By gosh, that thing was going to turn if it cost me the mother of all crick-in-the-necks!

With my strength draining and my blood pressure rising, I summoned one final assault on the valve. I waited, summoned all my strength, and launched: One—two—three—Yaaahhh! And with that final push for victory . . . I suffered defeat. The valve wouldn't budge, and instead a small leak began to dribble out. I raised the white flag of defeat and went to the couch to rest from my supreme effort.

The next day, I called a plumber, who fixed the problem. You know what they say, "It's never too late to learn." I paid extra, but I learned a life lesson that day, and resigned myself to a future maxim of "To every job, its expert, to every expert, his or her job."

---

1. P. J. Dowling, *The Hedge Schools of Ireland*, (Cork, Ireland: Mercier Press, 1968).

15

SIGNIFICANT QUOTES

QUOTATIONS

The following quotes express perfectly what I seek to do every day I live my life or lead a group on a tour. Think about these quotes and how they can inspire or challenge you to be your best self or live your best life.

For me, leading a tour is like going on stage. Telling the story of a place is like singing a song of that place, and when I tell a story, I want to tell the story so magically and so well that, as Springsteen says, it explodes to life!" That is what I am searching for when I lead a tour.

Bruce Springsteen, Musician and Singer

> *"That first step onstage is an unusual feeling. You have a very sober feeling in your gut that tells you that something is at stake, something that matters. You're taking a risk. It's not an entirely comfortable feeling but it's a necessary one."*

"What I am searching for from the moment I put my foot on stage until I walk off is the invisible thread of energy and inspiration or soul, or whatever you want to call it, that is going to take me to that place where a song can explode to life. That thread is between me and the audience every night. Always. I've got to grab it out of the air and physicalize it into something they can hear. Sometimes it's like catching a wave that can take you through all twenty-five songs. Sometimes it will take you through ten and then you have to re-find it. Sometimes you're looking for it again after one. A big part of what I'm experiencing when I'm performing is that search."

"I'm always asking myself, "How can I wring as much music and meaning as possible out of those six strings? . . ." With the correct presentation and playing style, you can summon up an orchestra with only a guitar."[1] *(Born to Run)*

Corrie ten Boom, Christian Writer

"Every experience that God gives us, every person He puts in our lives is the perfect preparation for a future that only He can see."[2]

C. S. Lewis, Christian Writer

"It would seem that Our Lord finds our desires not too strong, but too weak. We are half-hearted

creatures, fooling around with drink and sex and ambition when infinite joy is offered to us, like an ignorant child who wants to go on making mud pies in a slum because he cannot imagine what is meant by the offer of a holiday at the sea. We are far too easily pleased."[3]

Elizabeth Barrett Browning, Writer

"The earth is crammed with heaven and each common bush is afire with God. Those who see it, take off their shoes while the rest sit around picking blackberries."[4]

Eugene Peterson, Writer

"What a waste it would be to take these short, precious, eternity-charged years that we are given and squander them in cocktail chatter when we can be, like Jeremiah, vehemently human and passionate with God".[5]

Billy Casper, Pro Golfer

"The fact is, I had a talent I worked hard to perfect, and that brought a great deal of satisfaction to my family, my friends, and me."

Danny Meyer, Restaurateur

> *"Business, like life, is all about how you make people feel. It's that simple and it's that hard."*[6]

I like this quote because it boils things down to the basics. In the end, it's about how you make people feel. You must create a compelling customer experience, and you do that first and foremost by making people feel loved and welcomed and embraced.

Ken Burns, Documentary Film Maker

> *"It makes me think about how much atmosphere and feeling can I wring out of this story, this passage, this church, this landscape . . . a magical brew of place, story, voice inflection, emotion, memory, etc."*

Hugh Jackman, Actor

> *"Your acceptance and embracing of the possibility that you may fail miserably and die is commensurate with the only hope that you may succeed greatly and live."*
>
> *"Every moment on stage is pursued like it was the first time. We should approach life and every moment and relationship like it is the most important thing and for the first time."*

Winston Churchill, Statesman

"Success is the ability to go from one failure to another with no loss of enthusiasm."[7]

Mark Batterson, Lead Pastor of National Community Church, Washington DC

"Jacob was a cheater, Peter had a temper, David had an affair, Noah got drunk, Jonah ran from God, Paul was a murderer, Gideon was insecure, Miriam was a gossiper, Martha was a worrier, Thomas was a doubter, Sara was impatient, Elijah was moody, Moses stuttered, Zacchaeus was short, Abraham was old, and Lazarus was dead. God doesn't call the qualified, He qualifies the called!"[8]

Kevin Costner, Actor

"There's a lot of people in Hollywood who would measure their success based on the box office gross. . . . I have worked really hard not to do that. There is a real maturity you have to go through if you are really serious about your work. . . . You can make every decision on money and demographics, on what is safe and predictable or you can try to faithfully follow who you are."

"I'm really interested in the storytellers of our era, and I'm not interested in the story norms of our era. Many movies are contrived corporate

story lines built on what has been successful in the past. I can't do that. . . . I can't make a movie for a specific age group or a certain demographic. I wouldn't know how to. I can only make a movie that matches up with my own sensibility, and if I step away from that, I'm sure to lose myself."

Marilyn Monroe, Actress

"Trying to be someone else is a terrible waste of who you are."[9]

"Sometimes good things have to fall apart in order for better things to fall together."[10]

The Union Square Café Cookbook

"A profound wine is usually produced when a winemaker is courageous enough to cut back his vines, sacrificing a large grape production and potentially valuable crop in favor of a smaller harvest with fewer, better nourished, and more intensively flavored grapes. No matter how good a winemaker is, it's the quality of the grapes that will most determine the quality of the wine."[11]

Jack Welch, Businessman

"Be yourself, believe in your dream, grab life with a passion, don't be a dabbler, have a focus and grab life, pursue your vision and don't let the bureaucracy get you down."

Warren Buffet, Investor

"Success is doing what you love and doing it well and being loved by the people you want to be loved by."

"The real key is finding something you are passionate about and pursuing that. Bill Gates and I would have done what we did if all we had gotten was peanut butter and jelly sandwiches pushed under the door every night."

Adelaide Procter

"No true painter ever set on canvas all the glorious vision he conceived."[12]

Robert D. Kaplan

"In an age of mass tourism, adventure becomes more and more an inner matter where prodigious reading can transport you to places that others only a few feet away will never see."[13]

Richard Branson of Virgin Atlantic, Businessman

"To me, business isn't about wearing suits or pleasing stockholders. It's about being true to yourself, your ideas, and focusing on essentials."[14]

Sumner Redstone, Businessman

"Most people who succeed in significant areas do not succeed because of a desire for money."

"I don't believe in letting history get in the way of the future."

"Success is not built on success. It is built on failure. It is built on frustration. Sometimes it is built on catastrophe."

"The only thing that counts is competence. Not race. Not gender. . . . Competence."[15]

Jean-Pierre de Caussade, Monk & Writer

"There is nothing trivial about our passing moments, as they enclose the whole kingdom of holiness and [they are] the food on which angels feed."[16]

Sir Ken Robinson

"We are not robots, we are people who are driven by feelings, imagination, and a sense of possibility. Creativity is the essence of humanity. It is not an incidental part of being human, it is distinctly human."

Me

I find it so hard to sometimes break away and explore something new, because I want to go deeper and deeper into the heart and beauty and soul of these fascinating places and the people who live there. It takes a while to meet people who can help you go deeper.

Andrew Wyeth, the great painter, once said, *"People have asked me why I haven't moved beyond realism and into abstract. They say we have gotten to the end of realism and we want to move beyond." Wyeth said to them, "You may have gotten to the end of your own mind, but you have not yet begun to explore the depths of the subject."* That is how I feel. I have begun and been blessed with this fascinating journey into what appears a limited subject, and yet it seems to contain the inexhaustible riches of Aladdin's cave. The Lord has truly blessed me beyond all I could ever hope or dream of. He has taken me to a place I could never have found on my own, or even conceived, and all I can do is sit here in wave of thankfulness and gratitude.

The original temptation of Adam and Eve had been repeated down through time in many forms, but in the end, it boils down to the fact that Satan convinced them, and he tries to convince us, that God is withholding something good from us. (My version of a statement by Steve McVey in his book *Grace Walk*.)

You want to change the world? Do the responsibilities that lay at hand right before you.

Be the best you can be with the Lord's help and guidance, walking with him and building that future quietly, seemingly undramatically, moment by moment, day by day.

People often ask me if I get bored going to the same places all the time. To them, I say, fascinating places are like fascinating people, and you would never say, "I met the most interesting person last night, and I hope I never meet them again. No, fascinating places are inexhaustible. You never get to the bottom of them.

In the end, I am so thankful that the Lord has been in control of my life. He has taken my hand and led me through a series of doors that opened and doors that closed. Sometimes, when a door closed, he provided a bridge to move on, but in the end, he led me to a Garden of Eden job and vocation that I could have neither conceived of nor found on my own.

Know yourself, love yourself, be yourself.

---

1. Bruce Springsteen, *Born to Run*, (New York, Simon & Schuster, 2017).
2. Corrie ten Boom, *The Hiding Place*, (Ada, Mich: Baker Publishing Group, 2006), 12.
3. C.S. Lewis, *The Weight of Glory* (New York: HarperCollins, 2001), 26.

4. Elizabeth Barrett Browning, *Aurora Leigh*, (New York: C.S. Francis & Company, 1857), 304.

5. Eugene H. Peterson, *Run with the Horses*, (Colorado Springs: InterVarsity Press, 2009), 88.

6. Danny Meyer, *Setting the Table: The Transforming Power of Hospitality in Business*, (New York: HarperCollins, 2006), 3 7.

7. Victor C. X .Wang, ed., *Encyclopedia of Strategic Leadership and Management*, (Hershey, Pa.: IGI Global, 2016)437

8. Mark Batterson, *The Circle Maker: Praying Circles Around Your Biggest Dreams and Greatest Fears*, (Grand Rapids, Mich.: Zondervan, 2016), 78.

9. "29 Real Marilyn Monroe Quotes," https://brightdrops.com/marilyn-monroe-quotes, (accessed Feb. 22, 2023).

10. "29 Real Marilyn Monroe Quotes"

11. Danny Meyer, *The Union Square Cafe Cookbook* (New York: HarperCollins, 2009).

12. Adelaide A. Procter, "Unexpressed," *The Poems of Adelaide A. Procter*, (Boston: Ticknor and Fields, 1864), 172.

13. Robert D. Kaplan, *The Ends of the Earth*, (New York: Knopf Doubleday Publishing Group, 2014).

14. Keith Patching, *Leadership, Character and Strategy Exploring Diversity*, (London: Palgrave Macmillan, 2006), 158.

15. "I Am American Business," Sumner Redstone, https://www.cnbc.com/id/100000726 (accessed Feb. 22, 2023) .

16. Jean-Pierre De Caussade, *Abandonment to Divine Providence*, (New York: Crown Publishing Group, 2012), 52.

16

SPIRITUAL ESSAYS

The following spiritual essays are written from my heart to tell you some of the things that have meant most to me on my spiritual journey. These essays are meant to stand alone. For this reason, some may seem repetitive and repeat favorite quotes, and some have been lifted out of the body of the autobiographical part of this book. Nevertheless, from a spiritual point of view, these essays cover much of the heart and soul of who I am. I pray that you will read them, meditate on them, and use your Bible to back-check what I say.

CONVERSION

During my freshman year at Gordon Junior College, a lot of things were working toward a spiritual awakening in my life. I was like a tree during winter when it looks like nothing is happening, but internally things are lining up for a change as spring approaches.

Because of my loving father, I had a desire to be good, but it was more out of love and admiration for him rather than any knowledge of Christianity or Christ. I also had a vague romantic desire to seek the truth. Sunday school and church made little effect on me. I never thought much about the possibility of knowing God on any intimate level. Christianity seemed to be more of a philosophy of doing good in memory of God and Jesus. I was reading a little of the Bible, but it didn't have much impact on me.

During the summer of 1973, after high school graduation and before going to junior college, I took a step closer to something spiritual when Billy Graham came to host a crusade at the Atlanta stadium. I had seen Billy Graham on TV as my father liked to watch him, but we never talked about what we saw or heard, and nothing seemed to make any substantial impact. I must have absorbed a vague sense of what Graham was saying, and maybe this was floating around in my subconscious, perhaps waiting for what the Bible would call "the fullness of time," as seeds are planted, watered, and bearing fruit.

When Graham came to the Atlanta stadium, I went to see him and even answered his call to come forward to receive Christ, but I don't believe it was yet the fullness of time. I would call that night a "creeping closer."

Then in February of 1974, when I was a freshman at Gordon Junior College in Barnesville, Georgia, George Ford, my neighbor and friend from high school, asked me if my brother Doug and I would like to meet with a few people at West Side Park in Thomaston to talk about the Bible. He pitched it more like a chance to talk rather than a formal Bible study. We went, and I am not even sure there were any believers there among the five of us. We were more like seekers who were sharing things we had heard along our short journey in life.

In the end, it did not matter whether there were any real believers there or not because we were honestly seeking, and the Holy Spirit was there. That night I heard a lot of the things I had no doubt heard many times before—that God wanted to have a personal relationship with me and that it was possible through Christ. The words are a little vague in my memory, but their impact was not.

As I sat there, what I had no doubt heard so many times before suddenly meant something. That night I guess you could say Jesus performed a modern miracle. I, who had been blind and deaf to spiritual truth, could suddenly see and hear it for the first time. In the twinkling of an eye, I believe God gave me the grace to believe and see that Jesus was the answer to life's questions. It was as if I had been living in a dark room, and God suddenly turned the lights on.

As I sat there, an image came into my mind: If the cup of life was half full of mystery, Jesus was the only one who could fill that cup or explain that mystery. I saw in Him a big "Yes." In essence, He was saying to me, loud and clear, what He had said to the disciples, "I am the way, the truth, and the life" (John 14:6).

Even today, I don't know all I might want to know about life, but I am satisfied with what was revealed to me that night and in the years to come. God may not tell us all we *want* to know, but He tells us all we *need* to know to have peace, a sense of purpose, love, forgiveness, and perspective.

That night I truly feel that God gave me the gift of faith in Jesus Christ. It was as if a veil had been taken away, and there was Christ, who revealed Himself to me. This is described perfectly in the first chapter of Galatians where Paul says, "For I neither received it of man, neither was I taught it, but by the revelation of Jesus Christ . . . *when it pleased God*, who separated me from my mother's womb, and called me by his grace, to *reveal* his Son in me" (1:12, 15–16, italics added).

That night I went home, knelt beside my bed, and prayed, "Lord, I don't know if you are in my life or out of my life, but

I know you are the answer. If you are in, stay in, if you are out, come in now."

In John 17:3, Jesus said, "And this is life eternal, that they might know thee, the only true God, and Jesus Christ, whom thou hast sent." That night, a new relationship was born in my heart and mind and being. That night Jesus came in in the form of the Holy Spirit and took up residence in the manger of my heart. In John 14:23 Jesus talks about how he and his Father will come and make their abode with the believer. Before that night, it was *me*. After that night, it was *us*. In a very real way, I had been "born again," and in the best possible sense, my life would never be the same again.

This is the single most important event in my life, and it came out of the blue when I least expected it. It was like walking on a dusty, endless plateau through scrub pines and rocks, and suddenly coming upon the Grand Canyon of Life. What an incredible blessing.

When the Holy Spirit comes in, you begin not only to desire to read God's Word, but through the guidance and interpretation of the Holy Spirit, the Bible suddenly means something, and you can understand it.

Our group had gathered with George that night not expecting another meeting, but something dramatic had happened, and now we wanted to meet on a regular basis. We needed a teacher to lead the Bible studies, but there was just us. And so, Doug and I became the initial leaders. That was an incredible blessing, because it forced us to study the Bible and teach it to others. We were babes in Christ feeding on the "milk of the Word" and growing. In time, others would help lead the Bible study. It lasted about six months, but it fed us, and when it ended, we were strong enough to walk on our own.

As I have previously said, sometimes in life you are walking along with the days passing in a seemingly uneventful manner, but then you turn a corner and *bam*! Something happens, and you are never the same again. When George Ford asked Doug and me to come to a meeting at West Side Park in Thomaston, I had no idea my life would change forever. George thought enough of Doug and me to invite us, and I am forever grateful that he acted on that impulse. For him, it may have seemed like a very small thing to ask us, but God used him to change our lives forever.

AN IDEA ABOUT WHAT GOD MEANS FOR OUR FUTURE DESTINY

In reading John 14–17, as well as through the help of C. S. Lewis, I have begun to get an idea of what God has in store for us as believers. In these mortal bodies and minds, we see His plans dimly. He hasn't told us all we want to know, but He has told us all we need to know to begin the process of what it means to be transformed into his image.

In the beginning, God, as the Trinity, said, "Let us make man in our image." God was a tri-part being, so He made us tri-part beings with a mind, body, and spirit. The Trinity existed in a creative, dynamic fellowship of love and glory that was so wonderful they didn't want to keep it to themselves. They wanted to share their wonderful existence with others, so they created humans.

This act of creating humans took the holy fellowship from three to four, and by extension, many. I used to think of God's making humans in His image as a concept conflicted with the idea of ego. Now I see it as it should be seen—as an unselfish act of love, sharing, and giving.

Because of man's fall, sin had to be dealt with. The act of bringing humans back into the relational fellowship of personality, glory, and love would require all three parts of God's identity. The Father orchestrated the architectural plan that is clearly laid out in Romans 8:29–30. The Son made the plan a reality through creation and later by dying for us to redeem and restore the plan when humans sinned. The Holy Spirit, by indwelling the believer, made possible the realization of bringing man *literally* inside the Trinity's circle of fellowship, love, and glory.

The coming of the Holy Spirit was a sea-change experience in God's purpose and plan for mankind. Prior to the coming of the Holy Spirit, mankind was a creation once removed from God. Adam and Eve communed with God in the garden, Moses met God in the burning bush, and the disciples walked with, followed, and heard God through Jesus's presence. With the coming of the Holy Spirit, God would finally fulfill His initial desire to bring humanity inside the circle of fellowship by indwelling him. In John 14:17, Jesus said to the disciples, "Even the Spirit of Truth . . . you know Him, for he dwelleth with you and shall be in you."

This is a sea-change event and gives us the ability, through faith, to literally enter the Trinity's sacred circle of love, glory, and fellowship.

In John 14–17, Jesus laid out details about our eternal future in the next life, when God's desire for us will be brought to its fullest realization. But these chapters also show us that the possibility of evolving toward that plan begins in this life. Jesus showed the here and now of the plan when He defined eternal life in John 17:3, "And this is life eternal, that they might know thee, the only true God, and Jesus Christ, whom thou hast seen."

By Jesus's definition, eternal life is sharing in the life of the eternal Father, Son, and Holy Spirit. This is incredibly exciting for the believer. That sharing of life happens both now—and it stretches into eternity in a never-ending relational experience of love and glory and beauty. This relationship begins now and will last forever. It will never end (John14:16).

In the here and now, we are experiencing this glory and wonder with our earthbound senses, but after death, when we are made like Him in all its completeness, we will need a new body to handle and process all that awaits us.

The more I meditate on what is both my present and my future, the more I get a glimpse of the beauty, glory, and majesty of what we are experiencing in our "becoming." The Bible is a bird's eye view of the master plan from beginning to end, and as believers, our lives fit into that template. We were created, and we are being transformed into His image.

Jesus said He was the Alpha and the Omega, the beginning and the end. He must be our beginning and our end, our way, our truth, and our life.

He has given us all we need to fulfill our creative purpose and identity. We were created by Him and for Him (Colossians 1:16). Romans 8:29–30 shows that through his life, death, and resurrection, Jesus has called us and redeemed us. In John 14–17, Jesus reveals the rest of the plan with the great revelation of the Holy Spirit.

Once we are made holy by Christ's redemptive death and resurrection, the Holy Spirit comes to indwell the believer and begin the process of changing us "into the same image from glory to glory, even as by the Spirit of the Lord" (2 Corinthians 3:18).

The purpose of the Holy Spirit is to indwell us in order to bring us into that circle of love, glory, and fellowship. The death and resurrection of Christ makes us ready to enter the fellowship of the Trinity, *and the Holy Spirit takes us inside that fellowship and makes it a reality*. Through belief in the death and resurrection and the Holy Spirit, we are literally "born again" into the purpose for which we were created, fellowship with the Trinity.

Through abiding in Him and through the various actions of the Holy Spirit, we are becoming like Him. Through the transforming miracle of belief, God indwells us.

In John 14:17 Jesus told the disciples about the nature of the Holy Spirit, "Even the Spirit of truth, whom the world cannot receive, because it seeth him not, neither knoweth him: but ye know him; for he dwelleth with you, and shall be in you."

Later, in John 14:13, Jesus said that through the miracle of the Holy Spirit, God the Father and Jesus the Son will make their abode with the believer. That is an incredible revelation, that just as we live and have our being within God's created world, the purpose of God is for us to be one with Him and experience the love, glory, and fellowship that the Trinity had among themselves before the foundation of the world.

In Romans 8:22–23 we see that with the first taste of what we are becoming, we yearn for the completion of the process. "For we know that the whole creation groaneth and travaileth in pain until now. And not only they, but ourselves also, which have the first fruits of the Spirit, even we ourselves groan within ourselves, waiting for the adoption, to wit, the redemption of our body."

Our purpose has begun now, and it will be completed in eternity. In his book *The Weight of Glory*, C. S. Lewis spoke to this in how our minds and bodies yearn for our true home. "We do not want merely to see beauty, though God knows, even that is bounty enough. We want something else which can hardly be put into words—to be united with the beauty we see, to pass into it, to receive it into ourselves, to bathe in it, to become part of it."

Right now we have the first fruits of that experience through the indwelling Holy Spirit. But we are in the process of being turned from water into wine. We are at the same time *in that fellowship* of love and glory for which we were created, but we are also *being transformed deeper and deeper toward the perfection of that oneness* with the Trinity. The thought of who we are as believers and where we are headed is incredibly exciting!

C. S. Lewis continued, "We cannot mingle with the splendours we see. But all the leaves of the New Testament are rustling with the rumor that it will not always be so. Someday, God willing, we shall get in."

I disagree with Lewis. I believe that through the indwelling Holy Spirit, we are already in, and through the transforming work of the Holy Spirit, we are, at the same time, both in and also evolving from glory to glory into the image of Christ. To use a metaphor from my friend, Will Vaus, this process is like a tea bag steeping in a cup of hot water. As the tea bag abides in the water and the water in the presence of the tea bag, the water is being transformed from glory to glory into the full strength of tea. In the process, the water ceases to be water alone and becomes one with the tea.

In time and eternity, we will become like Him. But let us also enjoy the glory and the wonder of what we are now experiencing in our passing moments for, as Jean-Pierre de Caussade wrote in *Abandonment to Divine Providence*, "There is nothing trivial about our passing moments, for each contains the whole kingdom of holiness and [they are] the food on which angels feed."

In the end, Jesus gives us a glimpse of the glory that awaits.

> Father, I will that they also, whom thou hast given me, be with me where I am, that they may behold my glory, which thou hast given me: for thou lovest me before the foundation of the world. O righteous Father, the world hath not known thee: but I have known thee, and these have known that thou hast sent me. And I have declared unto them thy name, and will declare it: that the love wherewith thou hast loved me may be in them, and I in them. (John 17:24–26)

In the end, Jesus reveals the original wish in the mind of the Trinity at creation when He prays to the Father in John Chapter 17,

"That they all may be one; as thou, Father, art in me, and I in thee, that they also may be one in us" (John 17:21).

The process has begun, and when we die it will be finished! It is the "happily ever after" that is the truth that God is whispering in our heart!

EVERY GOOD ENDEAVOR

When I was little, I was afraid to sleep away from home. I was the little boy who was too scared to leave home—and yet travel, much of it alone, both overseas and in this country, was a future that God designed for me. It shows you that if God calls you to a future, He will uniquely prepare you for that future. As the saying goes, "God doesn't choose the qualified, he qualifies the chosen." Timothy Keller, in his book, *Every Good Endeavor*, says, "All human work is not merely a job but a calling."

The Latin word "*vocare*," "to call," is at the root of our common word "vocation." When God chose a leader for the people of Israel, he looked through all of David's brothers, many of whom, to the world, seemed far more qualified. Yet God chose David because God saw David's heart. And, because of his heart, God saw not what David was, but what David *could become* when empowered by Him.

When I look in the rearview mirror of my life, I can see how God was working all along the way, preparing me to design and lead tours to Western Europe and North American. From my childhood and then all through the years, God was preparing me and leading me through open doors, shut doors, bridges, passions, and interests to a place that only He could see. A place where I would be most fulfilled. A place that would give me meaning.

A place where He would maximize my whole being and maximize my opportunity to glorify Him.

We are spiritual beings made by him and for him (Colossians 1:16). All vocations are callings that give us opportunities to serve others and glorify Him. And those callings create a stage upon which we grow and evolve into His likeness. Our vocations are also opportunities to build up and encourage others, and lead them to Christ.

Every second in our life is a spiritual moment. We are as spiritual when we are at work or when we are taking out the trash as we are when we are on our knees praying. Jean-Pierre De Caussade wrote, "There is nothing trivial

about our passing moments, as they enclose the whole kingdom of holiness and [they are] the food on which angels feed."

Sunday school, church, Bible study, and prayer are ways God uses to equip and use us. But He also uses all the "secular" moments in our lives to fill us and lead us into the mission field that lies before us in the passing moments of our life.

God is an efficient craftsman in our life. He uses each moment and each event to sculpt us into the image of Christ. There is no excess dust surrounding the evolving image that is our life. He has no excess to be swept up and thrown away. He uses it all.

A GOOD LESSON LEARNED—AND A SPIRITUAL WATERSHED EXPERIENCE

When I worked in Bar Harbor, I really enjoyed the books I read, whether Bar Harbor or Acadia history or biographies about Franklin or Theodore Roosevelt. As always, whether I read about people or nature, I drew parallels and insights about the sculpting of my life views. Over the summer, my enthusiasm and excitement in my "secular" reading seemed to burn hotter and brighter than my Bible reading. I seemed to be learning as much spiritually from biography as I was from the Bible. This bothered me at first and finally led to a true spiritual revelation.

I was very disciplined in my physical and spiritual routine. Every day I ran, did push-ups and sit-ups, read my Bible, prayed, and read for pleasure. I was also taking nature hikes and learning from ranger walks. I took these years of resort work very seriously. It was at the same time, a serious endeavor and a joyful endeavor. C. S. Lewis talked about this kind of life in *The Weight of Glory, "We must play, but our merriment must be of that kind (and it is, in fact, the merriest kind) which exists between people who have, from the outset, taken each other seriously.*"

And so, I struggled with the fact that I was finding more excitement from my "secular" interests than I was from my "spiritual" interests. One morning, as I got on my knees to pray, a true revelation of the Lord came to me. I said,

> *"Lord, I know you are leading me in this thought path. You said you came that we might have life and have it more abundantly, but I don't feel I am experiencing an abundant joy in my Bible reading. At the same time, I do feel an abundant*

> *joy in my reading of biography and my walks in nature. I have more of a desire to read biography than the Bible. I have always been taught to consider all my desires guilty until proven innocent. I have also fallen into the view that certain activities, such as reading biography, running, or taking nature walks, are non-spiritual in nature, and others pursuits, like reading the Bible and praying, are more spiritual in nature. So, I feel guilty about my joy in the secular activities and my lack of enthusiasm in my Bible reading and prayer. From this day forward, I will assume all my desires, unless strictly forbidden in the Bible, as God-given as an integral part of your process of shaping my personal identity into the image of Christ. From this day forward, I will assume my good secular desires innocent until proven guilty instead of guilty until proven innocent."*

Yes, God means us to pray and read His Word, but He is also working out His sculpting process in our lives through the desires and interests He gives us.

As I worked through these thoughts in my prayer, an amazing joy of assurance immediately welled up within me—an assurance that this was God's will for me.

Since then, I have thought that this revelation was pictured in the story of Lazarus. When Christ raised Lazarus from the dead, that is a spiritual picture of Christ's saving someone for eternity, and that is wonderful, but Christ wants so much more for us. Everyone was joyful when Christ raised Lazarus from the dead, but Jesus told the people to loose the graveclothes that were binding Lazarus.

Similarly, we need to be loosed from whatever hinders our living a full life in both our spiritual and our secular potential.

Christ is to be our Savior for all eternity, but He is also our Lord both now in the immediacy of our passing moments and going forward into eternity. Eternal life is not just *then*; it is also *now*! Here and now in our passing moments, through both our spiritual and our secular interests, we are being sculpted into the image of Christ so that our personal potential might blossom into its highest fruition.

Colossians 1:16 says we are made by Christ and for Christ. The potential of this thought is amazing when we realize that God wants to work in concert with us, His creation, to both achieve His own ends and, in the process, bring our personal potential to its ultimate and fullest realization. We need to meditate and marinate on this because if it is true, and I believe it is, this is the truest source of our passion, our fulfillment, and our reason for being.

GOD WANTS US ALL TO REALIZE THE FULLEST POTENTIAL OF OUR IDENTITY

God wants all of us to realize the fullest potential of our personal uniqueness and identity. As Tim Tebow said, *"The beginning of knowing who we are is knowing whose we are."* It is an incredible thing to realize that the God of creation wants to work in concert with us to bring our personal identity, as well as His purposes, to their fullest possible fruition.

Our identity is discovered when we know our Creator. In Colossians 1:16, Paul wrote of Jesus, *"all things were created by him, and for him."* This strikes at the heart of who we are. We were created by Jesus, and so our identity begins and is bound up in our relationship with Him. The verse also says we were created *for him.* It is absolutely futile to try to understand our identity and purpose without knowing our Creator. Also, our Creator has given us an owner's manual—the Bible.

Fortunately, our Creator is loving and wants a relationship with His creation. In Psalm 8:3–4, David wrote, *"When I consider thy heavens, the work of thy fingers, the moon and the stars, which thou hast ordained; What is man that thou art mindful of him? and the son of man, that thou visitest him?"*

Wow! Think about that. The God of all creation wants to spend as much time with us as we will give Him. He created us uniquely with certain gifts and talents, and He wants to work with us to make us all He created us to be! We have no way of knowing what He created us to be, but He does. Only through Him can we discover our true identity.

If the President of the United States asked you to make time to talk with him, you would probably put everything aside and let him name the time and place. And yet, the God of all creation is in the waiting room of your life, patiently waiting for you to make time for Him in your busy schedule. How crazy is that? But also, what a blessing, privilege, and wonder it is that God is indeed extending to us this very invitation in each passing moment of our lives!

God has revealed who He is through Jesus. In John 14:9, Philip asked Jesus to show him what the Father is like, and Jesus' answer was, "Have I been so long a time with you, and yet hast thou not know me, Philip? He that hath seen me hath seen the Father."

In John 17:3, Jesus revealed the source of our identity, and the necessity that it must be planted in the soil of a relationship with our Creator. Jesus prayed to His Father, "And this is life eternal, that they might know thee the only true God, and Jesus Christ, whom thou hast sent."

In Jeremiah 1:5, God revealed Jeremiah's purpose to him, "Before I formed thee in the belly, I knew thee; and before thou camest forth out of the womb I sanctified thee, and I ordained thee a prophet unto the nations."

Similarly, through a relationship with God, He will reveal to us our identity and purpose. Much of this is revealed in the Bible. From there, in concert with the Holy Spirit, we are to work out our individual identity in "fear and trembling" (Philippians 2:12) through our personal relationship with Him.

In Romans 8:28–30, Paul said that we are "called according to his purpose." Those verses show how God works that purpose out in our lives. We have been called and justified though Christ's death on the cross. He died for our sins that we might be restored to a relationship with our Creator. God's purpose is to make us into the image of Christ, and the sculptor is the Holy Spirit (2 Corinthians 3:18). With this purpose as the end game,

He uses everything in our life to accomplish His work. This is why Paul says in Romans 8:28, "All things work together for good to them that love God, to them who are the called according to his purpose."

Now if we are all being made into the image of Christ, you might think that would result in a homogenized sameness for all people. But it is quite the opposite. In *Mere Christianity*, C. S. Lewis wrote,

> *"The more we get what we now call "ourselves" out of the way and let Him take us over, the more truly ourselves we become. There is so much of Him that millions and millions of "little Christs," all different, will still be too few to express Him fully. He made them all. He invented, as an author invents characters in a novel, all the different men that you and I were intended to be. In that sense our real selves are all waiting for us in Him. It is no good trying to "be myself" without Him.*
>
> *Imagine a lot of people who have always lived in the dark. You come and try to describe to them what light is like. You might tell them that if they come into the light that same light would fall on them all and they would all reflect it and thus become what we call visible. Is it not quite possible that they would imagine that, since they were all receiving that same light, and all reacting to it in the same way (i.e., all reflecting it) they would all look alike? Whereas you and I know that the light*

> *will in fact bring out, or show up, how different they are."*

In this way we see that, through Christ our individuality is actually brought to its fullest expression and development. Two purposes are served at the same time. He is most glorified when we allow Him to bring our identity to its fullest fruition by abiding in Him. Lewis further explained,

> *"Or again, suppose a person knew nothing about salt. You give him a pinch to taste and he experiences a particular strong, sharp taste. You then tell him that, in your country, people use salt in all their cookery. Might he not reply, "In that case I suppose all your dishes taste exactly the same: because the taste of that stuff you have just given me is so strong that it will kill the taste of everything else." But you and I know that the real effect of salt is the opposite. So far from killing the taste of the egg or the tripe or the cabbage, it actually brings it out. They do not show their real taste till you have added the salt."*[1]

Again, in the illustration of salt, being made in the image of Christ will enhance and make a person's individuality more distinct, vibrant, and vivid.

Father, Son, and Holy Spirit created humans to share the wonder, beauty, and love that they shared with each other before the foundation of the world. In John 17:21–26, Jesus expressed this beautifully in His prayer to the Father. In those verses, Jesus showed that the ultimate purpose of the Holy Spirit is to bring us into a oneness of fellowship with the Father, Son, and Holy Ghost.

C. S. Lewis fleshed out the wonder of these verses when, in *The Weight of Glory*, he spoke of one aspect of heaven. "We do not want to merely to see beauty, though God knows, even that is bounty enough. We want something else which can hardly be put into words—to be united with the beauty we see, to pass into it, to receive it into ourselves, to bathe in it, to become part of it"

Furthermore, in *The Problem of Pain*, C.S Lewis suggested that God created individuality so that each person would highlight a different part of God's glory.

> *"Surely, that each of the redeemed shall forever know and praise some one aspect of the Divine beauty better than any other creature can. Why else were individuals created, but that God loving all infinitely, should love each differently? And this difference, so far from impairing, floods with meaning the love of all blessed creatures for one another, the communion of the saints. If all experienced God in the same way, and returned Him an identical worship, the song of the Church triumphant would have no symphony, it would be like an orchestra in which all the instruments played the same note".*[2]

This dream of realizing our fullest potential is a work in progress. It has already begun, and in the passing moments of our lives, God is molding us into who He created us to be. In that process we are evolving more and more into the image of Christ. One day, when we die, the process with be complete, for the Bible says that when we see Him, we shall be like Him.

"Beloved, now are we the sons of God, and it doth not yet appear what we shall be: but we know that, when he shall appear, we shall be like him; for we shall see him as he is" (1 John 3:2).

This knowledge of God's work in us should fill us with hope and joy, meaning, and wonder!

HOW PHILOSOPHY, HISTORY, AND ART AFFECT THE DESIGN OF MY TOURS

Wayne Gretzky once remarked that playing a variety of sports during his youth had actually helped him in his ultimate mastery of hockey. As a young boy, it had been a toss-up as to whether his future would be in baseball or hockey. He loved both sports. In the end, the muscles, skills, and hand-eye coordination he developed in baseball, helped him in hockey. He came to feel that focusing on only one sport in youth would have adversely affected his long-term proficiency in hockey.

I see a direct application of this theory in how I design a tour. Whenever I see on the internet a list of the ten worst college degrees to have for a good financial future, I am quietly amused. For me, the great success of my tours has had a lot to do with how seemingly unrelated subjects helped in the design of my tours.

God has blessed me with a ravenous curiosity about almost everything in life. I got degrees in both history and literature in college, and I also took lots of courses in speech and education. Since college, I have studied extensively in art, literature, philosophy, and Christianity. My design of a tour, and my business plan for it, are almost totally a construct of my passion for all these subjects.

My love of biography led me to a passion for travel and to my working in resorts for five years after college. I wanted to see the places I had read about, and resort work paid my way. During those years, not only did I come to know the places where I would eventually lead tours, but the intangible skills I learned from living on the spot, built a mind for what I would do in ways that nothing else could have. As I kept journals and worked out my belief systems, God built in me a mind that could gather information, organize it, and make design decisions that would be of invaluable help in my future tour business. Those years that some might have seen as "wasted" were the best possible graduate school for what I would eventually do in life. God has used all of my wide interests quite efficiently in the course of my life. There were no scraps to be thrown away.

While I could never list all the sources that have helped me in the process of design and creation, here are just a few and how they have helped me.

My Christian Faith

My Christian faith gives me the superstructure, the dry-dock, the shipyard, if you will, to create my trips. It is the "dream factory" from which I seek to create transformative experiences. Not only are the Father, Son, and indwelling Holy Spirit my inspiration and my internal designers, but They are the power source into which I tap to create the magic of a golden moment.

Also, my relationship with the Lord calls me to be loving, caring, honest, genuine, and authentic in all my dealings with my clients. It also calls me to be honest in the way I run my business.

Gerald Murphy, American Painter

Through the study of art, my mind and spirit have been drawn to the creative design we can discover everywhere around us. Part of the creative design of a walk is to open the mind of the traveler to a new way of seeing that enjoys the beauty of life on a deeper level. All artists and writers have been mentors to me in heightening my sensibility so that I might help heighten others' sensibility. Gerald Murphy, an American painter during the twentieth century, is a great example of someone from whom I have learned so much. Gerald's daughter Honoria wrote of her father,

> *"It was as a painter that close friends preferred to remember Murphy, as John Dos Passos did when he wrote The Best of Times in 1966. He described a walk along the Seine with Gerald and Fernand Leger in 1924 – it was only the second time Dos Passos had met Murphy. "As we strolled along," he wrote, "Fernand kept pointing out shapes and colors . . . Gerald's offhand comments would organize vistas of his own. Instead of the hackneyed and pastel-tinted Tuileries and bridges and barges, . . . we were walking through a freshly invented world. They picked out winches, the flukes of an anchor, coils of rope, the red funnel of a towboat, half a woman's face seen behind geraniums through the casement window of the cabin of a barge. . . . The banks of the Seine never looked banal again after that walk".*[3]

Through reading passages like these, studying art on my own, and reading about art and artists, I have been trained to see and to think in new ways with new perspectives. As a result, the shapes and colors of my passing moments are enhanced and transformed. When I lead a tour, I hope to pass this trained sensibility on to others.

In a lot of ways, I feel I was as profoundly affected by that walk along the Seine as was Dos Passos. I feel that God has used Gerald's life, as well as the lives of other artists and writers, to strike that magic vision in me, that artist's heart and vision which, amidst the banality of everyday life, is able to organize vistas visually and experientially so that I have come to walk through a "freshly invented world." Thus, the quality of everyday life is heightened, and I have learned the magic of inventing the golden moment.

Some special moments just happen in life, but if you know enough about yourself, about the human spirit, and about the qualities of life, then so many times all the right ingredients are waiting for the sensitive person to "invent" the golden moment. On a tour, I constantly strive to take the ingredients of any given moment and to make that setting or that moment burst to life. Through the power and magic of the Holy Spirit, I am constantly trying to take the common water of a given moment and turn it into wine of the finest quality . . . living water that feeds the spirit of my fellow travelers.

Gerald Murphy has also given me a sense of the holiness and beauty of the potential of the "golden moment" if you will. As his granddaughter Laura reflected, *"that ability to see beauty in the simplest things and to turn the simplest things into a thing of beauty for others."*

Lin Yutang, the Chinese philosopher, spoke of how art tends to restore in us a "freshness of vision" and a more "vital sense of life." He spoke of life and the artist's duty:

> *"As we grow older in life, our senses become gradually benumbed, our emotions become more callous . . . and our vision of life is warped by too much preoccupation with cold, trivial realities. Fortunately, we have a few poets and artists who have not lost that sharpened sensibility, that fine emotional response and that freshness of vision,*

> *and whose duties are therefore to be our moral conscience, to hold up a mirror to our blunted vision, to tone up our withered nerves."*[4]

This has certainly been the effect of Gerald's life on my sensibilities. Here are a few more passages that help round out my picture of Gerald Murphy

In October 1975, Peg Mcleish wrote to Honoria about an Easter party that Gerald helped organize.

> *"I know that what Dow did that Easter in his garden in Snedens was so magical and enchanting that never again will . . . I sit in a beautiful garden without thinking of him. . . . An artist can do this with his painting, a poet with his poem – that capturing of the essence of a moment—but, somehow, Dow's special gift seems to have been in the very doing itself, so that the record is left not in any concrete form that can be examined by others, as a painting or a poem can be, but is simply held in the minds of those who were present at the moment of creation. . . . He certainly knew the value of "the golden moment," which he shared so willingly and joyously with others..."*[5]

Later, Gerald's granddaughter, Laura, would remember,

> *"As I remember Grandpa, one thing that stands out in my mind is the manner in which he did even the smallest task. He was a perfectionist, a very meticulous person in every respect. Every*

> *morning during the summers in East Hampton, I would trot over to his house just to watch him shave. . . . Each time the routine was just the same, but it was done like a miniature concert. . . . I also sensed-or maybe I only realized it when I got older-that he had the ability to see beauty in the simplest thing and to turn the simplest thing into a thing of beauty for others.*[5]

All this would later contribute to the way I design a day on a tour. In my thought process, we would not just walk from the hotel to the Louvre, but I would give thought to what route would visually unfold to the eye and the spirit of my clients in the most beautiful way with the best storyline to feed their spirits. In an attempt to create a transformative moment, I would take everything into account. Everything was analyzed in my mental laboratory and in concert with the Holy Spirit, in an effort to create the golden moment from common things through an alchemy of the mind.

Henry David Thoreau, Philosopher and Writer

In *Walden*, Thoreau said, *"It is something to be able to paint a particular picture, or to carve a statue, and so to make a few objects beautiful, but it is far more glorious to carve and paint the very atmosphere and medium in which we live and through which we look. To affect the quality of the day, that is the highest of arts."*

This is what I am constantly striving for and seeking—to transform the very quality of the moment. To make a walk or a museum visit into a transformative spiritual experience on which the soul of a person feeds. Such an experience also fills a spiritual reservoir of memory from which a person may drink and feed for the rest of his or her life.

Sheldon Vanauken and C. S. Lewis, Christian Writers

Most of my ideas about timelessness and timeless moments I first learned from Sheldon Vanauken. My study of C. S. Lewis has, in recent years, added to and informed these ideas. When I connected those ideas with the Christian idea that our spirits and souls are eternal, then there was obviously an intersection and meeting point where I realized that I could try to set up a stage on which the possibility of "golden timeless moments" could happen.

When I scout out a place, I seek to experience as many things as possible. I am like a painter or writer who is seeking to know his subject. Once I know my subject, I seek to get a spiritual feel for which experiences are the most valuable. Once I determine that, I seek to lay those experiences out in such a way that there is enough time to let these experiences have their effects on a person's soul. When you get the right moment and feel and combine that with the right traveler and the right amount of time, you get the real possibility of a golden transformative moment that people will feed on for the rest of their life whether they know it or not.

Lin Yutang, Chinese Philosopher

In his book, *The Importance of Living*, Lin Yutang taught me some very important design principles.

One of the most important was that of building in substantial blocks of free time. Many tour companies build a tour based on the premise of "the more things seen, the better." They cram a lot of things into a day and leave almost no time for personal time or shopping. One of the main frustrations many people have on most tours is that they wish they had had more time to look around that quaint little village or linger over their meal at that charming restaurant.

Lin Yutang devoted an interesting chapter to "The Importance of Loafing." Here are some of the fascinating concepts I discovered:

> *"Time is useful because it is not being used. Leisure in time is like unoccupied floor space in a room. Every working girl who rents a small room where every inch of space is fully utilized feels highly uncomfortable because she has no room to move about, and the moment she gets a raise in salary, she moves into a bigger room where she has a little more unused floor space, besides those strictly useful spaces occupied by her single bed, her dressing table, and her two-burner gas range. It is that unoccupied floor space which makes a room habitable, as it is our leisure hours which make life endurable. . . . I understand there is a rich woman living on Park Avenue who bought up a neighboring lot to prevent anybody from erecting a skyscraper next to the house. She is paying a big sum of money in order to have space fully and perfectly made useless, and it seems to me she never spent her money more wisely. . . . Figuratively speaking, we too, are so cramped in our life that we cannot enjoy a free perspective of the beauties of our spiritual life. We lack spiritual frontage."* [6]

I think this is a great metaphor of why I think it is far better to design a day to have two or three great experiences and then more time to linger and spiritually soak in those experiences rather than to psychologically clutter the day and the mind of the traveler with as much activity as possible. Someone might say, "But look at all you could see if you moved faster and saw more." I would reply, "I am not interested in sightseeing, I am interested in sight-experiencing." If a person is only interested in seeing things, he or she could go to Barnes and Noble and buy a book. That way they could see more and save both time and money.

Another Christian principle I pair with this to back up my design philosophy is the fact that we are eternal beings and that our true home is timeless. When I create fewer experiences, but allow more time, I allow the spiritual and psychological margin in a day to create a sense of timelessness that I am convinced the human spirit recognizes and responds to. It is always better to allow too much time for an experience rather than not enough.

You may say, "I doubt whether or not most people get any of these ends to which you are striving." But I feel these mystical and spiritual "contrivings" are valuable, for I am convinced that the traveler is fed and enriched whether he or she realizes it or not.

Ernest Hemingway, in talking about a different subject, clearly defined what I mean here. "If a writer of prose knows enough about what he is writing about, he may omit things that he knows and the reader, if the writer is writing truly enough, will have the feeling of those things as strongly as though the writer had stated them. The dignity of movement of an ice-berg is due to only one-eighth of it being above water."

So too, whether or not the traveler is aware of what I am striving for, the level of the experience is heightened and the traveler enriched.

I might add that the principles I have discussed here are equally applicable to how we live in our personal lives.

KNOW YOURSELF, LOVE YOURSELF, BE YOURSELF

One of the greatest truths that God has taught me in life is what I call the philosophical trinity: "Know Yourself, Love Yourself, Be Yourself." I developed this over time through keeping my journals during my resort work after college. I would read biographies and then write in my journals what I learned or felt about what I had read. If I was reading a biography on Franklin Roosevelt, for example, I invariably compared his thoughts or character to mine and thought through whether it was something I should adopt for my life. Over time I realized that I didn't want to *be* these people, but I wanted to distill the best of what I could get out of their lives and graft it into my life.

From reading history and biography, I developed a vision to travel and see the places I had studied. I wanted to visit the places were the historical people who had meant something in my life had lived. I wanted to see what they saw and touch what they touched; to commune with the spirit of those people in those places. I wanted to drink deeply from those biographies and experiences, to take it all in and let these lives, places, and settings inspire me, drive me, and have their effect on me. I wanted to think about life, to take it in, and let it make its mark on my individuality.

I would later read Henry David Thoreau and Ralph Waldo Emerson and see that many of my thoughts were very much like their writings. This seemed to indicate that these things I was learning were universal truths that lay just below the surface of life, waiting to be discovered by anyone taking the time be alone, look within themselves, and think about the important things of life.

So I kept coming back to a philosophical trinity: "Know Yourself, Love Yourself, and Be Yourself." Each of the three parts is a challenge.

Know Yourself

Henry David Thoreau wrote in *Walden*, as Plato did a millennia earlier, "Know thyself." When I came upon this trinity, I had not read *Walden*, but I feel that so many of the great thoughts "discovered" down through the ages are basic truths that lie just below the surface of our consciousness. All that is required to unearth these truths is for a person to be quiet, to get alone, and to begin to think about life. In line with that, Romans 1:19–20 says that what is known of God is evident in nature.

Three factors helped me get to know myself in those years of travel: (1) I traveled alone, (2) I traveled as a newborn Christian, and (3) I kept a detailed journal of my daily actions and thoughts.

It is so important to get to know yourself. The fast pace of life keeps a person from looking inward. We wake up, full of the demands of the day in mind, and it is easy to rush off, leaving a knowledge of ourselves behind. To get to know yourself, you need to be quiet and be alone. The Bible tells us a lot about ourselves and what it means to be human, but we also need to be quiet and get to know who we are as unique individuals.

Among the many things to note are the things we like, have a passion for, are drawn to, and conversely, the things we don't like and are not drawn to. Reading biography and studying the lives of others naturally gave me a looking glass and mirror to discover who I was and who I was not.

In looking at the life of another person, particularly one you admire and wish to emulate, you can naturally compare and contrast that person with yourself. Inevitably, in this compare-and-contrast examination, you come to define yourself and to see who you are and who you are not.

Love Yourself

Once we get to know ourselves, we need to learn to love ourselves. This is not always easy because when we discover who we are, we invariably learn that we are a curious combination of strengths and weaknesses, talents and flaws. When we look at others, we see some who are more talented in areas where we are weak. They may be better looking, smarter, or more talented. How do we come to terms with this ever-present reality? This is where I found that God's Word and truth was the best psychology.

When I go to God's Word, I find the issue fully fleshed out. On one side I am sinful and broken, but on the other side I am made in God's image. In Psalms, David, who was said to be "a man after God's own heart," wrestled constantly with his dual nature. He often belabored his sinful nature, but he also reveled in being made in God's image. In Psalm 139:14, David says of God, *"I will praise thee; for I am fearfully and wonderfully made."*

So, we find this dual nature fighting within us and challenging our self-image. God's truth solves this problem when we find that God has loved us unconditionally, and He has solved the problem of our sinful nature. In John 3:16, He tells us that He loves us so much that He sent His son to die for our sin. So even though we are flawed, imperfect, and sinful, God loves us completely and unconditionally. He accepts us as we are. He found us so valuable that He was willing to send Jesus to die and pay the debt of our sins so our relationship with Him could be restored. This relationship is what we were made for.

Colossians 1:16 says of the relationship between mankind and Christ, *"We were made by him and for him."*

So, when properly understood, I can embrace myself in my unique individuality. Yes, I am broken and sinful, but God also loves me enough to give His Son to die for me. When properly understood, these two perspectives should keep our ego in a proper balance. I am unique, called by God to serve Him in a unique way for which only I am designed.

We may not be as strong, as smart, as talented, or good-looking as others, but we are unique, and no one else has our specific nature. God made us unique because we were meant to play our part in the world, to play our part in the body of Christ. The Bible talks about how the eye should never say that it has no need of the foot or vice-versa. God is all things to all people, and we are made in His image; therefore, we can be easily lured into the trap of trying to be "all things to all people."

We are made in God's image, but we are not God. A healthy self-image comes from the fact that we don't need to be God. We only need to be uniquely ourselves and who God created us to be—to play our part, which only we, in our unique alchemy of strengths and weaknesses, can play. Also, a big part of our uniqueness is the road of life we have travelled and the experience we bring with us. God has used these things we've been through, both good and bad to sculpt us into the unique individuals we are becoming. Often, from the hard times we have been through, we find healing words and perspectives that may help another person.

When we look at the identity of humans, we see that we were created by God and for God. To find true meaning and purpose in life, we must find it in that context. We were created to run on the fuel of a loving relationship with our Creator. When Jesus was asked what the greatest commandments were, He said, *"Love God with all your heart, mind, and strength and love your neighbor as yourself."*

Many people find that loving themselves is the hardest challenge. Thinking through the philosophical trinity of know yourself, love yourself, and be yourself is a good path toward embracing and loving who you are without being egotistical.

I have a saying that seems egotistical, but actually embraces the psychological/spiritual trinity: "If I weren't myself and I met myself, I would want to be myself."

Be Yourself

The final hurdle in the trinity is to be yourself. Once you know who you are and who you are not, then you embrace that uniqueness, in all its glory and in all its flaws and weaknesses. Having done this, we complete the last hurdle when we walk out on the stage of life, stand in the spotlight big enough for only us, face God and those whose lives cross our paths, and be all of the person we were created to be. That is our gift through God to others, and living out our identity in Christ is the surest way to find joy, meaning, purpose, and fulfillment.

In conclusion, the words of Marylyn Monroe remind us that, *"Trying to be someone else is a terrible waste of who you are."*

OUR IDENTITY MUST BE BUILT ON WHO GOD SAYS WE ARE.

Our identity must be built not on who we think we are, but rather on who God thinks and says we are. He knows us far better than we know ourselves, and because of that, His dreams for us are far better than our dreams for ourselves.

Below are some of the wondrous things God has revealed about us. As you read these verses, keep these thoughts in mind: God knew us before we were born, and He knows what we will become. We were made by Him and for Him.

Jeremiah 1:4–10

> *"Then the word of the LORD came unto me, saying, before I formed thee in the belly, I knew thee; and before thou camest forth out of the womb I sanctified thee, and I ordained thee a prophet unto the nations."*
>
> *Then I said, "Ah, LORD God, behold, I cannot speak: for I am a child."*
>
> *But the LORD said to me, "Say not, I am a child: for thou shalt go to all that I shall send thee, and whatsoever I command thee thou shalt speak. Be not afraid of their faces: for I am with thee to deliver thee."*
>
> *Then the LORD put forth his hand, and touched my mouth. And the LORD said unto me, "Behold I have put my words in thy mouth. See, I have this day set thee over nations and over the kingdoms, to root out, and to pull*

> *down, and to destroy, and to throw down, to build, and to plant."*

In speaking to Jeremiah, God was also speaking to us. He knew us before we were born. His relationship with us is that intimate, that wonderful! He is the beginning and the end, and He knows both what we are and what we will be.

Like Jeremiah, we are to seek him and allow God to transform us into all that we can be. God gives us desires, interests, passions, and skills. God prepared me over a long period for my future work. He transformed me over time from who I was to who I became. He used all the experiences and circumstances along the way, and in the fullness of time, He gave me my life's calling. When I was little, I wouldn't even go next door to spend the night, but now I fly all over, and many of my richest moments come when I am traveling alone.

Psalm 139

Here David speaks about how intimately God knows us. Read all of it. Meditate on each verse and let it sink in and show you how intimately God knows you. Verses 13–14 say,

> *"Thou hast possessed my reins: thou hast covered me in my mother's womb. I will praise thee; for I am fearfully and wonderfully made: marvelous are thy works; and that my soul knoweth right well."*

God knows us thoroughly, and we are to revel in who we are and in who we are becoming in him.

John 3:16

Jesus expresses the depth and breadth of God's love for us.

> *"For God so loved the world, that he gave his only begotten Son, that whosoever believeth in him should not perish, but have everlasting life."*

Colossians 1:16

> *"All things were made by him and for him."*

In all these verses and many more, God reveals the depth and breadth of His love for His creation. We were made by Him and for Him. As Tim Tebow said, "We cannot begin to know who we are without knowing *whose* we are." In these verses, God reveals that He knows us intimately, in fact, He knows us far better than we know ourselves. He knew us in eternity before we were conceived. He values us and loves us so much that He gave His Son to die for us while we were still sinners and not caring about Him. He wants a relationship with us so much that He gave his Son to die so that we might be restored to a right relationship with Him.

He also has designed us for a specific calling that He knows we can accomplish, even if we don't know it ourselves. In His calling, in order to accomplish His will, He gives us authority to build up and to tear down. How amazing that the God of all creation desires to have a relationship with us and gives us the privilege of working in concert with Him to help accomplish His plans in the world.

Think on these things. Meditate on these things. Read all of Psalm 8 and Psalm 139. Let them soak into you mind, body, and spirit. It is the ultimate fairy-tale come true. It is, in fact, the fountainhead and source from which all dreams and fairy tales spring forth.

THE ROD THAT BUDS
WHAT I SEEK TO DO WHEN I DESIGN A TRIP

We are "sub-creators," made in God's image. We find meaning and fulfillment as we work in concert with the Holy Spirit to create—out of the secular clay of our careers and our everyday lives—something spiritual, eternal, and transformative that God uses both in our lives and in the lives of those whom He brings across our paths.

We are created and called to a relationship with God and with others. We are created for the purpose of having an intimate relationship with a personal God. Jesus said in John 17:3, "This is eternal life, that they might know thee, the only true God and Jesus Christ whom thou hast sent."

As I seek to design a tour, I work with a palette of biography, landscape, cuisine, art, history, and more to design an earthly experience that God will take and transform it into something living and eternal, something that Christ transforms into "living water" that feeds the mind and senses but also something spiritual that feeds the soul.

When C. S. Lewis was a small boy, his brother, Warnie, took the lid off a tin container of biscuits. He used moss, twigs, grass, and sticks and made a magical miniature garden on it. When the young Lewis saw it, he said it was such a thing of mystical beauty and magic that it transported him into a spiritual realm of loveliness and something he could not quite put his finger on. But he knew that whatever the experience was, he wanted to have it again.

Lewis said the toy garden experience caused him to feel things the real garden could not. The toy garden transported him to a spiritual realm, and he knew he wanted to return. Something about the make-believe garden had gained access to his imagination and caused him to feel things more deeply than a real garden could. Later he would create the imagery stories of the Chronicles of Narnia to help people see and feel spiritual truths and concepts.

In a similar way, I seek to create an experience for the traveler, using the palette of history, biography, a sense of place, and landscape, along with art and cuisine. I work in concert with the Holy Spirit to create a magical, transformative experience that takes the people who are with me to an eternal moment of truth and beauty that feeds them in a deep way.

In the Middle Ages, people studied the primitive science of alchemy in hopes of extending life and magically turning base metals into gold. Likewise, I am trying to take the basic elements of a place and experience, and work in concert with God to transform that common experience into a golden, eternal experience that will feed not only the mind, but also the spirit. I take the cauldron of the moment and add biography, landscape, art, history, and whatever is at hand to create, through God, a magical experience that mentally and spiritually transports those with me into another realm of the eternal that them on the deepest level.

Artists of all kinds have a sense of this. Bruce Springsteen spoke of this when he said,

> *"That first step onstage is an unusual feeling. You have a very sober feeling in your gut that tells you that something is at stake, something that matters. You're taking a risk. It's not an entirely comfortable feeling but it's a necessary one. What I am searching for from the moment I*

put my foot on stage until I walk off is the invisible thread of energy and inspiration or soul or whatever you want to call it that is going to take me to that place where a song can explode to life. That thread is between me and the audience every night. Always. I've got to grab it out of the air and physicalize it into something they can hear. Sometimes it's like catching a wave that can take you through all twenty-five songs. Sometimes it will take you through ten and then you have to re-find it. Sometimes you're looking for it again after one. A big part of what I'm experiencing when I'm performing is that search.

I'm always asking myself, "How can I wring as much music and meaning as possible out of those six strings? . . . With the correct presentation and playing style, you can summon up an orchestra with only a guitar."

These ideas and these types of experiences are what I strive to create. I feel I am an architect of transformative experiences, and the laboratory in which I strive to create these moments is travel. The artist Gerald Murphy has been a role model for the kind of experience I am trying to create. It was said of Gerald Murphy:

"I know now that what Dow did that Easter in his garden in Snedens was so magical and enchanting that never again will . . . I sit in a beautiful garden without thinking of him. . . . An artist can do this with his painting, a poet with his poem—that

> *capturing of the essence of a moment—but, somehow, Dow's special gift seems to have been in the very doing itself, so that the record is left not in any concrete form that can be examined by others, as a painting or a poem can be, but is simply held in the minds of those who were present at the moment of creation. . . . He certainly knew the value of "the golden moment" which he shared so willingly and joyously with others."*[7]

John Dos Passos described a walk along the Seine with Gerald and Fernand Leger in 1924. It was only the second time Dos Passos had met Murphy.

> *"As we strolled along, Fernand kept pointing out shapes and colors. . . . Gerald's offhand comments would organize vistas of his own. Instead of the hackneyed and pastel-tinted Tuileries and bridges and barges . . . we were walking through a freshly invented world. They picked out winches, the flukes of an anchor, coils of rope, the red funnel of a towboat, half a woman's face seen behind geraniums through the casement window of the cabin of a barge . . . the banks of the Seine never looked banal again after that walk."*[8]

The following quote by Henry David Thoreau in *Walden* seems to capture the special quality or ability that I am trying to create in a moment. *"It is something to be able to paint a particular picture, or to carve a statue, and so to make a few objects beautiful; but it is far more glorious to carve and paint the very atmosphere and medium through which we look. . . . To affect the quality of the day, that is the highest of the arts"*

"No true painter ever set on canvas all the glorious vision he conceived." This quote by Adelaide Procter is on the ceiling of the Library of Congress. I can never perfectly create the exact transformative experience I strive to create, but the very act of striving for it changes the atmosphere of the experience.

God has blessed me with a deep sense of the drama of our passing moments. Our passing moments are epic, because our eternal God is laced through the base metals of each of them, no matter how common they may seem. When we tap into His presence, even a common moment is, through God's alchemy, transformed into gold. In his book *Abandonment to Divine Providence*, Jean-Pierre de Caussade said, *"There is nothing trivial about our passing moments, as they enclose the whole kingdom of holiness, and [they are] the food on which angels feed."*

This is the world I live in and the world I seek to take people into through the vehicle of travel. I am trying to tap into and actually create the moments the great art teacher and artist Robert Henri spoke of in his book *The Art Spirit*,

> *"There are moments in our lives, there are moments in a day, when we seem to see beyond the usual. Such are the moments of our greatest happiness. Such are the moments of our greatest wisdom. If one could but recall his vision by some sort of sign. It was in this hope that the arts were invented. Sign-posts on the way to what may be. Sign-posts toward greater knowledge.*

> *There seem to be moments of revelation, moments when we see in the transition of one part to another the unification of the whole. There is a sense of comprehension and of great happiness. We have entered into a great order and have been carried into greater knowledge by it. This sometimes in a passing face, a landscape, a growing thing. We may call it a passage into another dimension than our ordinary. If one could but record the vision of these moments by some sort of sign! It was in this hope that the arts were invented."*[9]

Even though my travelers may not be aware of all my thoughts and efforts, they can still be blessed by them. We bring the water, but God alone has the power to turn that water into wine. I bring together the makings of a day on tour, and then I pray that God will bless those moments and make the finest wine out of them.

WHAT WILL HEAVEN BE LIKE?

I think in heaven we will finally be truly in the image of God and also one with God. Father, Son, and Holy Spirit created humans to share the wonder, beauty, and love They shared with each other before the foundation of the world. This desire makes the creative purpose a thing of love and sharing, rather than an egotistical desire to make a god-like mini-me. In essence, the Holy Trinity did not want to keep what They experienced within Their private circle. They created humans to share the wonder, the love, and the glory They had with newly created beings.

In Romans 8:28–30, Paul says that we are *"called according to his purpose."* Those verses continue to show how God works that purpose out in our lives. We have been called and justified though Christ's death on the cross. He died for our sins that we might be restored to a relationship with Him. God's purpose is to make us into the image of Christ, and the sculptor is the Holy Spirit (2 Corinthians 3:18). With this purpose as the end game, He uses everything in our lives to accomplish this purpose. This is why Paul said in Romans 8:28, *"All things work together for good to them that love God, to them who are called according to his purpose."*

As we evolve more and more into his image, we abide in Him and become more and more one with Him. This is a work in progress that will only be completed in heaven. Jesus talks about this evolving oneness that includes Father, Son, Holy Ghost, and the believer. In John 17:19–23, Jesus prays to the Father,

> *"And for their sakes I sanctify myself, that they also might be sanctified through the truth. Neither pray I for these alone, but for them also*

> *which shall believe on me through their word; That they all may be as one; as you, Father, art in me and I in thee, that they also may be one in us: that the world may believe that thou hast sent me. And the glory which thou gavest me, I have given them; that they may be one, even as we are one: I in them, and thou in me, that they may be made perfect in one; and that the world may know that thou hast sent me, and hast loved them, as thou hast loved me."*

Father, Son, and Holy Spirit created humans to share Their oneness, and the wonder, beauty, and love that They shared with each other before the foundation of the world. In John 17:24, Jesus expressed this further in His prayer to the Father about what we will share with Them in heaven. *"Father, I will that they also, whom thou hast given me, be with me where I am; that they may behold my glory, which thou hast given me: for thou lovedst me before the foundation of the world."*

C. S. Lewis fleshed out the wonder of these verses in *The Weight of Glory*, when he wrote of one aspect of heaven. *"We do not want to merely to see beauty, though God knows, even that is bounty enough. We want something else which can hardly be put into words—to be united with the beauty we see, to pass into it, to receive it into ourselves, to bathe in it, to become part of it."* Imagine being one with the Father, Son, and Holy Spirit and passing into the fellowship of Their love and joy and the beauty of Their holiness. This is the incredible future of the believer!!!

In this world, many things transport us emotionally and physically into feelings of joy and other-worldly wonder and ecstasy. But Lewis wrote that in this world, *"We cannot mingle with the splendors that we see. But all the leaves of the New Testament are rustling with the rumor that it will not always be so. Someday, God willing, we shall get in. When human souls have become as perfect in voluntary obedience as the inanimate creation is in its lifeless obedience, then they shall put on its glory."*

Lewis chose his words carefully: "pass into," "put on its glory," "receive it into ourselves," and "become part of" the person and glory of God. This experience will be so amazing and joyful that we will need a new body to handle it. Lewis adds, "As Augustine said, the rapture of the saved soul will 'flow over' into the glorified body."

As a young boy, Lewis had experienced moments of otherworldly joy, the source of which he could not identify. Those heavenly intimations of joy and ecstasy led Lewis on a lifelong journey in search of their source. In the end he found the true source of that joy to be found in Christ. In *Surprised by Joy*, Lewis writes,

> *"I was now approaching the source from which those arrows of Joy had been shot at me ever since childhood. . . . No slightest hint was vouchsafed me that there ever had been or ever would be any connection between God and Joy. If anything, it was the reverse. I had hoped that the heart of reality might be of such a kind that we can best symbolize it as a place; instead, I found it to be a Person."*[10]

In Revelation 21:6 Jesus said, *"I will give unto him that is athirst of the fountain of the water of life freely."* When Lewis contemplated what drinking joy from the true fountain might be like, he concluded, *"In the light of our present specialized and depraved appetites, we cannot imagine the torrens voluptatis, and I warn everyone most seriously not to try."* This is again the reason why we will need a new body to safely and completely experience what God means to give us. For those who do try it, Lewis contemplated the joy of this experience. *"What would it be like to taste at the fountainhead that stream of which even these lower reaches prove so intoxicating. Yet that, I believe, is what lies before us. The whole man is to drink joy from the fountain of joy."*

Furthermore, Lewis suggested that, in heaven, God will use our fully realized individuality so that each person would highlight a different part of His glory. As we worship God in the fullness of our individuality, we will enter into and realize our true purpose.

> *"Surely, that each of the redeemed shall forever know and praise some one aspect of the Divine beauty better than any other creature can. Why else were individuals created, but that God loving all infinitely, should love each differently? And this difference, so far from impairing, floods with meaning the love of all blessed creatures for one another, the communion of the saints." If all experienced God in the same way, and returned Him an identical worship, the song of the Church triumphant would have no symphony, it would be like an orchestra in which all the instruments played the same note."*[11]

This dream of fully realizing our fullest potential is a work in progress. It has already begun, and in the passing moments of our life, God is sculpting us into who He created us to be. In that process we are evolving more and more into the image of Christ. One day, when we die, the process with be complete for the Bible says that when we see Him, we shall be like Him. Also, Jesus tells us that we will pass into the love, beauty, and joy of the Holy fellowship of the Father, Son, and Holy Spirit. In the joy of all of this worship experience I have described, there will be no sadness or sorrow and no memory of tears. We will sing a "new song" (Revelation 5:9).

First John 3:2 says we can't really grasp what our lives in heaven will be like. For sure, it will have elements of what both the Bible and Lewis, as well as others, have intimated, but it will be so much more wonderful. I also believe it will be the ultimate reality of what "home" means to us. It will be so incredible that we will need a new body to experience it all!! This knowledge of God's work in us, and the future of the believer, should fill us with hope and joy. It is, without question, the ultimate fairy-tale come true. I pray this journey will be your "happily ever after." To God be all the praise, the honor, and the glory!

---

1. C.S. Lewis, *Mere Christianity*, (New York: HarperCollins, 2009).
2. C.S. Lewis, *The Problem of Pain*, (New York: HarperOne, 2001).
3. Honoria Murphy Donnelly, *Sara & Gerald, Villa America and After*, (New York: Holt, Rinehart, and Winston, 1984).
4. Lin Yutang, *The Importance of Living*, (New York: HarperCollins, 1998).
5. Donnelly, *Sara & Gerald.*
6. Yutang, *Importance of Living.*
7. Donnelly, *Sara & Gerald.*

8. John Dos Passos, *The Best Times: An Informal Memoir*, (La Vergne, Tenn: Open Road Distributing, 2015).
9. Robert Henri, The Art Spirit, (New York: Basic Books, 2007).
10. C.S. Lewis, Surprised by Joy, (San Diego: Harcourt Brace, 1956).
11. Lewis, Problem of Pain

POSTSCRIPT

THE BEST DECISION YOU COULD EVER MAKE!!!

You may have read parts or all of this book and maybe thought that I have some kind of special relationship with God, and maybe wondered if you could have that kind of relationship. Yes, you can!! Let me say this; what I have is offered to you also. Jesus said, *"Behold, I stand at the door and knock. If anyone hears My voice and opens the door, I will come in to him and dine with him, and he with Me."* (Revelation 3:20) Maybe you have already opened the door and let Jesus into your heart, but if you haven't, you can begin that journey right now. This is the relationship you were created for. Jesus said, *"And this is eternal life, that they might know thee the only true God, and Jesus Christ whom thou hast sent."* (John 17:3) You can begin your personal journey with God to work out His plan for your life right now. It will give you peace, purpose, joy, and meaning for this life and the next. You may have heard all these verses before, but maybe they have never moved from your head to your heart. The journey can start right now!!

God Loves You

"For God so loved the world, that He gave is only begotten Son, that whosever believeth in Him should not perish, but have everlasting life." John 3:16

"But God commendeth his love toward us, in that, while we were yet sinners, Christ died for us." Romans 5:8

We are all Sinners

"For all have sinned, and come short of the glory of God." Romans 3:23

"As it is written, There is none righteous, no, not one." Romans 3:10

God's Remedy for Sin

"For the wages of sin is death; but the gift of God is eternal life through Jesus Christ our Lord." Romans 6:23

"But as many as received Him, to them gave He power to become the sons of God, even to them that believe on his name." John 1:12

"For I delivered unto you first of all that which I also received, how that Christ died for our sins according to the scriptures; And that he was buried, and that He rose again the third day according to the scriptures." I Corinthians 15: 3-4

You Can Be Saved Now and Begin Your Relationship With God

> *"Behold, I stand at the door and knock. If anyone hears My voice and opens the door, I will come in to him and dine with him, and he with Me."* Revelation 3:20

The Prayer to Receive Christ into Your Heart

> *" Dear Jesus, I know that I am a sinner. I am sorry for my sin. I want to turn from my sin and follow you. Forgive me. I believe you died on the cross for my sin. I want you to come into my heart and be both my savior and the Lord of my life."*

I pray you will open that door and let Jesus into your heart and life. This is where the journey begins.

If you have any questions or if you want to talk to me, here are my contacts:

Russ Head
P.O. Box 1126
Thomaston, GA 30286
E-mail: russhead@windstream.net
Cell # 706/656/8808

www.ingramcontent.com/pod-product-compliance
Lightning Source LLC
Chambersburg PA
CBHW020846090426
42736CB00008B/256
* 9 7 8 1 9 6 3 6 1 1 1 4 4 *